KT-482-805

HAMLET'S MOTHER

GENDER AND CULTURE

Carolyn G. Heilbrun and Nancy K. Miller, EDITORS

HAMLET'S MOTHER

AND OTHER WOMEN

CAROLYN G. HEILBRUN

COLUMBIA UNIVERSITY PRESS

NEW YORK

Columbia University Press
New York   Chichester, West Sussex
Copyright © 1990 Carolyn G. Heilbrun

LIBRARY OF CONGRESS CATALOGING-IN-PUBLICATION DATA

Heilbrun, Carolyn G.
Hamlet's mother and other women / Carolyn G. Heilbrun.
p. cm. — (Gender and culture)
Includes bibliographical references.
ISBN 0-231-07176-0 (cloth)
ISBN 0-231-07177-9 (paper)
1. English literature—Women authors—History and criticism.
2. American literature—Women authors—History and criticism.
3. Women and literature.
4. Women in literature.
I. Title.   II. Series
PR111.H45 1990   820.9'9287—dc20   89-49208

Columbia University Press books are printed on permanent and durable acid-free paper

Printed in the United States of America
c 10 9 8 7 6 5 4 3 2 1
p 10 9 8 7 6 5 4 3 2 1

FOR JIM
WHO LIVED THROUGH IT ALL

Contents

Preface to the Paperback Edition (2002)

WHEN I was a small child in the early 1930s, the First World War was still alive in everyone's mind, and there used to be an image that became a popular saying, or metaphor. A boy looks up at his father and asks: What did you do in the Great War, Daddy?

Should a grandchild demand of me what I had done in the great feminist movement in the last quarter of the twentieth century, I could hand her this book. I think it pretty well covers the efforts and risks of certain of us, academics mostly, in the time of that struggle for women's right to their own lives. What we have here may be little more than a piece of history—except my hope is that any girl or woman awakening to the gender constraints upon her and her aspirations might find some encouragement, or anyway some hints, in these selections. When I was a girl, if one wished for something beyond the assigned female destiny, there was no reading on the subject to be had, nothing to confirm that the wished-for destiny ever existed in the realm of possibility.

Yes, in these essays I was bearing witness to my own times and the battles central to my generation. Those struggles, however, may be recognizable not only to my peers, but to anyone finding herself in a similar place. In fact, many women just beginning to question their assigned role in life may find that the writings of my generation speak with startling exactness to their condition. I once responded deprecatingly to a compliment on my book *Towards a Recognition of Androgyny*, a compliment delivered thirty years after the book's publication. "I would not write it that way now," I said. "I'm not in that place anymore, and doubt my ancient view of it." "We are in that place now" was the answer I received.

I also hope that those who doubt the necessity for feminism then or now might be persuaded to read what it was like back then. I well remember asking my young mother, like so many children, what life was like in old-fashioned times when she was my age. My mother thought that funny then, but alas, the feminist reformations we fought and suffered for may today seem just as old-fashioned as my mother's girlhood seemed to me.

I fear that, unlike the engagements of the First World War, the battles of the feminist conflict will have to be reenacted again and again; there will be no armistice, not even a temporary one. For the struggle for female equality is non-ending, and in places ruled by some religious orders, women's control of their own destiny starts today further back than we, in America, have ever experienced. The fight continues everywhere.

One of the odd errors that has taken hold in the decade since this book first appeared is that feminism has somehow outlived its purpose and even its usefulness. That the younger generation today is said to scorn the old-hat feminism of their mother's generation is both true and false. When has a daughter ever failed to belittle her mother's hard-won certitudes? I have long since noticed that the only mistakes new mothers do not make with their children are the missteps promulgated by their own female progenitors. Thus it seems that for women in the Western democracies, the accomplishments of feminism have become ordinary, expected, taken for granted. "Who worries about that sort of thing now?" these women ask from their places in law, medicine, the military, and beyond.

So the poet Maxine Kumin, who is my age, is "significantly challenged" by her daughters. "I confess it," she writes; "each of [my] daughters has taken me aside to say that the women's movement is too narrow, does not address the global issues. Hunger. Survival. The absence of hope in refugee camps everywhere. Zero population! Nuclear freeze! Humane resettlement policies, immediate distribution of surplus foods; put that in your poetry, they are saying. Get with it, Ma. Write about the Love Canal, the challenge to safe abortion, food stamp cutbacks. Clitoridectomies. Poseidon submarines."

Who can argue with that?

In a recent novel by Susan Isaacs, *Long Time No See*, one woman in her fifties says to her old comrade: "May I inquire precisely why we went through a revolution in women's rights, why we bothered to have our consciences raised? So our daughters could sit on a bench in a playground and talk about whether Pampers or Huggies hold poopy better?"

I couldn't have put it better, or half as well. In the richer suburbs today, one could hardly guess there had been a revolution; so many young women have again embraced the exclusive roles of housewife and mother. Yet while I complain of this in exactly the same tone as Isaac's character, I think I have an answer that goes a little way to ameliorating the outrage and pride we old combatants feel.

Young women, particularly if they are rich and thin and using the latest in hair colors, are at the height of their attractiveness and their imprisonment in romantic illusions. No feminist teacher of college women can quite doubt this, and the responses of her students can become distinctly depressing. There are, of course, always some young women who "get it" from the very beginning; their numbers, however, are not legion.

The saving grace is this. In time, these women discussing diapers on park benches—as we did in the terrible fifties when there were neither Huggies nor Pampers but cloth diapers that had to be washed—these women will age as we aged. They will meet up with the problems women face in growing old, the pitfalls in even the most perfect marriages, the outrageous and tedious demands of children, the appalling disdain of adolescents, and, if they take a job, the discrimination that is still flourishing and is easy neither to endure nor fight. The future of feminism does not lie with the young but rather with the gray battalions, whether or not the gray is transformed to a brighter color.

There is another denunciation often made of feminism today: that it is an upper or upper-middle class phenomenon and hasn't helped the poor. Believe me, women from the working class are not discussing poop, nor are they sitting on benches. They are laboring in the world, and their opportunities for self-defense, like their options regarding jobs, are far greater than they were fifty years ago, before the recent women's movement. Gloria Steinem, for example, discovered that while her classmates from Smith College were loath to embrace or endorse concepts such as sexual harassment or birth control or legal abortion, the working-class girls she grew up with in Toledo, Ohio, got the message fast enough. It is, however, often the case that revolutionary ideas about women's place in the world do not begin with those who suffer the most. Though all classes benefit, such ideas usually begin with those for whom money and time are the available tools.

It was, incidentally, during the time of feminism in my life that the phrases "sexual harassment," "date rape," "child abuse," and "domestic violence" were formed. These phrases had not existed before because the crimes they describe had not, before feminism, been recognized clearly enough to be named. Today, Islam, for example, does not recognize these phrases. As a religious principle, it too often believes in enslaving women more than does any other religion, however restrictive. This, like all forms of slavery, cries out for reform.

Then there is tennis: when Billy Jean King and Martina Navratilova came along, women could not have credit cards, could not take out a mortgage without a man's signature, could not, in many places, control their own money or serve on a jury or on an equal basis with men in the military. Today, with feminism at their backs, women tennis champions earn as much as the men, which was not the case before Billy Jean King took up the fight. This past year, the Williams sisters played each other for the championship in prime time, a media triumph that the men have not yet achieved. And both

Venus and Serena Williams tell us how much they enjoy shopping and using the credit cards they earned by playing brilliant tennis.

Young women take all this for granted. Well, why not? But if you read works by women writers or interpret the canon from a less white-male viewpoint, *Hamlet's Mother and Other Women* relates how some of us went about achieving that. We took up the literature that was "theirs" and asked new questions of it. Oh, we were threatening, all right, but we prevailed. I look back now on what took so much courage then, and consider myself fortunate to have taken part in that great struggle. We American feminists who are old saw the last century out knowing that, while women elsewhere in the world are still shackled, we did demonstrate the possibility of a woman's right to personhood. We began the new millennium having shown that women could make their own decisions about how they would live—and that nothing terrible would follow except the transformation of the old order where men made all the rules.

Foreword

THERE ARE three kinds of people, as Carolyn Heilbrun herself might well say: those ahead of their time, those of their time, and the belated. We will not bother with the last group. Looking back now over the history of feminist criticism of the past two decades, it is not hard to determine in which of the first two categories to place Carolyn Heilbrun. If only for the 1957 date of "The Character of Hamlet's Mother"—but we are not uniquely dependent on chronology here— Heilbrun is a woman ahead of her time.

In the histories of feminist criticism that now abound, there is a slight hesitation over which work to place at the beginning of the remarkable out-pouring of books and essays about women and literature, gender and culture, that has come to constitute this new field: Mary Ellmann's 1968 *Thinking About Women,* or Kate Millett's 1970

Sexual Politics? Preference is often given to *Sexual Politics,* perhaps because of its academic origins—a Ph.D. thesis at Columbia—and I will
take it up here as a point of departure because it is a book whose
importance to the new field Carolyn Heilbrun helped define. Jonathan
Culler, for instance, in the chapter of his book *On Deconstruction* called
"Reading as a Woman," cites Heilbrun's 1971 review of Millett's accomplishment, "Millett's *Sexual Politics*: A Year After": "Hers is not
meant to be the last word on any writer, but a wholly new word, little
heard before and strange. For the first time we have been asked to
look at literature as women; we, men, women and Ph.D.'s have always
read it as men. Who cannot point to a certain overemphasis in the
way Millett reads Lawrence or Stalin or Euripides. What matter? We
are rooted in our vantage point and require transplanting."

This analysis is characteristic of Heilbrun's reviewing and writing
style: its insights are generous and meant to capture the originality of
another's project; Heilbrun here, for instance, recasts the aim and effects of Millett's explosive rereadings both in order to counter a public
reception that seems to be missing the point—and to bring out the
implications of the work for those who might otherwise resist them.
At the same time, Heilbrun moves the discussion forward by adumbrating a critical strategy for the future: in this case, what will be called
several years later in the discourse of deconstruction: "reading as a
woman." As is also often the case, the formulation in language, as she
likes to put it (revising Marianne Moore), that "cats and dogs can
read," tends to prefigure with bracing clarity and utter conviction (is
it unfair of me to point out that "wholly" is Heilbrun's favorite ad-
verb?) the terms of debate subsequently rehearsed in fancier dress.

Here, as throughout her career as a critic, Heilbrun is attracted to
the apocalypse, to acts of revelation and naming, but her diction always keeps track of human ordinariness: our potted plant root-bound
nature; the cat (again) chewing on the phonecord she evokes in the
introduction to this volume. Finally, there is the touch of wit that
wards off the always threatening cliché of all cultural criticism: men,
women, and the third term that rescues the reader from the litany:
Ph.D.'s as a possible third sex.

"The Character of Hamlet's Mother" was published in 1957. It seems
possible, without succumbing entirely to the temptations of typolog-
ical thinking, to suggest that this first published article, which reads
Shakespeare, shall we say, as a woman, announces the themes of the

later work: the critical engagement with psychoanalytic theory; the demystification of what Mary Ellmann was to call the use of "sexual analogy" by establishment critics; the revolt against stereotypes of gendered identities; the reclaiming of freedoms—notably sexual liberation (avant la lettre)—for women; the intersecting and irreducibly complicated relations between literature and life, both of which constrain a culture's imagination about women and their place in the world. In this instance, Heilbrun ends by suggesting quietly, but as it turns out radically, an apparent contradiction in terms (a favorite trope): that Gertrude could be both passion's slave and intelligent (an oxymoron reserved, it seems, for women only).

These strands in the writing could be pulled together more tightly to summarize Heilbrun's overriding interest as a critic, palpable throughout the different genres of her literary production—books, essays, reviews, addresses, detective fiction—a passion for the life in texts. Whether reading *Little Women* or *Plant Dreaming Deep,* the *Odyssey* or *The Years,* Heilbrun presses and exposes the mediations binding life and text in the work of culture. This is not a matter of taking the one *for* the other, but rather seeing the one *in* the other. Put another way, from the beginning Carolyn Heilbrun has been writing the biography of literature. I will return to the question of biography.

I want to backtrack first to the notion of timing: of the century, or even the decade one is born into. In an important essay on Joyce and Woolf that she is publishing here for the first time, Heilbrun works her way through the tangled esthetic and social ties linking Woolf, T. S. Eliot, and Joyce. She cites in particular Lionel Trilling's disagreement with Eliot about the place of Joyce's work in a history of modernism, Trilling's claim that "Joyce was entirely 'a man of the generation into which he was born.'" If we were to transpose this question into a history of feminism, we would have to say that Heilbrun was entirely *not* of the generation into which she was born. Or rather, that her life was spent writing herself out of the generation into which she was born. She made such a good job of it, that she seems ahead of herself; this impression comes perhaps from the fact that she had such a vivid sense of what might lie ahead. As she puts it in *Writing a Woman's Life,* when she describes the birth in 1963 of Amanda Cross and her heroine, Kate Fansler: "Amanda Cross could write, in the popular, unimportant form of detective fiction, the destiny she hoped for women, if not exactly for herself: the alternate life she wished to

inscribe upon the female imagination." In the essays on detective fiction collected here Heilbrun as Heilbrun analyzes a genre not generally
thought of as concerned with imagining new plots for women for the
possibilities it offers both of social critique and cultural innovation.

For feminists of my generation—and I feel that I am very deeply
of the generation that came to writing, as the French feminist phrase
goes, in the 1970s—it has always seemed that Carolyn Heilbrun was
already there, there for us, and yet still somehow ahead. She wrote,
in a book that was not very well understood, *Reinventing Womanhood*
(1978), that she was "born a feminist." This of course did not mean
that she had forgotten the lessons of Simone de Beauvoir: for if one
is not born, but becomes a woman, one also becomes a feminist. To
feel oneself born a feminist, I think, is to sense, without having the
language in which to express it, that there is an alternate life for women.
It is this insight that drives the feminism Heilbrun learned through
the women's movement as it took shape in the late sixties and early
seventies.

If it is nice for us, who are only of our own generation, to have
had Carolyn Heilbrun's work laying the ground for us to dance on,
and occasionally trample ungraciously, it has not, I know, always been
as nice for her. What she says of Woolf in her fifties is not a little
autobiographical: "My aim is to suggest, in the light of my own experience of being in one's fifties, how it was that in middle age Woolf
found herself uniquely urged toward an artistic act of great courage.
These professional women of my generation who became frank feminists in their fifties are few enough, and they had the support of a
growing women's movement. This meant practically that, though they
would be derided, they would not be altogether isolated."

Heilbrun spoke in *Reinventing Womanhood* of feeling an outsider
and the extent to which being an outsider—like Woolf's Society of
Outsiders—was constitutive of feminist projects. I want to suggest,
though the terms in their etymology contradict each other, that this
sense of eccentricity is in fact central to Heilbrun's work from the beginning: the exemplary women, women in literature and history she
writes of in this volume, her favorite sleuths, all in some crucial way
share the sense of not completely (I'm tempted to write, wholly) fitting. It is the representation of that voluntary displacement that at-
tracts her to May Sarton's writing, movingly described here: the exile

of "the woman artist, alone in a house." This margin of distance is always marked in Heilbrun's thinking.

Woolf in her fifties, Kate Fansler in her forties, Carolyn Heilbrun in her sixties. Of Fansler, Heilbrun writes: "she has become braver as she has aged, less interested in the opinions of those she does not cherish, and has come to realize that she has little to lose, little any longer to risk, that age above all . . . is the time when there is very little "they" can do for you, very little to fear, or hide, or not attempt brave and important things."

It is perhaps in the addresses collected here that we have the most vivid sense of what becoming braver means for a woman who also has chosen to be a feminist in the profession of literature. In these addresses Heilbrun both speaks for women—to those who might not have heard what we've been saying—and to women who share the struggle at different places in their lives. (This is also often the occasion for the belated to discover what feminism—for better or for worse—might come to mean for them.) Although to many Heilbrun's highly visible signs of public recognition—chaired professor, former president of the MLA, recipient of honorary degrees, etc.—make her seem an insider to the institution she addresses, her language and its resistance to the stereotypes of privilege and comfort keep alive the difference of view that defines the outsider.

It is both characteristic of Heilbrun's rhetoric of self-definition and bolder than it might seem on paper that she should open her University Lecture, "The Politics of Mind: Women, the Tradition, and the University," in the rotunda of Low Library (the home of Columbia University's central administration) by an act of resistance to its protocols (in the introductory note that frames this section of essays she acknowledges the intense anxiety of the moment for her): "I have been a member of the Columbia University community for more than thirty-five years, and I can only consider myself to be speaking as what Lionel Trilling called an opposing self, opposed to culture, in this case the culture of the university." The reference to Trilling, her teacher and then colleague, which punctuates her writing throughout these essays, is here the shorthand for an older and now superannuated view of what academic community means for its members: Trilling's "life of the mind," revisited from a feminist perspective as "the politics of a wholly male-centered culture and university."

What then of life—in the sixties, hers, in the nineties, ours—and what is next? Heilbrun has written powerfully in *Writing a Woman's Life* about the freedom of being old, of life after closure, as she puts it; and of breaking the general silence about the pleasures that might exist in getting beyond most definitions of a woman's life. And so it is perhaps not altogether astonishing that her current project involves writing the biography of a woman's life; the invented, various, and exemplary life of a woman and a feminist now in her fifties, Gloria Steinem. It seems somehow fitting that having written so movingly about biography, the new biography of women, Heilbrun should finally practice it; or rather return to biography as a mode of reading the world, since this was also the genre of her first book. She will now have the occasion to review and even rewrite the history of the second wave of feminism to which she came ahead of her time, her generation, but which also came in time for her to become an exemplary representative of ours.

But despite the fact that to many of us Heilbrun seems to fit the category of exemplary women, she has resisted the impulse to mythologize herself. In fact, even in the current moment when autobiography has become fashionable, Heilbrun continues to prefer to write about the lives of others. This book ends with Harriet Vane at Oxford, and thoughts about the life Sayers invented for herself and that we can guess at through Harriet's independence and outrageousness.

In *Hamlet's Mother and Other Women* we find juxtaposed for us pieces from a life of writing: 1957–1988. The result is a surprising tapestry of feminist argument in tonic prose—more cheerful and engaging, on the whole, in the figures of its representation, than the pattern, one presumes, of Penelope's shroud (Penelope is a favored reference here)—about the future of women's lives. We have displayed in these essays the remarkable heterogeneity of Carolyn Heilbrun's preoccupations from Ariadne to Harriet Vane, Shakespeare, Homer, Sophocles, Freud, Vera Brittain, Winifred Holtby, Louisa May Alcott, May Sarton, Virginia Woolf, P. D. James, teaching, institutional politics, English department doldrums, male academics, modern British fiction, feminist criticism, marriage, art, mothers and daughters, plot, friendship between women, aging, detectives—the list is a long one. As other women, and readers, how not to feel this book is for us?

Nancy K. Miller

HAMLET'S MOTHER

Introduction

EXCEPT FOR the first essay which provides its title, all the pieces in
this collection were written between 1972 and 1988, that is within my
life as a declared and dedicated feminist.* "The Character of Hamlet's
Mother" was composed and hopefully sent forth in the 1950s, and is
my first publication, academic or other (if one doesn't count a story
I wrote in college to which the *Atlantic Monthly* awarded a prize and
printed in some sort of college supplement). About this first essay, I
remember only that I sent an offprint to Lionel Trilling, whom in
those days I admired from a respectful distance. He responded with a
one line postcard mentioning his amazement in discovering that there

*In attaching dates to these essays, I have adopted this rule: if a paper was first presented as a speech,
I have used the date of the speech, if first presented in published form, the date of publication, if
not a speech and not previously published, the date of writing.

had been so much obfuscation on the matter of Hamlet's mother. I can't find that postcard, my only communication from him, but I like to think that it is somewhere among the papers I have stored rather than among those I decided, as my mother-in-law says, to "pitch." That first essay, in any case, does indicate that I was gnawing at the idea of women as misunderstood and wrongly condemned, though not, as I then thought, by Shakespeare. In short, I was a feminist waiting for a cause to join, or maybe just waiting for the cause this article adumbrated to be named.

Between 1957, when the *Shakespeare Quarterly* published my first article, and 1972 when the second essay in this volume appeared, I was not unpublished, but I was still wandering in the wilderness or, as Trilling (after Dante) liked to put it, in a dark wood. I published a biography of the Garnett family (of which I had, last year, to renew the copyright, an act designed to make one feel like her own grandmother), a critical monograph on Christopher Isherwood, and a number of essays and reviews indicating to me as my eye scans the titles in my *curriculum vitae* that I was simultaneously closing in on my feminist commitment and admiring men, like E. M. Forster, who didn't seem to equate manliness with the subjection of women. But, as my 1972 essay on Dorothy L. Sayers, "Sayers, Lord Peter, and God," indicated, I admired feminists but wasn't sure I ought to say so in public.

In 1973 I published *Toward A Recognition of Androgyny* which caused a minor stir (the word "androgyny" was still largely unknown though highly suspect). I thought of including in this volume several attempts I have made to keep the idea of androgyny from being altogether destroyed by its critics, although many of their objections to the concept seem to me sensible. I have decided, however, not to bother with all that anymore (with the exception of my remarks on androgyny and detective fiction), partly because the book itself can still speak to those at that special point in their lives when androgyny is a liberating concept, and partly because I have lived long enough to see androgyny on its way back. Certainly writers like Sandra Bem have done a fine job examining the concept both theoretically and experimentally, and I am content to leave the field to her while cheering her on.

Between 1964 and the date when these essays begin, I also published four detective novels in secrecy under the name Amanda Cross. The essays in this volume with the heading "Detective Fiction" reflect, not my own experience as a writer in the genre, but my thoughts on detective fiction as it has engrossed and fascinated me over the years. Here, as everywhere, I am a feminist, and I ought, I dare say, to define that term. I recognize that it is a frightening word to many women otherwise eager to make their way in the world. To these simultaneously brave and frightened women the label "feminist" evokes various unsightly images altogether disturbing and likely to frighten the males in the middle distance: radical, disruptive, strident, shrill, even, especially, lesbian. I am particularly pained to find younger women deriding feminism even though the positions they now occupy would not have been open to them without the efforts of others who dared to call themselves feminist. But such are the pains of those who fight revolutions and live to see their early, though partial success. A feminist, as I use the word, questions the gender arrangements in society and culture (all societies and cultures) and works to change them; the desired transformation gives more power to women while simultaneously challenging both the forms and the legitimacy of power as it is now established.

If I have had a model for the form this volume of essays will take, it is Ursula LeGuin's collection *Dancing at the Edge of the World*. And this is odd because LeGuin and I are wholly different kinds of writers, although as I once wrote in an essay (not reproduced here) called "Why I Don't Read Science Fiction," we have a great deal in common for two people who have never met. (She writes in her wonderful story "Sur," "It is very difficult for women to meet, when they live as far apart as we do.") We were both born in the twenties, which gives us the same squint on life. We each have a long marriage and children, which means we both bought into the nuclear family and somehow, by luck or brains, made it work for us. We each have a cat who chews the telephone cord. She has said: "I write science fiction because that is what publishers call my books; left to myself I would call them novels." I had always thought it was chiefly the different categories in which we write that, talents apart, made LeGuin and me different kinds of writers.

But in the introduction to her recent collection of essays, I came on a phrase that further distinguishes us; like so many of her phrases, it reverberates for me: "My goal being always to subvert as much as possible without hurting anybody's feelings." That was always my goal too, but I have not been able to achieve it. I attribute this, not only to the fact that LeGuin may be and probably is a nicer person than I, but also to the fact that she is not part of an institution, that she does not find herself always and repeatedly up against a kind of recalcitrance that kindness alone, that wonderful female virtue, cannot penetrate. Nonetheless, I admire her goal, and have tried to come as close to it as my different world allows. (Neither of us, it might be observed, has discovered a way to make the cat stop chewing the telephone cord.) To subvert with kindness may almost be a contradiction in terms, an oxymoron; nonetheless, I honor and pursue it as a goal.

Except for the opening one on Hamlet's mother, these essays are arranged not chronologically but by subject; the date of first public appearance is given at the end of each essay. A short introductory note before each category describes the circumstances under which the essays were first presented, as well as revisions I have made for this volume. I have rewritten nothing, but have sometimes joined two essays together, or removed repetitions. All such changes have been noted.

In recent years, a number of articles, published and not published, have been written about me. Almost all of them mention that I began (and some lament that I have remained) a conservative. I find this interesting, partly because conservatives, when I was a girl, were not, as they are today, reactionaries wishing radically to transform our society, in my opinion for the worse; conservatives were those who identified with what in a society was worth conserving, that is, what I then thought worth conserving. I am no longer, I believe, a conservative, but I started from there, and now find a particular delight in being simultaneously condemned as a conservative and damned as a (radical) feminist. It is a position between ideologies that I am not unwilling to claim, though much of my conservatism seems to me to be little more than a function of when I was born and came to consciousness.

My friend Nancy Miller who edits with me the series Gender and Culture in which this volume appears, suggested for it the title "Hamlet's Mother." We had also thought of "Essays Awaiting the Revolution," as a subtitle, but eventually abandoned it. There is a sense in which the revolution I fought in and for has already been replaced by a new and somewhat different one. Few early revolutionaries recognize everything in the revolution their efforts helped eventually to bring about. That is probably just as well. Perhaps these essays ought, therefore, to be called "A Stage in the Revolution." Although I shall certainly continue cheering and taking part, feminism will eventually shift it aims; it has already begun to do so. My words, then, are for those who can now be inspired by, or wish to remember, the relative clarity of a revolution in its earlier years.

Jennifer Crewe, the editor of this and all but the earliest books in the series Gender and Culture, has been a model of encouragement, courtesy, and efficiency. It was she who first plowed through the ungainly and irregularly reproduced collection of my essays, choosing the ones she thought best for this volume. I am old enough to remember the days when editors and publishers were the friends, not the brokers, of writers; Jennifer reminds me pleasantly of those publishing days, providing me with one of the very few occasions when I care to indulge that highly over-rated emotion: nostalgia.

I

THE

CHARACTER

OF

HAMLET'S MOTHER

The Character of Hamlet's Mother

THE CHARACTER of Hamlet's mother has not received the specific critical attention it deserves. Moreover, the traditional account of her personality as rendered by the critics will not stand up under close scrutiny of Shakespeare's play.

None of the critics of course has failed to see Gertrude as vital to the action of the play; not only is she the mother of the hero, the widow of the Ghost, and the wife of the current King of Denmark, but the fact of her hasty and, to the Elizabethans, incestuous marriage, the whole question of her "falling off," occupies a position of barely secondary importance in the mind of her son, and of the Ghost. Indeed, Freud and Jones see her, the object of Hamlet's Oedipus complex, as central to the motivation of the play.[1] But the critics, with no exception that I have been able to find, have accepted Hamlet's word "fraility" as applying to her whole personality, and have seen in her not one weakness, or passion in the Elizabethan sense, but a character of which weakness and lack of depth and vigorous intelligence are the entire explanation. Of her can it truly be said that carrying the "stamp of one defect", she did "in the general censure take corruption from that particular fault" (I.iv.35—36).

The critics are agreed that Gertrude was not a party to the late King's murder and indeed knew nothing of it, a point which on the clear evidence of the play, is indisputable. They have also discussed whether or not Gertrude, guilty of more than an "o'er-hasty marriage," had committed adultery with Claudius before her husband's death. I will return to this point later on. Beyond discussing these two points, those critics who have dealt specifically with the Queen have traditionally seen her as well-meaning but shallow and feminine, in the pejorative sense of the word: incapable of any sustained rational process, superficial and flighty. It is this tradition which a closer reading of the play will show to be erroneous.

Professor Bradley describes the traditional Gertrude thus:

> The Queen was not a bad-hearted woman, not at all the woman to think little of murder. But she had a soft animal nature and was very dull and very shallow. She loved to be happy, like a sheep in the sun, and to do her justice, it pleased her to see others happy, like more sheep in the sun. . . . It was pleasant to sit upon her throne and see smiling faces around her, and foolish and unkind in Hamlet to persist in grieving for his father instead of marrying Ophelia and making everything comfortable. . . . The belief at the bottom of her heart was that the world is a place constructed simply that people may be happy in it in a good-humored sensual fashion.[2]

Later on, Bradley says of her that when affliction comes to her "the good in her nature struggles to the surface through the heavy mass of sloth."

Granville-Barker is not quite so extreme. Shakespeare, he says,

> gives us in Gertrude the woman who does not mature, who clings to her youth and all that belongs to it, whose charm will not change but at last fade and wither; a pretty creature, as we see her, desperately refusing to grow old. . . . She is drawn for us with unemphatic strokes, and she has but a passive part in the play's action. She moves throughout in Claudius' shadow; he holds her as he won her, by the witchcraft of his wit.[3]

Elsewhere Granville-Baker says "Gertrude who will certainly never see forty-five again, might better be 'old.' [That is, portrayed by an older, mature actress.] But that would make her relations with Claudius— and *their* likelihood is vital to the play—quite incredible" (p. 226). Granville-Barker is saying here that a woman about forty-five years of age cannot feel any sexual passion nor arouse it. This is one of the mistakes which lie at the heart of the misunderstanding about Gertrude.

Professor Dover Wilson sees Gertrude as more forceful than either of these two critics will admit, but even he finds the Ghost's unwillingness to shock her with knowledge of his murder to be one of the basic motivations of the play, and he says of her "Gertrude is always hoping for the best."[4]

Now whether Claudius won Gertrude before or after her husband's death, it was certainly not, as Granville-Barker implies, with "the witchcraft of his wit" alone. Granville-Barker would have us believe that Claudius won her simply by the force of his persuasive tongue. "It is plain", he writes, that the Queen "does little except echo his [Claudius'] wishes; sometimes—as in the welcome to Rosencrantz and Guildenstern—she repeats his very words" (p. 227), though Wilson must admit later that Gertrude does not tell Claudius everything. Without dwelling here on the psychology of the Ghost, or the greater burden borne by the Elizabethan words "witchcraft" and "wit," we can plainly see, for the Ghost tells us, how Claudius won the Queen: the Ghost considers his brother to be garbage, and "lust," the Ghost says, "will sate itself in a celestial bed and prey on garbage" (I.v.54– 55). "Lust"—in a woman of forty-five or more—is the key word here. Bradley, Granville-Barker, and to a lesser extent Professor Dover Wilson, misunderstand Gertrude largely because they are unable to see lust, the desire for sexual relations, as the passion, in the Elizabethan sense of the word, the flaw, the weakness which drives Gertrude to an incestuous marriage, appalls her son, and keeps him from the throne. Unable to explain her marriage to Claudius as the act of any but a weak-minded vacillating woman, they fail to see Gertrude for the strong-minded, intelligent, succinct, and, apart from this passion, sensible woman that she is.

To understand Gertrude properly, it is only necessary to examine the lines Shakespeare has chosen for her to say. She is, except for her description of Ophelia's death, concise and pithy in speech, with a talent for seeing the essence of every situation presented before her eyes. If she is not profound, she is certainly never silly. We first hear her asking Hamlet to stop wearing black, to stop walking about with his eyes downcast, and to realize that death is an inevitable part of life. She is, in short, asking him not to give way to the passion of grief, a passion of whose force and dangers the Elizabethans are aware, as Miss Campbell has shown.[5] Claudius echoes her with a well-reasoned argument against grief which was, in its philosophy if not in its language, a piece of commonplace Elizabethan lore. After Claudius' speech, Gertrude asks Hamlet to remain in Denmark, where he is rightly loved. Her speeches have been short, however warm and loving, and conciseness of statement is not the mark of a dull and shallow woman.

We next hear her, as Queen and gracious hostess, welcoming Rosencrantz and Guildenstern to the court, hoping, with the King, that they may cheer Hamlet and discover what is depressing him. Claudius then tells Gertrude, when they are alone, that Polonius believes he knows what is upsetting Hamlet. The Queen answers:

> I doubt it is no other than the main,
> His father's death and our o'er-hasty marriage. (II.ii.56–57)

This statement is concise, remarkably to the point, and not a little courageous. It is not the statement of a dull, slothful woman who can only echo her husband's words. Next, Polonius enters with his most unbrief apotheosis to brevity. The Queen interrupts him with five words: "More matter with less art" (II.ii.95). It would be difficult to find a phrase more applicable to Polonius. When this gentleman, in no way deterred from his loquacity, after purveying the startling news that he has a daughter, begins to read a letter, the Queen asks pointedly "Came this from Hamlet to her?" (II.ii.114).

We see Gertrude next in Act III, asking Rosencrantz and Guildernstern, with her usual directness, if Hamlet received them well, and if they were able to tempt him to any pastime. But before leaving the room, she stops for a word of kindness to Ophelia. It is a humane gesture, for she is unwilling to leave Ophelia, the unhappy tool of the King and Polonius, without some kindly and intelligent appreciation of her help:

> And for your part, Ophelia, I do wish
> That your good beauties be the happy cause

Of Hamlet's wildness. So shall I hope your virtues
Will bring him to his wonted way again,
To both your honors. (III.i.38–42)

It is difficult to see in this speech, as Bradley apparently does, the gushing shallow wish of a sentimental woman that class distinctions shall not stand in the way of true love.

At the play, the Queen asks Hamlet to sit near her. She is clearly trying to make him feel he has a place in the court of Denmark. She does not speak again until Hamlet asks her how she likes the play. "The lady doth protest too much, methinks" (III.ii.240) is her immortal comment on the player queen. The scene gives her four more words: when Claudius leaps to his feet, she asks "How fares my Lord?" (III.ii.278).

I will for the moment pass over the scene in the Queen's closet, to follow her quickly through the remainder of the play. After the closet scene, the Queen comes to speak to Claudius. She tells him, as Hamlet has asked her to, that he, Hamlet, is mad, and has killed Polonius. She adds, however, that he now weeps for what he has done. She does not wish Claudius to know what she now knows, how wild and fearsome Hamlet has become. Later, she does not wish to see Ophelia, but hearing how distracted she is, consents. When Laertes bursts in ready to attack Claudius, she immediately steps between Claudius and Laertes to protect the King, and tells Laertes it is not Claudius who has killed his father. Laertes will of course soon learn this, but it is Gertrude who manages to tell him before he can do any meaningless damage. She leaves Laertes and the King together, and then returns to tell Laertes that his sister is drowned. She gives her news directly, realizing that suspense will increase the pain of it, but this is the one time in the play when her usual pointed conciseness would be the mark neither of intelligence nor kindness, and so, gently, and at some length, she tells Laertes of his sister's death, giving him time to recover from the shock of grief, and to absorb the meaning of her words. At Ophelia's funeral the Queen scatters flowers over the grave:

Sweets to the sweet; farewell!
I hop'd thou shouldst have been my Hamlet's wife.
I thought thy bride-bed to have deck'd, sweet maid,
And not t' have strew'd thy grave. (V.i.266–269)

She is the only one present decently mourning the death of someone young, and not heated in the fire of some personal passion.

At the match between Hamlet and Laertes, the Queen believes that Hamlet is out of training, but glad to see him at some sport, she gives him her handkerchief to wipe his brow, and drinks to his success. The drink is poisoned and she dies. But before she dies she does not waste time on vituperation; she warns Hamlet that the drink is poisoned to prevent his drinking it. They are her last words. Those critics who have thought her stupid admire her death; they call it uncharacteristic.

In Act III, when Hamlet goes to his mother in her closet his nerves are pitched at the very height of tension; he is on the edge of hysteria. The possibility of murdering his mother has in fact entered his mind, and he has just met and refused an opportunity to kill Claudius. His mother, meanwhile, waiting for him, has told Polonius not to fear for her, but she knows when she sees Hamlet that he may be violently mad. Hamlet quips with her, insults her, tells her he wishes she were not his mother, and when she, still retaining dignity, attempts to end the interview, Hamlet seizes her and she cries for help. The important thing to note is that the Queen's cry "Thou wilt not murder me" (III.iv.21) is not foolish. She has seen from Hamlet's demeanor that he is capable of murder, as indeed in the next instant he proves himself to be.

We next learn from the Queen's startled "As kill a king" (III.iv.30) that she has no knowledge of the murder, though of course this is only confirmation here of what we already know. Then the Queen asks Hamlet why he is so hysterical:

What have I done, that thou dar'st wag thy tongue
In noise so rude against me? (III.iv.39–40)

Hamlet tells her: it is her lust, the need of sexual passion, which has driven her from the arms and memory of her husband to the incomparably cruder charms of his brother. He cries out that she has not even the excuse of youth for her lust:

O Shame! where is thy blush? Rebellious hell,
If thou canst mutine in a matron's bones,
To flaming youth let virtue be as wax
And melt in her own fire. Proclaim no shame
When the compulsive ardor gives the charge,

Since frost itself as actively doth burn,
And reason panders will. (III.iv.82–87)

This is not only a lust, but a lust which throws out of joint all the structure of human morality and relationships. And the Queen admits it. If there is one quality that has characterized, and will characterize, every speech of Gertrude's in the play, it is the ability to see reality clearly, and to express it. This talent is not lost when turned upon herself:

O Hamlet, speak no more!
Thou turn'st mine eyes into my very soul,
And there I see such black and grained spots
As will not leave their tinct. (III.iv.88–91)

She knows that lust has driven her, that this is her sin, and she admits it. Not that she wishes to linger in the contemplation of her sin. No more, she cries, no more. And then the Ghost appears to Hamlet. The Queen thinks him mad again—as well she might—but she promises Hamlet that she will not betray him—and she does not.

Where, in all that we have seen of Gertrude, is there the picture of "a soft animal nature, very dull and very shallow"? She may indeed be "animal" in the sense of "lustful." But it does not follow that because she wishes to continue a life of sexual experience, her brain is soft or her wit unperceptive.

Some critics, having accepted Gertrude as a weak and vacillating woman, see no reason to suppose that she did not fall victim to Claudius' charms before the death of her husband and commit adultery with him. These critics, Professor Bradley among them (p. 166), claim that the elder Hamlet clearly tells his son that Gertrude has committed adultery with Claudius in the speech beginning "Ay that incestuous, that adulterate beast" (I.v.41ff). Professor Dover Wilson presents the argument:

Is the Ghost speaking here of the o'er-hasty marriage of Claudius and Gertrude? Assuredly not. His "certain term" is drawing rapidly to an end, and he is already beginning to "scent the morning air." Hamlet knew of the marriage, and his whole soul was filled with nausea at the thought of the speedy hasting to "incestuous sheets." Why then should the Ghost waste precious moments in telling Hamlet what he was fully cognisant of before? . . . Moreover, though the word "incestuous" was applicable to the marriage, the rest of the passage is entirely inapplicable to it. Expressions like "witchcraft", "traitorous gifts", "seduce", "shameful lust", and "seeming virtuous" may be noted in passing. But the rest of the quotation leaves no doubt upon the matter. (p. 293)

Professor Dover Wilson and other critics have accepted the Ghost's word "adulterate" in its modern meaning. The Elizabethan word "adultery," however, was not restricted to its modern meaning, but was used to define any sexual relationship which could be called unchaste, including of course an incestuous one.[6] Certainly the elder Hamlet considered the marriage of Claudius and Gertrude to be unchaste and unseemly, and while his use of the word "adulterate" indicates his very strong feelings about the marriage, it would not to an Elizabethan audience necessarily mean that he believed Gertrude to have been false to him before his death. It is important to notice, too, that the Ghost does not apply the term "adulterate" to Gertrude, and he may well have considered the term a just description of Claudius' entire sexual life.

But even if the Ghost used the word "adulterate" in full awareness of its modern restricted meaning, it is not necessary to assume on the basis of this single speech (and it is the only shadow of evidence we have for such a conclusion) that Gertrude was unfaithful to him while he lived. It is quite probable that the elder Hamlet still considered himself married to Gertrude, and he is moreover revolted that her lust for him ("why she would hang on him as if increase of appetite had grown by what it fed on") should have so easily transferred itself to another. This is why he uses the expressions "seduce," "shameful lust," and others. Professor Dover Wilson has himself said "Hamlet knew of the marriage, and his whole soul was filled with nausea at the thought of the speedy hasting to incestuous sheets"; the soul of the elder Hamlet was undoubtedly filled with nausea too, and this could well explain his using such strong language, as well as his taking the time to mention the matter at all. It is not necessary to consider Gertrude an adulteress to account for the speech of the Ghost.

Gertrude's lust was, of course, more important to the plot than we may at first perceive. Charlton Lewis, among others, has shown how Shakespeare kept many of the facts of the plots from which he borrowed without maintaining the structures which explained them. In the original Belleforest story, Gertrude (substituting Shakespeare's more familiar names) was daughter of the king; to become king, it was necessary to marry her. The elder Hamlet, in marrying Gertrude, ousted Claudius from the throne.[7] Shakespeare retained the shell of this in his play. When she no longer has a husband, the form of election would be followed to declare the next king, in this case undoubtedly her son Hamlet. By marrying Gertrude, Claudius "popp'd in between th' election and my hopes" (V.ii.65), that is, kept young Hamlet from the throne. Gertrude's flaw of lust made Claudius' ambition possible, for without taking advantage of the Queen's desire still to be married, he could not have been king.

But Gertrude, if she is lustful, is also intelligent, penetrating, and gifted with a remarkable talent for concise and pithy speech. In all the play, the person whose language hers most closely resembles is Horatio. "Sweets to the sweet," she has said at Ophelia's grave. "Good night sweet prince," Horatio says at the end. They are neither of them dull, or shallow, or slothful, though one of them is passion's slave.

ENDNOTES

1. William Shakespeare, *Hamlet,* with a psycholoanalytical study by Ernest Jones, M.D. (London: Vision Press, 1947), pp. 7–42.

2. A. C. Bradley, *Shakespearean Tragedy* (New York: Macmillan, 1949), p. 167.

3. Harley Granville-Barker, *Prefaces to Shakespeare* (Princeton: Princeton University Press, 1946), 1:227.

4. J. Dover Wilson, *What Happens in Hamlet* (Cambridge: Cambridge University Press, 1951), p. 125.

5. Lily B. Campbell, *Shakespeare's Tragic Heroes* (New York: Barnes & Noble, 1952), pp. 112–113.

6. See Bertram Joseph, *Conscience and the King* (London: Chatto and Windus, 1953), pp. 16–19.

7. Charlton M. Lewis, *The Genesis of Hamlet* (New York: Henry Holt, 1907), p. 36.

II

EXEMPLARY

WOMEN

Introductory Note

THE ESSAY on Margaret Mead was written for a journal of criticism put out by the graduate students at Columbia. As far as I know, it was never read or noticed, although I took that assignment as seriously as any other. The fact is, I accept assignments when I have something I want to say and welcome the opportunity to publish it, or speak it. I refer to a talk by Sandra Gilbert and Susan Gubar given at a Columbia conference that year; their words have since become part of their three-volume *No Man's Land,* the first substantial work to analyze and reveal the centrality of newly empowered women's voices to modernist literature.

"Freud's Daughters" was inspired by the biography of Anna Freud by Elizabeth Young-Bruehl, particularly as that life compared to the work of other women analysts who knew or worked with Freud. It appeared in the *Yale Review,* a journal I especially enjoy writing for, despite the fact that the date on the journal is always many months earlier than the actual date of its appearance.

The essays on Vera Brittain were written for American editions of *Testament of Friendship* and *Testament of Experience,* here one day and gone the next as is the wont of books commercially published in America. I have cut the essay on the friendship between Vera Brittain and Winifred Holtby (and given it the title "Winifred Holtby") to avoid repetition with already published ideas on this friendship in *Writing a Woman's Life.* I had at one time hoped to write a biography of these two, but that was already planned by the literary executor of their estates. I still await, with unabated eagerness, his efforts.

The essay on Virginia Woolf and James Joyce was written for a centenary volume on James Joyce, to be edited by Hugh Kenner and Tom Staley. Because of various academic catastrophes, the centenary volume never appeared. I am pleased to be able to publish this essay here for the first time. "Virginia Woolf in her Fifties" was written for a volume Jane Marcus was editing: *Virginia Woolf: A Feminist Slant.* I remain grateful to her for this chance to record something about Virginia Woolf I had long wanted to say.

2

Margaret Mead and the Question of Woman's Biography

SANDRA GILBERT and Susan Gubar, speaking at the Poetics of Gender Colloquium at Columbia, identified the problem women face in contemplating their "powerful aesthetic foremothers."[1] Gilbert and Gubar were concerned with the female precursors of women writers, but the problem is not confined to literary types. For women, to search for a tradition of past female autonomy and influence is to enter a problematic realm, full of anxiety and ambivalence.

Probably no famous woman represents this anxiety and ambivalence better than Margaret Mead. She was, with the possible exception of Eleanor Roosevelt who came to fame through marriage, the most famous professional woman of her day. Mead made it wholly on her own, as a single gifted female. Her three husbands, her lovers male and female, her child, her friends and crowds of loved ones all bear contradictory evidence of her qualities, personality, genius. Mead's case offers theorists of biography, as well as theorists of female psychology, a rare example of the problematic relation of women to a prominent foremother.

We must begin by asking what paradigm we have for the relation of feminist women today toward matrilineal and patrilineal inheritance. For Gilbert and Gubar, Freud's model of the family romance is particularly useful. They see the choice a woman must make as being between what Freud calls "mature" renunciation of the mother and "regressive" identification with her (4–5). Since the woman is, for Freud, defined as castrated and incapable of a satisfactory oedipal struggle, she is destined either to subdue her own desire for the mother into a desire for the father's power in the form of a baby boy, or, accepting the mother, to become a woman who is defined by the patriarchy as regressive, to some degree monstrous. While feminists may quail at this unhappy choice, the anxiety they and all women feel in the face of the patriarchal culture Freud was recognizing, describing, and supporting is inevitable. To the degree that Mead, as a mother figure, represents claims against the "family romance," all women must, inevitably, regard her with anxiety. It is my contention that the anxiety women feel toward foremothers, literary or not, is inevitable because either the foremothers were denied full autonomy or else were too efficiently punished for having achieved it. Identification, in either case, is perilous. As is the human wont, we blame the foremother for her inevitable failure.

If the boy is anxious in coming to terms with his actual or spiritual father, yet there is a recognizable satisfaction in the quest. The girl, on the other hand, must, as Gilbert and Gubar recognize, make an enormous investment of psychic energy as she becomes involved in an arduous process of self-definition, and finds frightening and inadequate the few female models available to her. "Female artists," Gilbert and Gubar write, are "haunted and daunted by the autonomy of such figures" as their accomplished female predecessors, experiencing "mingled feelings of rivalry and anxiety" (11). Intimacy with the mother threatens the daughter with a share in the mother's subordination; disdain of the mother threatens the daughter with the bitter rewards of the female intruder into the patriarchy. As Nancy Chodorow has demonstrated, the daughter is left in a no-win position, figuring out not "how to be feminine, but how not to be her mother," how, that is, not to be diminished, not to suffer as her mother has suffered. As Chodorow writes, we do not know "what self would look like in a non-gendered society."[2]

The effects of this inevitable ambivalence and anxiety on the part of the "daughters" have been noticeable on women's biographies of women. Before the current women's movement, it was difficult to find a woman's biography of an accomplished woman that was not palpably terrified of making any unseemly claims on behalf of the woman subject. Avoiding large claims was no doubt made easier by the fact that the subjects themselves were usually unable to express with full honesty the exemplary meaning of their lives, and because of their own anxieties, were inclined to protect themselves by trying to palliate the patriarchy. Betty Friedan's comments on Mead suggest the sort of problem this has created for biographers.

In *The Feminine Mystique,* Friedan recounted Mead's many accomplishments and innovations on the whole question of gender. Yet, Friedan concluded, "this is not the vision the mystique took from Margaret Mead, nor is it the vision she continues to offer. Increasingly, in her own pages, her interpretation blurs, is subtly transformed into a glorification of women in the female role—as defined by the sexual biological function." Friedan identifies the central irony of female models: "the role of Margaret Mead as the professional spokesman of femininity would have been less important if American women had taken the example of her own life, instead of listening to what she said in her books."[3]

Much the same might have been said of Helene Deutsch and George Eliot, for example, or, indeed, of Jane Austen, who herself avoided the marital conclusion so imperative for all her heroines. What happens with all these women is that we desire of them greater courage and imaginative originality than was possible: as Margaret Atwood has remarked, "there are a lot of things that somebody looking back at us will be able to see that we just don't see because it's not a choice for us to see it. It's not part of our vocabulary."[4] Jane Howard reports in her biography of Mead that Friedan, who had accused Mead of "incredible vacillation" regarding the women's movement, was moved at Mead's funeral to "pay my respects. I felt that Mead, who was born twenty years before me, had gone as far as she could with feminism and that I, in reacting to her, took it a step further and was in a way her heir. I felt part of a procession."[5]

We can, I therefore conclude, mark a distinction between what I might here call the Gilbert and Gubar theory of female attitudes toward foremothers, and the response toward predecessors that has emerged since the establishment of the modern women's movement within the last fifteen years. As Bell Gale Chevigny has put it, in an essay vital to this discussion, "our education and general culture lay so much greater stress on our understanding of men than of women that we approach the lives of our . . . foremothers with few and arbitrary tools." But even as we grapple today "with some aspect of this ignorance which is so costly to ourselves," we are, I believe, escaping from the "family romance" into a new understanding of motherhood, and of our relations to our mothers and foremothers. I think we are learning to experience female autonomy "without a sense of abandoning the mother," just as we have grown able to forgive our foremothers and our women friends their inevitable ambivalence and fears.[6] I do not agree with Gilbert and Gubar, therefore, that Maxine Kumin's attitude toward Anne Sexton in her poem "How It Is" is characterized with the same ambivalence and anxiety Woolf or Dickinson or earlier women felt toward precursors. In understanding the anxieties the patriarchy inevitably arouses in women, we enable ourselves, with whatever pain, to love, forgive, and admire those women who preceded or accompanied us on the way to female autonomy.

Of the two current biographies of Margaret Mead, one is virtually without value, except for the anecdotal plums to be plucked from it to suit purposes such as mine. Jane Howard is a snapper-up of inconsidered trifles from whoever was available, or living, or ready to talk. The result is the sort of journalistic jumble of impressions, errors, and occasional insights characteristic of *People* or the newsmagazines. Mead's daughter tells us that her mother was "barely five feet tall," her father "just over six foot five,"[7] while Howard calls Bateson "nearly a foot taller."[8] This is the least of it. What is far worse is that anyone who talked about Mead, particularly if what she or he said was "sexy," or nasty, or titillating, is solemnly recorded, as though knowledge of a person might be compiled from a collection of all available anecdotes. So Mead's first husband, the only one to survive, is allowed remarks on her which in a rejected husband and octogenarian are certainly questionable and biased. Survival does not insure truthfulness. Howard has accumulated "facts" wholly unaware of the narrative imperatives of biography: As David Bromwich recently demonstrated, the pictures we have of Keats and Joyce are the creations of their biographers, and not necessarily true.[9] Enthusiasm has engendered them. Doubtless, we shall take a long time to admit that biographies are fictions necessary to the biographer, but such I believe inevitably to be the case. Apart from all other considerations, the chance involved in what "facts," documents, memories survive has been far too little credited: we dislike admitting that the results of our scholarship, while rewarding, may be far from conclusive. Howard, avoiding any purpose other than the desire to be widely read, leaves the question of women's biographies just about where it was.

We have, at the same time, in *With a Daughter's Eye,* a memoir of Mead and her second husband, Gregory Bateson, a work that considerably advances the question both of women's biography and of daughters' attitudes toward mothers and foremothers. There is a self-consciousness in the book, the effect of, among much else, feminist criticism, that marks it as an advance over the stage of anxiety and ambivalence described by Gilbert and Gubar. As Mary Catherine Bateson reports: "Because I have not wanted to make myself available to biographers, I have felt an obligation to put my experience down in my own words" (227). If we recall two phrases of Chevigny's in connection with women writing the biography of women, we perceive the milestone we have in the Bateson book: Chevigny realized that her biographic subject, Margaret Fuller, was offered no precedent by nineteenth-century society for "what Fuller was groping to become." Bateson, of course, had such a "precedent" in her own mother. When Chevigny suggests that "it is nearly inevitable that women writing about women will symbolically reflect their internalized relations with their mothers and in some measure re-create them,"[10] the uniqueness of the Bateson testimony becomes clear.

I do not wish to claim for Bateson, or anyone, total awareness of all internalized ideas; nonetheless, the pattern of father-son relations, that is, the more open acknowledgment of ambition, destiny, and love-rivalry, is evident in this daughter's account. We hear the echo of a certain male acknowledgment of the harsh demands of fathers in Bateson's account of her birth as recorded "with a series of neurological tests and manipulations that are disturbing to see on the film today, with our growing sense of the importance of tenderness in the delivery room. . . . My friends ask whether it makes me angry to see that, and I respond, no, here I am, I'm okay" (26).

Because in Bateson's family, as she tells us, "we never simply live, we are always reflecting on our lives" (20) (or, as all writers discover, nothing has really happened until it has been written down), this biography permits Bateson to repossess her life. She realizes that the innovations Mead "made as a parent were actually greater than they now seem because so many have since been incorporated in the patterns of society" (33). These innovations" were possible, Bateson writes, because they "came out of a certainty of her own love, a sense that she had been loved and could trust herself to love in turn, with a continuity of spontaneous feeling even where she was introducing variation. She was prepared to take responsibility because she did not suspect herself of buried ambivalence either toward me or toward her own parents" (32). The result for Bateson was a choice of life and loving that represented many models, not the single one prescribed by convention: "I might have built on materials I was offered any of many life-styles: marriage with children or marriage without children, marriage open or faithful, transient or sustained, home-making or outside career, solitude or commitment, the love of men or the love of women. It seems to me that most of what she taught me about how to behave was rooted in the specifics of individuals or households rather than in general principles" (72–73).

Stephen Toulmin, reviewing these books, has chosen to emphasize Mead's "daemon," her vocation to "bring the human sciences to the American consciousness. Those who were repelled by the manipulative aspects of her daemon often saw her work for the advancement of science as self-advancement. Yet this was the price she was ready to pay."[11] Her daemon also enlarged, by example, and by her daughter's testimony, the possibilities of female lives. To make mistakes, to be sneered at, to be ludicrously popularized, as by Howard, is a small enough price, and one we can be certain she, and those whose lives she has enabled, painfully but gladly pay for the chance to revise society's expectations of women. Despite the care she took not to offend the American cult of motherhood in the fifties—how outspoken revolutionary women can ever be is central to the question of female anxiety and ambivalence—she made new female destinies possible, providing when the time came the model Fuller had lacked. That her biological daughter should testify so believably to the praise and honor, beyond anxiety and ambivalence, she feels for her mother, is not only an important tribute, but the herald of an important change in the hearts of women as they look back upon their women predecessors.

1985

ENDNOTES

1. Sandra Gilbert and Susan Gubar, "'Forward Into the Past': The Complex Female Affiliation Complex," unpub. essay, p. 2.

2. Nancy Chodorow, *The Reproduction of Mothering: Psychoanalysis and the Sociology of Gender* (Berkeley: University of California Press, 1978), pp. 137n. and 218.

3. Betty Friedan, *The Feminine Mystique,* 10th anniv. ed. (New York: Norton, 1974), pp. 137, 145.

4. Margaret Atwood, "Interview with Margaret Atwood," *River Styx* (1984), 15:21.

5. Jane Howard, *Margaret Mead: A Life* (New York: Simon & Schuster, 1984), p. 426.

6. Bell Gale Chevigny, "Daughters Writing: Toward a Theory of Women's Biography," *Feminist Studies* (1983), 9:94, 95, 96.

7. Mary Catherine Bateson, *With a Daughter's Eyes: A Memoir of Margaret Mead and Gregory Bateson* (New York: Morrow, 1984), p. 20.

8. Howard, *Margaret Mead,* p. 253.

9. David Bromwich, "The Uses of Biography," *Yale Review* (1984), 73:161–176.

10. Chevigny, "Daughters Writing," pp. 89, 80.

11. Stephen Toulmin, "Margaret Mead's Daemon," *New York Review of Books,* December 8, 1984, 31:9.

3

Freud's Daughters

"For the sake of euphony, and to avoid clumsy locu-
tions like 'his/her' or, worse, 's/he,' I have used the
traditional masculine form to apply to both sexes."
—Peter Gay, *Freud: A Life for Our Time,* 1988

"For the first time I had a daydream or a story with a
female main person in my head."
—Anna Freud to Lou Andreas-Salomé, 1922

FREUD EXPLAINED to the poet H. D., when she came to him for
analysis, that she had "two things to hide, one that you were a girl,
the other that you were a boy." Furthermore, Freud told her, not only
did she want to be a boy, she wanted to be a hero. Thus succinctly
did Freud enunciate the dilemma with which his new "science" endowed all young women not easily devoted to what he saw as the
"purely feminine" type. Anna Freud, like her father, associated public
or professional achievement with masculinity; feminine achievement
consisted in being "a pretty enough girl really to be attractive to men,"
like Mathilde, Freud's oldest daughter, who loved dancing. Marie Bonaparte saw her own writings as her potency; when she was using her
head "she was male, and she fantasized that her head was male." For

Anna Freud, her writing was a boy, her "penis child." All intelligent women had to choose between what Freud, and Anna Freud after him, defined as distinctly a masculine or feminine destiny. As a result, Freud's women followers teetered uncertainly between two destinies, clearly the rightful possessors of neither. Anna Freud honored the memory of her friend Marie Bonaparte exactly as her father had honored the memory of Lou Andreas-Salomé, by praising her work as the perfect blending "of feminine charm, intuition and longings with the relentless sharpness of a masculine intellect." Yet this "perfect blending" was never explicitly recommended nor was it achievable in any but the most exceptional cases. In short, all accomplished women were deviants, part of a puzzle none of them, with the remarkable exception of Karen Horney, saw any point in solving.

With the publication of *Anna Freud* by Elisabeth Young-Bruehl we have a chance to review the lives of all those major women who accepted Freud as the father of a new science and the father of their minds and hearts. That in doing so they had to accept his binary view of human nature, masculine versus feminine, left them, and his daughter most of all, poised on a contradiction they managed to live while failing to narrate or confront. Peter Gay's refusal to grapple with what he considers clumsy or uneuphonious language in order to rescue women from the category of "other" emphasizes the recalcitrance of Freud's followers, men as well as women, boldly to reconsider one major aspect of his theory. It is, among much else, to Young-Bruehl's credit that she does not observe Gay's allegiance to the "traditional masculine form," managing nonetheless to write with precision as well as grace. Although never polemical, she is at least ready to set forth the problem.

In *Anna Freud*, Young-Bruehl has discovered and, further, created a life almost perfect in its navigation between the poles of Freud's greatness and his theories of womanhood. Anna Freud, because she was Freud's actual daughter and because he willingly made her the keeper of his life and works, never lost her father's love and never needed the love of another man. Freud called her his Antigone, but, in her birth, she was Athene: no woman birthed her, although women not her mother nurtured her in infancy and throughout her life. She did not marry, but lived what both she and Freud recognized as a "masculine" life, thriving on the love of women and never questioning

Freud's definitions of "masculine" and "feminine." She had early found the perfect man, and did not bother to seek another. Her mother was easily the least significant person in her life.

One of Freud's analysands had said: "Well, look at her father. This is an ideal that very few men could live up to, and it would surely be a comedown for her to attach herself to a lesser man." To this Gay adds: "If Freud had fully recognized the measure of his power over his daughter, he might have hesitated to analyse her." The more relevant and vibrant question, surely, is not Freud's failure to recognize the measure of his power over his daughter, but to face, with greater pain and generosity, even at the risk of losing her adoration, the essential conflict of the life into which he had, with however benign intention, led her. He might in the light of *her* life have reconsidered his absolute division of all lives between the masculine and the feminine. As it was, his paternal devotion falls somewhere between that of Margaret Fuller's father, who deserted her at adolescence leaving her no path in life, and of Marianne Thornton's father, well described by another devoted student of Freud, Lionel Trilling.

Trilling, writing in the 1950s about Marianne Thornton, an aunt of E. M. Forster whose biography Forster had just published, remarked: "There seems never to have been any question of her marrying. Mr. Forster does not suggest that her father was a possible barrier to matrimony. Yet Marianne's relation to her father was exactly of the sort that often makes it difficult for a girl to marry. . . . He took her very seriously; he wrote her charming and loving verses, and he also taught her to examine her life and to mend it. . . . He taught her to understand public affairs and to discuss them with him; . . . he engaged her as 'a sort of secretary' as soon as she could write legibly. Add that he was a handsome man, of perfect integrity, heroic in his notions of work, and magnanimous in all his acts. It would have been hard for her to look upon his like again."

Having, like Marianne Thornton, accepted her father absolutely, Anna Freud was never distracted from her life work by worries about possible romantic attachments. But neither did she reach even Gay's compromise with Freud's gender distinctions, or his ambivalence toward women's achievements. That Freud "did not conceal his wry distrust of the feminist movement," Gay writes, "beautifully illustrates this confusion of alliances and positions. He might hold to the sweet, competent housewife as his ideal, but he never obstructed—on the contrary, he fostered—aspiring female psychoanalysts, and took their views seriously." Yet while writing to Ernest Jones that in "my experience you have not to scratch too deeply the skin of a so-called masculine woman to bring her feminity to light," he did not ever seek to question or analyze the terms "masculine woman," and "femininity," the nonsense of which his statement demonstrates. It is, therefore, debatable that he took the views of women analysts seriously, unless one amends it to read "certain of their views." Since neither Anna nor (with one exception) any of those women who had studied with Freud or were of European origin ever dared to challenge his sharp gender distinctions, we must assume they knew how violently such a challenge would be dismissed as heresy. Here is Anna at the end of her life:

Freud "was convinced that anatomy determined whether predominantly male or female qualities would be developed and prepare the individual for his or her differing future life tasks. As little as the sexual manifestations of boys and girls differ from each other in the oral and anal phases, as significant is the marked dissimilarity in the phallic phase during which the anatomical equipment of the female child puts her at a disadvantage in relations to the possessor of the phallus. . . . [T]he girl in turn develops penis envy and the wish for a substitute for what has been withheld from her, a wish that ultimately culminates in the wish to have a child." Young-Bruehl goes on to remark, as Gay does not, that the "professional success of women analysts—including Anna Freud herself—had never been taken by Freud as reason to recant his general remarks, just as he had never advanced the hope that women analysts would be a vanguard of cultural change."

Anna Freud developed into a most effective and lovable human being, able to administer without bitterness and to struggle without overt hostility. She had a love for children that was not personal: can hundreds of children replace a phallus? If one plucks from her biography her remarkable personality traits, they form the portrait of an enormously appealing individual. To me and probably to many female readers she seemed an inevitable alter ego, partly recognizable, partly hidden, wholly admirable.

None of Freud's other "daughters," Helene Deutsch, Melanie Klein, Lou Andreas-Salomé, Margaret Mahler, Marie Bonaparte—to name only a few who have come recently before us in biographies or memoirs—escaped any more than did Anna their acceptance of and suffering with his fatal gender bifurcation. Only one of those who both knew Freud personally and gave their lives to psychoanalysis challenged Freud's view of women; her fate was to be thrown out of the psychoanalytic establishment. As Robert Coles put it, "For years I have heard various psychoanalysts dismiss her ideas out of hand, or scorn them as of little value or interest." Her name was Karen Horney, and her biography, *A Mind of Her Own: The Life of Karen Horney,* has recently been published. Its author, Susan Quinn, puts the matter emphatically enough: "She had discovered that there was little room in psychoanalysis for what could be called the loyal opposition. Her attempts to be a critic from within, taking Freud to task for his views on female sexuality, had been written off by Freud and forgotten by nearly everyone else. Nor was she content to be called, as she so often was, 'a good clinician.' Everyone knew this was a subtle put-down, often applied to females with 'good instincts' but no intellectual rigor." As Quinn's biography makes clear, "there were many other women in psychoanalysis who did not react as Horney did to Freud's ideas about them. Only Karen Horney possessed the right history, and temperament, to take up the challenge."

What was that history, what was that temperament? Two facts leap to the foreground: Horney was not a Jew, and she did not love her father. Indeed, she profoundly disliked him, finding him, as she wrote, "simply unbearable. He is low, stupid, materialistic, without self-discipline and self respect, and a hypocrite besides."

Her disdain for her father is the easier of the two facts to ponder; certainly it distinguishes her sharply from her female psychoanalytic peers. Margaret Mahler and Helene Deutsch both adored their fathers, and scorned their mothers. Both were treated like "sons" by their fathers, although Mahler alone seems to have resented her father's refusal to consider her as a potential or successful sex object for other men. Deutsch wrote of her father: "He was devoted to me and accepted me fully, not as a substitute for a boy but as his spiritual heir as well as his beloved girl with the beautiful eyes." Anna Freud might have used much the same words, both here and when Deutsch spoke of "one feminine type in particular: the daughter who adopts her father's ideals and fights on his behalf, along with him, for these goals." Together with the devotion to the father goes, it would seem inevitably, what Deutsch frankly called "my hate of my mother and horror of identification with her." Deutsch came to realize "how many of the positive ideals in [her] life are a reaction against her," but nonetheless fully embraced the view that the emancipated woman is masculinized. Anna Freud is less outspoken, but Young-Bruehl's biography makes brilliantly clear that Anna admitted no identification with her mother, forgot often even to mention her, and found women substitutes for her all her life. She wanted "to be judged by her father as more reasonable than the girls and women he had in analysis," while "Martha Freud's remarks about Anna's plainness and drab clothes and unattractive flat shoes were a source of tension, and Anna Freud had little patience with her mother's dedication to elegant dresses, coiffures, and cosmetics."

Horney, on the other hand, sympathized with her mother, and dreaded the times when her father, a sea captain, was home. Where biographical insights into the narratives of women's lives must intersect most sharply with Freudian dogma is precisely in the daughter's identification with the father as in Anna Freud's case. The astonishment that students of Helene Deutsch's work must inevitably feel is caused by her adamant refusal to identify herself as a woman, to see women's central problem, not in their "escape" into masculinity, but in their flight from the powerlessness, the aching dullness, of femininity. Karen Horney was able to face the dilemma of being a woman in a Freudian universe because she had not originally identified with her father, did not scorn or hate her mother, above all, found the courage and honesty to evaluate her own emotions by that method Quinn claims she found early and continued through her life: she tested them against her own experience.

What did it mean that Horney was not a Jew? How much should be made of this? Marie Bonaparte, a Princess of Greece, was also Gentile: she, however, was rich and powerful all her life, able to arrange for Freud's escape from the Nazis as for much else. Without a medical degree, she never had to struggle through all-male medical schools or societies that denigrated any but the most conventional careers for women. Certainly the likelihood, which Mahler and Deutsch make especially vivid in their memoirs, of being despised and hated simultaneously as a woman and a Jew forced upon these women a defensive move: they established themselves securely within the patriarchal fortress of psychoanalysis, which accepted them as acolytes as well as Jews. In a more benign atmosphere, as in the United States, less virulent anti-Semitism trained some women to the necessary experience of being outsiders. But the violent hatred of Jews even in pre-Nazi Austria and

Poland drained the courage needed to fight as a feminist. For Horney, this primary drain upon her courage did not exist.

Freud has often been placed with Darwin and Einstein as one of the great "fathers" of modern science, but in the case of the other two we know that the respect they inspire in those who succeeded them does not require strict allegience to every aspect of their work. Freudians, once they submerge themselves in his teachings, seem to have entered a labyrinth or maze from which there is no escape, only the continual study of the endless paths, all blind, all pre-charted. To know a convert to a religion who cannot see beyond it is to know doctrinaire Freudians, who distinguish themselves from more humble discoverers of universal truth only by their great intelligence and extensive educations. They fill us, therefore, with terror and pity; if we are women and not whole-hearted Freudians, more with terror.

In defending her father's every sacred word against all who would change any of it, Anna Freud often used the word "heresy." Young-Bruehl notes that it was just as intolerable to her "to think of any rearrangement of his theoretical house as it was to think of rearranging his study." After a lifetime that she thought of, certainly in her imagination, as "masculine" (she even imagined her female dog as male, so that it might better protect her) she could still, as we have seen, insist upon her father's definition of an inevitable "feminine" role.

Of Freud's "daughters," therefore, Horney alone was attracted early to feminism, Horney alone questioned Freud's edict that "we deal only with one libido which behaves in a male way." Sandor Rado, one of Freud's many Luther-like betrayers, pointed out that (as Quinn quotes him) analysis "was not the study of the life of a person, digging out what the turning points, what the problems were. . . . It was a search for opportunities to apply certain Freudian insights . . . castration complex, Oedipus complex, narcissism, oral eroticism, anal eroticism . . . the patient's production was very soon oriented by that, because he saw that what is fruitful is if he talks about these matters." When it came to the turning points and problems in the lives of women, rigor was even less appropriate or useful. Only in the very early days, when his first women patients helped Freud to understand repression and to provide what Bertha Pappenheim called "the talking cure," did he seem supple enough to construct a scheme not somehow dictated by the patriarchal structure of society or the male-centered appeal of the oedipus plot.

Yet Anna Freud, if one regards her life rather than her pronouncements of allegiance to the Freudian scripture, seems strangely guilty of great female accomplishment. She worked in an area, early childhood, upon which Freud had not written extensively, and where the demands of sex roles might, to some extent, be ignored. (When she worked with adults, particularly male homosexuals, she cast great light on the problems of women but not on her announced subject. She considered homosexuality to be an illness, to be curable, to be regrettable.) She found support and love from women and men in an extended family of remarkable range and devotion. She gave her life to a cause of great importance, and if she believed herself to be engaged primarily in defending her father's work, she expanded and modified it in places where his edicts had not been laid down. She was a person of high intelligence, great kindness, and endless courage and generosity.

What she was not was a model for a new female destiny. Like Freud's other "daughters," with the exception only of Horney, she never questioned Freud's entirely masculine grammar of the psyche. I take some comfort in learning that, toward the end of her life, she, who doted on detective fiction for relaxation, would read works with female heroes, even though she had never been able to imagine such creatures in her own fantasies, and had not previously cared to read about them. But there can be no comfort in the fact that Freud's latest biographer, Peter Gay, will not make the admittedly difficult effort to use less exclusive pronouns. For Monique Wittig was surely right when she recognized the pronoun as the most insidious of masculine claims to be the only subject. "It is," she writes, "without justification of any kind, without questioning, that personal pronouns somehow engineer gender all through language, taking it along with them quite naturally, so to speak, in any kind of talk, parley, or philosophical treatise. And although they are instrumental in activating the notion of gender, they pass unnoticed." In that part of the unconscious where ideas of gender lie buried, Freud's biographers, it seems, do not dare to tread.

1989

4

Vera Brittain's *Testament of Experience*

WHEN VERA Brittain was a tiny child in 1897 she watched, passively but one assumes with appreciation, the flags in the streets of Macclesfield flying for Queen Victoria's diamond jubilee. This may have been the last public celebration Brittain experienced without a sense of outrage: experience for her was early to become a head-on encounter with event. Youth is given to us; experience we pay for. But even Brittain's youth, disrupted by the war that was to claim so many of her generation, transformed itself from a time of happenstance to one of terror and anger. It would be the pattern of her life.

Testament of Experience was the third of Brittain's testaments, and by the time of its publication in 1957, she recognized that she was writing in one of the forms created and developed in the twentieth century, and unique to it. About 1930, she tells us, "John Grierson invented the word 'documentary,' which he later defined as 'the creative treatment of actuality.'" Nothing has more marked the literature of our time than the blurring of fact and fiction, the discovery that "fact" is difficult to establish, that "fiction" is by no means confined to the realm of fantasy, that both are contrived to provide us with story, the ordering of events into narrative. One need think only of James Joyce writing to a friend in Dublin to inquire whether a man of a certain height might let himself down from the railings at 7 Eccles Street and drop unharmed into the areaway. When institutionalized religion and the rationalization of patriotism had ceased satisfactorily to justify human pain, writers—the greatest and the least—set out to create a more honest "representation" of "reality," which "justified" nothing. All became relative and quotidian. All became experience.

As a writer Vera Brittain stands apart from her contemporaries on two counts. First, her rendering of experience, her "documentation," did not comfortably assume (though she was a while learning this) the form of the novel. Second, because she was a woman, Brittain's record of what had happened to her in the larger world of events was not only different, but adjudged insignificant. At the time she wrote *Testament of Youth* nobody supposed that the public would be interested in another war book, let alone a war book by a woman. Yet it became a best-seller and made her famous.

Brittain was not a great novelist. But she understood the terror of the world she lived through; she did not, as many have done, protect herself from that terror and anxiety by turning her back on the implications of events, or adopting the unexamined commandments of a narrow creed. She was willing, above all, to admit that being a woman gave her a special insight into the cruelty of nationalistic actions, and permitted her to report them in a new way.

She was, unlike her friend Holtby, a "typical woman"; she did not stride the earth like an oversized Diana. Rather, she must have seemed—and in some degree this determined her fate—like any womanly woman from the middle class, pretty, small, often frightened. Men seemed to fall in love with her on sight, and in droves. (The reader may guess at her demeanor and features from the fact that, on a speaking tour of the United States after the success of *Testament of Youth*, she was taken for the Duchess of Windsor—the abdication was a recent event—

because they were both small and wore their dark hair parted in the middle. Brittain denied any further likeness, but in a 1949 photograph of her the resemblance is undeniable.)

But however suited by looks to a womanly life, she fought that definition from her earliest days. Her whole experience can be seen as an attempt not to be defined by any of society's strictures on women. It is too concise but not inaccurate to say that she devoted her life to a redefinition of women and peace. Looking about us today, we cannot claim that she was successful in either struggle. But struggles interest us less for their success than for their purpose and meaning. And one of the sad consolations of failure is that one speaks as poignantly to a later age which one's efforts have failed to transform.

Her first fight, as the daughter of an overwhelmingly conventional middle-class business family, was to be permitted to attend Oxford. But it is characteristic of her that, once there, she fought, not to stay for the sake of her studies, but to leave for the sake of war. When she returned to Oxford after the war, after the deaths of her fiancé, two friends, and her brother, she was an outsider, isolated by her war experiences as a nurse and, she felt, derided by her fellow students in their postwar giddiness and desire to forget. In *Testament of Friendship* she gives an account of how she felt persecuted in the course of a college debate: she was to use this scene in her first novel, *The Dark Tide,* not having yet discovered her right form to be the documentary. She and Holtby, the only two women at Somerville College entitled to wear active service ribbons, met Queen Mary on her visit to Oxford; Brittain was to comment that "this was the first time since returning to Oxford I hadn't to feel ashamed of the War."

At Oxford, as at every point in her life to follow, Brittain found herself living two lives at once, the conventional and the revolutionary, the old life and the new. The Oxford to which she returned after the war was not the same Oxford she had left, nor was she the same person. Further than this, no one of her generation who mattered to her was left from that earlier life. The transformation she underwent between 1918, when her brother was killed, and 1920, when her friendship with Winifred Holtby began, was a complete one, as though she had been born again, yet was haunted by her former life.

How she and Holtby went to London to establish themselves as journalists and novelists has been told in *Testament of Friendship*. Holtby provided Brittain with that rarest of human experiences, a friendship nothing but death could sever—not distance, nor marriage, nor what cynics call, between professional women, competitiveness, nor their individual failures and successes. Yet, ironically, what strikes us today as most extraordinary about Brittain is precisely that she was, in an essential way, an ordinary person. Life which had shaped Holtby large, blond, goddesslike, and loving, formed Vera Brittain from the prescribed model for women. Yet this small, pretty, intelligent, but unexceptional woman lived out experiences as unusual today as they were then, and found the form—her "testament"—in which to write of them. She has not only offered us one of the rare accounts of women's friendship; she has also here described her refusal to live by any of the accepted scripts for women's lives. Those professional young women who today have children and work can find in her story a pattern for that brave undertaking. Of the two children born to her marriage, the daughter, Shirley Williams, early became a member of Parliament and, later, of the Labour government.

After the war and her return to Oxford, Brittain never expected to marry. Her life with Holtby in Doughty Street seemed to hold all possibility and vitality: it is nicely emblematic of the vigorous attitude of those two young women that the only disaster of the period—publishers' rejection slips for them spelled not disaster but experience—was the death of their pet tortoise, who died because they did not recognize his need to hibernate, but kept waking and feeding him. "I do hope," Brittain wrote to Winifred, who was back in Yorkshire, "that, after this lovely period of peace, some devastating male is not going to push into my life and upset it again. Just when things look so promising, too."

The "devastating male" was not a likely occurrence at this time. As Brittain was to write in *Testament of Youth*, she and Holtby were aware of being "superfluous women," and Brittain, again in a letter, reported to Holtby on the matter: "*The Times* is exciting itself over the surplus women, as revealed by the census—101 per 1,000, I believe, to be exact! They were quite nice to us in a leading article today, and said that women who had lost their husbands or lovers in the War couldn't be expected on that account to relegate themselves to perpetual widowhood or spinsterhood. But they suggested that women who were willing to seek work abroad would not only obtain for themselves a better chance of getting a husband but would be doing their country a service! It never seems to occur to anybody that some women may

not want husbands; the article even talked about 'finding the domesticity they desire'! Personally, I haven't the least objection to being
superfluous so long as I am allowed to be useful." Nor was her generation of women, Brittain has assured us, naive about the problems
of "sublimation": "We were now capable of the frank analysis of our
own natures, and the stoical, if reluctant, acceptance of realistic conclusions."

Frank about desire, they were analytic about marriage. Between
marriage and desire women have doomed themselves, as Brittain knew,
to domesticity and marginality. She wrote—and the words are no less
startling today—that she believed marriage irrelevant to the main purpose of life: "For a woman as for a man, marriage might enormously
help or devastatingly hinder the growth of her power to contribute
something impersonally valuable to the community in which she lived,
but it was not that power, and could not be regarded as an end in
itself. Nor, even, were children ends in themselves; it was useless to
go on producing human beings merely in order that they, in their
sequence, might produce others, and never turn from this business of
continuous procreation to the accomplishment of some definite and
lasting piece of work." Her view of marriage bore little relation to
those romantic ideas which for centuries—and today as much as ever—
underlay women's ideas about the purpose of courtship. Brittain spoke,
not of marriage divorced from love (not even friendship is divorced
from love, as all who ever wrote about it have known), but of "the
loyal, friendly emotion which arises between mutually respectful equals
of opposite sex who are working side by side for some worthwhile
end."

Brittain's perception of the delusions inherent in all institutions, but
especially the institutions of government and marriage, marks all her
work. She smelled out hypocrisy, and knew the suffering of its victims.
She noted that soon after the war, for example, while the medical hos-
pitals refused to take women for training as doctors because they could
not teach "certain unpleasant subjects of medicine to mixed audi-
ences," they simultaneously lowered the age of admission for nurses:
the shortage of nurses made this advisable; nor was nursing a profession for which men cared to apply.

But women have been clear-sighted about marriage before; they
have either, therefore, avoided it or forgotten their earlier trepidations.
Vera Brittain, typically, did neither. She married, but without forget-

ting or denying that she knew marriage to be death for women as individuals.

There is another point to be made. The love which Brittain had given to her dead fiancé she did not expect to recur, and it never would. This is a theme which is repeated in her novels. Both in *Honourable Estate* and in *Born 1925*, the woman protagonist loves (and passionately makes love to, once) a man who is killed in the war. The women feel for these early loves what Brittain felt for Roland Leighton: that she wanted nothing so much as to love him and bear *his* child.

The marriages which follow for these women are a compromise between passion and companionship. In *Honourable Estate*, Ruth Alleyndene ponders: "Only after their wedding had she fully realized the contrast which would confront her between that earlier union springing spontaneously from passion, and a marriage based upon tender affection and mutual respect. Her memory of desperate love made adjustment more difficult, she knew. Passion had been, for its brief duration, violent and abandoned, while affection was considerate and infinitely patient; yet the rapture in that passion had made everything easy and unpremeditated, whereas the relationship between herself and Denis involved a conscious co-operation which demanded as much from intelligence as instinct. Undoubtedly more difficult, but perhaps, in the long run, better worth-while?" Brittain knew that if men made the mistake of conflating marriage and desire, as in novels by Jane Austen and others they often do, at least they can still have their work in the world and their libraries at home. For women to lose themselves in marriage, particularly if there are children, is to lose their selves, probably beyond recall.

Brittain is unusual in not only writing of this, but living it. This, no doubt, is why the "documentary" form was essential to her. Great novelists like George Eliot can live what they cannot imagine for their women characters. Unravelers of experience like Brittain dare to live what is revolutionary, and write of it, but not in fiction. As the passage quoted from her novel demonstrates, her characters think as though they were taking part in a formal debate. In life, one may think clearly and act, not without great effort, upon those thoughts. But characters in novels move by intenser passions.

And so Brittain knew that the pattern for marriage was not romance in any of its forms, but friendship. And she knew this with a determination that shaped her life. Her friend Holtby, who *was* a novelist, has pictured that determination in a minor character in two novels: she was too wise to create a major character like Vera Brittain. Delia Vaughan, thus, speaks in Holtby's novel *The Crowded Street:* " 'Do you seriously intend to stay here all your life? To wash dishes that the next meal will soil, to arrange flowers that will wither in a week, to walk in fear and trembling of what Mrs. Marshall Gurney will say, although you know quite well that she hasn't got the intelligence to say anything worth saying?' . . .

" 'We can't all be clever,' she said, without much joy in the thought.

" 'Clever? Who said that we all had to be clever? But we have to have courage. The whole position of women is what it is to-day, because so many of us have followed the line of least resistance, and have sat down placidly in a little provincial town, waiting to get married.' " In Holtby's *The Land of Green Ginger,* the Brittain-like character is even more minor, but with decided opinions: "All you have to do is want enough," she says to the heroine before disappearing from the novel; "Look how I fought my parents to get them to let me try for Somerville. People will always give way to you if you really mean to do something, and all getting on in life is getting people to give way." This may not be how Brittain would have put it, but Holtby has caught some of the vigor necessary to an active life. Holtby realized, furthermore, that so few people know what they want from life that life, perhaps amazed at such clarity of purpose, occasionally grants their desire to those who can name it. As Brittain lived out with Holtby a friendship which only Holtby's death in 1935 ended (I have written of this in the introduction to *Testament of Friendship*), so she lived out a new kind of marriage.

But not in the beginning. Marriage began for Vera Brittain in extraordinarily unpromising circumstances: as a faculty wife in America. George Catlin had accepted, before his marriage to her, a professorship at Cornell University in Ithaca, New York. Had the role of isolated and unhappy wife not been experienced so early and so intensely by Brittain, her determination to go on working might have been weakened. As it was, her most salient characteristic, anger, was aroused. Her anger may have appeared cool, but it had an object—inhuman institutions like marriage and war—and it empowered her to attempt profound change.

Like many others, particularly writers of nonfiction, Brittain did not feel something had been experienced until it had been written about. Her marriage tempted her to record her honeymoon. Like many brides before her, she wondered how her "undiluted society" would satisfy her new husband. She need not have wondered, since it was never put to the test. But the book she wrote about her honeymoon turned out to be unpublishable: Brittain later explained, "Its ideas on marriage—now common to most intelligent people—were then uncongenial and even shocking to conventional minds."

Meanwhile, at Cornell, she pondered the condition of marriage in the United States. Her problems had begun with the American consulate in London, which refused to give her a passport in her own (that is, her maiden) name. They were interested in no fact about her but whether or not she was married. "Alas, I reflected," she reported in *Thrice a Stranger,* "that a simple ceremony, lasting for twenty minutes, should so easily transform an individual with qualities into a type having a status! . . . once let [a woman] agree to live with some man as his lawful spouse, and everyone conspires to rob her of [her] unbecoming individualism." This was good preparation for America, where she found that her role as faculty wife was identical to her mother's role of wife in provincial Buxton: "Although I had been an Oxford student I had never actually lived in a University city, and it had not occurred to me that 'Faculty wives' would fall as easily as any other kind of wife into the conversational traps provided by meals, babies, illnesses, and the delinquencies of the latest 'help.'" Cornell, she surmised, may have been an exception; it "was not disposed to encourage the intellectual pretentions of its female appendages. It was one of the few coeducational institutions where the status of the women students was definitely lower than that of the men, and its Faculty had displayed from the first a resolute intention to keep its wives and daughters in their place." She noticed not only the exclusion of wives and daughters from the clubs and academic events, but also "the contrast between its married women and its girl students, vital with the eager, confident youth which their teachers' wives had once possessed."

As the year in America ended, "a queer year of mixed pain and pleasure," Brittain wrote to Holtby that she came away with two conclusions: "1. That I would not now for the world not have married G., or want not to have met him. 2. That marriage in general is an unhappy state, and to be avoided by anyone who is already quite happy single unless they are *very* sure it is what they want, and have planned beforehand the conditions on which they intend to live together." In fact, as we learn in *Testament of Experience,* Brittain questioned the role of faculty wife at Cornell and the larger issue of a woman's obligation to sacrifice her professional life to domesticity.

Although she came to admire the United States, and to write well of it in *Thrice a Stranger,* she was outspoken in her letters to Holtby: "America is a civilisation whose members spend all their energy in adapting themselves to each other, and on the whole they succeed very well—I never met so many people with such a fear of originality, solitude and independent thought (all of which they dismiss in the one term 'highbrowism')." This, of course, was in 1926, when on a visit to Columbia University Brittain strolled with pleasure alone in Morningside Park, and described Harvard as "an extended Somerville." She suffered from a complaint perhaps outdated now: "There are too many women with nothing to do but kill time, who simply cannot grasp the fact that there are any women whose work is of more importance than theirs. One is bothered perpetually by social trivialities." But the sense that her work, and thus her life, was impossible with G. at Cornell is altogether contemporary.

We can read in *Testament of Experience* how Brittain and her husband determined to try out what she calls a "semi-detached" marriage, what we today call a commuter marriage. G. was lost without her at Cornell during the first months this new plan was put into practice, but soon realized with rare insight that he had married her precisely for that vitality he was, by keeping her at Cornell, asking her to nullify: "I do think that ours has been a perfect marriage. It has been just such a marriage as I could have wished, something hardening and yet *con amore.* I wanted somebody who adventured; I wanted somebody above all who would keep me keyed up to that pitch of vivid living and working which is the keenest and divinest of all experiences in life." To preserve that marriage they agreed to live separately for four months of the year, when he would be at Cornell, and she in London. In the end, what with world events and her husband's professional concerns, their regular separation became unnecessary; in fact, they were often separated by their work, his more than hers. Soon children were born to them.

Do we know very much of the man she married, beyond what she has told us in her books? She has told us little. Catlin himself disliked being portrayed, forcing her barely to mention him in *Testament of Youth,* turning him, she complained, into a cipher. He is always referred to by initial; in *England's Hour,* by another name. An intensely peripatetic man—he crossed the ocean eleven times during World War II, and was torpedoed twice—he used to meet up with her in unlikely parts of the world; once they met by accident in Chicago. In his own autobiography, published in 1972 after Brittain's death, he speaks of her little, referring to her as his "wife" more often than not. She was famous, and perhaps he did not feel the need to say more. Some comment on the marriage, however impersonal, would have been welcome, but all we get is this: "My world was not entirely Vera's, although they overlapped." Later he tells us how Brittain during World War II "put her whole literary standing in jeopardy by her integrity and unwavering stand on the absolute pacifist principle. . . . On one occasion she discussed with me whether it would not be politically better for me if we had a divorce. We had become more and more closely devoted to each other and I repudiated the idea. Admittedly it is easy to talk about 'standing on one's own feet'; but society has an instinct to feel in terms of guilty association. Nevertheless, I preferred to stand by my own reputation and to let the consequences ride."

Brittain wrote about the pacifist struggles, to which Catlin referred, in *Testament of Experience.* She was accused of everything from insanity to being in the service of the Nazis. Her experiences in World War I make her pacifism readily understandable; nor is it difficult to sympathize with her horror at the retaliatory bombing of German cities. Certainly, it was not easy to remain a pacifist in World War II; if ever war could be justified, Hitler seemed to have justified it. Unlike other English pacifists, or Englishmen like Somerset Maugham who were simply afraid, Brittain let neither fear of bombs nor dislike of war keep her from England. However, her children, like many others, were sent to America for the worst years of the English bombardment, when invasion seemed not only likely but imminent. Certainly it is easier to honor a pacifist than an aging militarist, not least because it is rarely the militarist who himself suffers or dies.

Yet if Brittain's character is clear in the light of her pacifism and her feminism, her personality is not an easy one to extract from her *Testaments.* It is still rare to discover a woman's involvement in war,

and then in peace, in friendship and a working marriage, in parent-
hood and fame as an author. The *Testaments,* it seems likely, will endure because they remain unique chronicles of the experience of a generation, and especially of its women. Brittain's are not, alas, experiences
which in their courage and unconventionality have become more usual
with the passing years.

But, for all this, their author is not revealed within them in any
very personal sense. We know Holtby far better; in her short life she
wrote and spoke with an openness Brittain never matched. Yet one
must concede that Brittain knew herself. As a pacifist in World War
II, she was urged by the Quakers to become one of them. "Amid the
pressures of wartime," she writes, "the Church of England seemed to
me to compromise precisely where a truly Christian body would stand
firm." But in the end she did not join the Society of Friends for reasons wholly characteristic of her in their honesty: She did not feel
herself suited to "the group-thinking which seemed to be an essential
part of the Quaker philosophy." In addition, she writes, "I thought
myself personally unsuited to the Quaker community. Frivolous clothes
and the use of cosmetics were not consistent with their sober habits,
yet I recognized these forms of vanity as too habitual to be eradicated.
Equally inconsistent with the Quaker way of life was my combative
disposition. This, within limitations, I could learn to discipline . . .
but I could not provide myself with a placid temperament or become
uncontroversial by wishing that I were. (And anyway, did I really wish
it?)"

She did not wish it; she had never wished it. A woman less con-
troversial would have accomplished nothing that remains to us of her
efforts, least of all her record of them. That television should have
offered her story of World War I ten years after her death, and more
than sixty years after the events described, suggests that there is something enduring about her combativeness. If she does not emerge from
her *Testaments* as wholly lovable, like her friend Winifred Holtby, she
won the friendship of this lovable woman, which is tribute enough.

Brittain was successful in her life, as after it. *Testament of Friendship,*
we should recall, sold 167,000 copies in its first year, before the era of
the "blockbuster" book; *Testament of Youth,* also a best-seller, brought
her 1,300 letters in the first four years after it was published; then she
stopped counting. Her novels sold well also, though they met odd

fates: the fact that the entire cheap edition of *Honourable Estate* was destroyed by bombs seems prophetic of the destiny of her fiction, and was perhaps not regrettable. Fiction was not her mode. Rather she was a witness of her times, who lives among us still as a writer of testaments, cantankerous both for her self and for noble causes.

1981

5

Winifred Holtby

THOSE WHO, like Winifred Holtby, die young, retain their promise;
they gain a kind of immortality untested by the ravages of age and
loneliness and decay. They do not live to see themselves superseded.
Laurence Binyon, in one of his war poems, captures this saving grace:
"They shall not grow old, as we that are left grow old./Age shall not
weary them, nor the years condemn." Vera was to say much the same
of Winifred, dead at thirty-seven of kidney disease: "Did she who loved
life so deeply that she endured indescribable pain and discomfort in
order to give herself a few more months of it, perhaps reflect that there
are worse things than dying young and beloved, with one's mind consciously in tune with all that is best in the life of one's time? Did she
remember that it is sadder still to grow old and lonely, to watch the
friends of a lifetime vanish like lighted candles blown out one after

another by the breath of an unseen presence; and saddest of all to reach the stage of crying doom upon one's epoch, condemning its youth and deploring that which is new and experimental because one's mind has died before one's body?"

But when all allowance has been made for the effect of an early death, which, more readily than the greatest biographer, can turn a life into art, there still remains something extraordinary about Winifred Holtby.

The Viscountess Rhondda, who was the editor of *Time and Tide,* ended an obituary notice of Winifred by saying: "People will say I am describing a saint. I am." Brittain comes close to saying the same thing. Both refer, as people usually do in considering saints, not to her marvelous vitality but to her generosity. She increased her joy in life by expending it, and those who needed her recognized her on sight. It was her talent to give as though the favor were received, not offered. Yet Brittain, who knew the full extent of Holtby's efforts on behalf of others, who had herself been the recipient of Holtby's gifts, felt that the tragedy of Holtby's life lay in the responsiveness of her generous nature, "her disastrous willingness to put aside her permanent interest for the temporary convenience of others." Because of Holtby's "humble readiness to estimate all those for whom she worked as her superiors," her great talents were late in ripening. As Lady Rhondda was to express it, only in *South Riding,* Holtby's last novel, which she kept herself alive by sheer will to finish, did she show "anything like the full stretch of her powers," only there was she able to find the form of her rare ability to "hold in her mind at the same moment—and even sympathize with—several conflicting and incongruous points of view." Yet even when Winifred was dying, blind, and with her mind already on the borderland of vagueness, she spoke to Lady Rhondda of someone who needed help in finding a job.

We do not, perhaps mistakenly, think of saints as feisty: Winifred was. Many have described her; here is Yorkshire novelist Phyllis Bentley's portrait: "This year [1929] I met Winifred Holtby for the first time, when she came to Halifax to give a course of University Extension lectures. I envied Winifred with all my heart. Tall and fair and handsome, with those wonderful blue eyes, that charm and gaiety and warmth, that lovely speaking voice, that precision of English, that flat in London, that post on *Time and Tide,* those interesting well-cut clothes, that Oxford degree! I loved her dearly—who did not love Winifred?

She stayed the night with us once or twice, and when she left it was as if brightness fell from the air."

Phyllis Bentley later was eager to do a long novel on the history of the textile trade in the West Riding; many said the book would be too somber, that she should write a short, bright novel. She consulted Winifred, who answered by postcard from London: "Do the long one. Stick to your own genre. A thousand tongues unite to sing about the Modern Girl. No one else is playing your game. Sage advice. Love, W. H." Bentley (who did write the long novel, a great success) was later to quarrel with Vera Brittain, because of private tensions that intervened between them, though they ended praising one another's generosity; but with Winifred, Bentley did not quarrel. Holtby quarreled only with those who tried to direct her life, and then she argued with patience, love, and understanding.

Lady Rhondda tells a revealing story about Holtby's personality. After Winifred had become a director of *Time and Tide,* and did every kind of job in connection with this exciting journal, a famous man said one day to Lady Rhondda, the journal's editor: Holtby "is the most brilliant journalist in London; *why* don't you get her for your literary editor?" "I rang her up," Lady Rhondda continues, "and told her what he'd said; 'Oh, *no,* Margaret, I'll do anything else in the world but *not* that, you *know* I can't say "NO" to people.' " Literary editor was the only post on *Time and Tide* Winifred did *not* fill. When Winifred's club, though it had no rules against Orientals, refused to take an Indian friend, she resigned. That is a common enough act today, but it was rare then. She had in common with saints an integrity of being, a centeredness: her desires, her words, her actions were not at war. Though her unselfishness took time from her talents, she did not, like most of us, give with half a heart what the other half resented giving.

There was an Artemis quality about her; she was not meek, but rather fiercely maiden, glorying in a golden freedom rare in women. Yet, for all that, she liked men, and was to help them as freely as she helped women. Her male peers were few; the man who might have been her lover or husband had been emotionally damaged in the war, made irresolute and afraid. Vera's brother, whom Winifred often thought she might have married, was dead with all the others. (When Vera went to America, she wrote Winifred with amazement of all the men one's age to be met there.)

It is not surprising, therefore, that the pattern for their new friendship at Oxford, their plans for the years ahead, should have been, even unconsciously, a male pattern. They looked forward, as young men did, to leaving the university for London, work, and "life." Winifred wrote to Vera of her delight in just such an account: "If you call yourself Rodney and me Peter it might almost be a glorified replica of some of our midnight conversations." There was no script for young women which seemed written to their needs. They, indeed, would write them.

But, we seem always to need to remind ourselves, one does not appear "male" simply because one eschews the accepted female life. And it was as "the young Diana" that Holtby first struck Brittain at their original meeting. They had been assigned the same tutor, the dean of Hereford College. In a manner not uncharacteristic of long friendships, this one began with mutual distaste. Brittain awaited the arrival of Holtby feeling "unaccountably antagonistic," partly because she wanted the dean to herself, and partly because after the losses and experience of the war, she felt isolated from the world in general, and from Oxford with its postwar gaiety in particular. "I was staring gloomily," she wrote in *Testament of Youth,* "at the Oxford engravings and photographs of The Dolomites which clustered together so companionably upon the dean's study wall, when Winifred Holtby burst suddenly in upon this morose atmosphere of ruminant lethargy. Superbly tall, and vigorous as the young Diana with her long straight limbs and her golden hair, her vitality smote with the effect of a blow upon my jaded nerves. Only too well aware that I had lost that youth and energy for ever, I found myself furiously resenting its possessor. Obstinately disregarding the strong-featured, sensitive face and the eager, shining blue eyes, I felt quite triumphant because—having returned from France less than a month before—she didn't appear to have read any of the books which the Dean had suggested as indispensable introductions to our Period." Holtby, on her side, found Brittain touchy.

Between the death of Edward, her brother, in 1918, the last year of the war, and the beginning of her friendship with Holtby in 1920, Brittain inhabited a land of isolation, resentment, and terror. She suffered from hallucinations that she was becoming a witch, or growing a beard, as a dark shadow seemed to spread across her face. She could not mention this even to Winifred, but it was Winifred's friendship that enabled her to recover, to agree to live and shed what we can now recognize as survivor guilt.

The remarkable friendship, beginning in 1920 and ending with Winifred's death in 1935, is preserved for us not only in *Testament of Friendship,* but in the letters they wrote to each other whenever they were apart. When the summer term in which they had met ended in 1920, Brittain and Holtby spent a fortnight walking in Cornwall and preparing their special subjects for the following term. They worked together in a cottage lent them in West Pentyre, the beginning of a "shared working experience." Winifred was later to write to Vera of a woman novelist who "said I hardly knew my luck, having someone with whom I could work who shared my taste and ambitions. But I think I know my luck—a little." To which Vera wrote back: "My dear—take care of yourself and don't let destiny require of me the last loss."

The early letters reveal also the narrowness of the young women's escape from an academic university life. Holtby almost had a First, which would certainly have condemned her to a college fellowship. Indeed, she was offered a tutorship at St. Hugh's College. And in congratulating her on refusing it, Vera turned for confirmation to a strange source: Robert Leighton, the father of Vera's dead fiancé, to whom Vera had introduced Winifred, spoke strongly of his fear of Winifred's deserting fiction for academe, counseling her that fiction is greater than scholarship, though scholarship is not to be deserted. "Mr. Leighton told me yesterday," Vera wrote Winifred, "(which I never knew before) that he knew George Eliot quite well in the last years of her life. He says she was very pleasant and charming to talk to, very approachable and more like a horse than anyone he ever met. She wasn't a bit early Victorian or old-fashioned, and when nearly sixty used to wear straw hats with blue flowers, and blue ribbons tied under her chin! She was very fond of blue."

So was Winifred. Both she and Vera took enormous pleasure in clothes, and clucked at professional women who allowed themselves to appear dowdy or unfashionable. They never missed a chance for gaiety. In *Letters to a Friend,* the youthful Winifred refers more to clothes she has bought or, more likely, made than to any other subject. Five feet ten, and with large feet, she liked to appear happily bedecked.

Through the hard grind toward publication, and the constant stream, at first, of rejected manuscripts and bad reviews, Holtby and Brittain sustained each other. Brittain's first novel, *The Dark Tide,* was to cause ructions at Oxford, which (as it would later do with Dorothy Sayers) took some time to forgive its author. Brittain, even while writing the book, feared for the suffering its publication would cause. Winifred, again home in Yorkshire as the convenient daughter, wrote to encourage her: "*Daphne* [*The Dark Tide*'s first title] is going to be a fine book—but that's not the end of it. You will be a finer person for having written it—but that's not the end, either. The world may possibly be a better place because you wrote it—and, if there is, as I believe, immortality of all things that are good and beautiful, then even that is not the end. My dear, go on and prosper. You have earned your right to be great. If there is yet a higher price to be paid, you will pay it; and if the achievement is worthy of the promise of *Daphne,* then no price will have been too high. You will say, I know, that the price can be too high—that a time comes when suffering defeats its own end, and becomes a corrupting, not a stimulating force. Your own work shows that for you the time has not come yet, and there is every reason why it should never come."

That same year, 1921, the two traveled together to Italy, for the joy of it, and to visit Vera's brother's grave. The account of this trip is in *Testament of Friendship;* it was to remain with them always as the best of times. Winifred wrote to Vera: "The journey would have been pleasant in most circumstances, and interesting in any, but because you were there it was wholly delightful. Whatever things may happen in the future of good or evil, at least we have had one perfect time which nothing can take away . . .

> Our actions all have immortality;
> Such gladness gives no hostage unto death.

Thank you, thank you, thank you, for being so completely satisfactory, you most sweet woman. And we will go again. There are heaps of lovely places to see, and things to do. Never doubt I want to see and do them, and that I ask no better travelling companion than you."

They write each other what may sound like love letters to a world attuned only to affection between courting men and women: "I find you in all small and lovely things [Winifred writes to Vera], in the little fishes like flames in the green water, in the furred and stupid softness of bumble-bees fat as laughter, in all the chiming radiance of warmth and light and scent in the summer garden. I love you for all small and silly things."

Unlike Vera Brittain, Holtby did not grow up fighting for her right to an education and permission *not* to be a "lady." Her parents, from Yorkshire yeoman stock, early recognized her talents and, despite their conservatism, encouraged her to apply to Oxford. Her "public" school had, rare in those days, assumed that its graduates would go on to a profession. She lost no one in the war who had been life to her. Her struggle, after the war and Oxford, was more for the right to go her own way, religiously, professionally, and, in politics, radically. She wrote to her mother in 1923, trying to explain why her aims were different than those of her parents. At Oxford, she wrote, "I read a great deal of the history of the Church, of the way in which creeds were built up by men . . . how year by year the original teaching of Christ became more and more set about with interpretations and symbols until the real meaning over and over was lost." Apparently, Winifred's mother had accused her of selfishness.

"Dear heart, when I say that I want 'to get on,' do you really think I just want fame? Don't you know that when I am in Bethnal Green I have a strong temptation to throw aside this climbing and to do what I always used to think I would do—just work in the slums among the poor people? But I believe that would be a coward's way of service. I believe that service lies in this—that each of us should use in the highest way, to the very widest possible extent, the abilities and powers they have been given. I believe that to be content with humbler service, when one is able to stand greater responsibility, is only cowardice. . . . To ladle soup in a slum kitchen when one should be defending Justice as a King's Councilor, or Truth as a writer or philosopher, is blind sacrifice, which may even be deliberate cowardice and fighting away from the light."

Holtby understood with great clarity the fears and anxieties that assault women who set forth into the world of experience. In the same remarkable letter, she tried to write her mother of how she felt: "Though I am a thousand times unfit to seek [my vision], though I know myself a coward, often to lie, always to shrink from unpleasantness, to dread unpopularity, to hate effort, yet I must go along the road I see. . . . You may think me selfish or inconsiderate. I may hurt you again. But still I count on your love, and love you. And if the methods I see are different from the ones you would have me choose, it is because my qualifications and abilities are different." In its love and hope for love, its insistence on her own rights while honoring the mother's, this letter is one that has passed between mother and daughter many times, when the daughter had courage, respect, and affection.

Before she died at the age of thirty-seven (George Eliot, Brittain reminds us, did not publish a novel until she was over thirty-eight), Holtby had published six novels, enough short stories to fill two volumes, and a book of poems. She wrote the first English critical study of Virginia Woolf's writing, two works of satire, two books of sociology, one on women, and a play. In addition, she lectured, made public speeches on behalf of parliamentary candidates, and worked for the rights of dispossessed Africans. Brittain reports how, at home nursing her infant daughter while Holtby was in Geneva, she took over Winifred's correspondence. "We had then no secretary so I opened and answered it as it came. I found that it consisted mainly of requests to speak, write, read manuscripts and perform many other unremunerated services: letters from Africans; 'fan mail' about her articles; multitudinous pressclippings; and a number of cheques from periodicals. Familiar as I was with the extent and persistence of the claimants on her time, their confident appeals to her benevolence revealed the diverse services which she managed to perform for individuals of whom each apparently believed that he or she was the only one."

6

Virginia Woolf and James Joyce:
Ariadne and the Labyrinth

IN THEIR separate ways, Joyce and Woolf divide the modern genius between them. The relationship between these two great writers has, to an extraordinary degree, been ignored. Only a very few critics have recognized Joyce and Woolf as part of the same "extended family," whose members quarrel with one another but close ranks against "them,"[1]—"them" being those writers whose idea of reality was, in Woolf's words, a series of gig lamps symmetrically arranged. Indeed, Woolf's most famous passage, the one which refers to life as a luminous halo, is followed by the name of Joyce. In their different ways, they both, Woolf knew, attempted to come closer to life. Yet almost all notice of commerce between them has been confined to a dismissal of Woolf's "snobbish" response, in her diary, to her first reading of *Ulysses*, and to accusations that she copied Joyce. Joyce's views on Woolf are nowhere, to my knowledge, mentioned, but *The Voyage Out* was among the books in his Trieste library in 1920. Joyce had stamped his name in it.[2]

At Joyce's death in 1941, Woolf noted in her diary that he was "about a fortnight younger than I am."[3] There were, in fact, only eight days between their births. Less than three months after she recorded his death in her diary, she took her own life. In the nearly fifty years since their deaths, critical attention in the first thirty centered upon Joyce, only in the last twenty upon Woolf. Hugh Kenner wrote in 1978: "As the great age of Modernism recedes, it grows increasingly clear that the decisive English Language book of the century was *Ulysses*, the first pivotal book in English since *Paradise Lost*."[4] The truth of this statement is sharpened in the light of the Joyce-Woolf relationship.

No critical display is more offensive than that which praises one author only by damning another, as though critical judgment were a seesaw on which one reputation cannot rise unless another is lowered. Certainly today the woman writer is rare who receives praise not bought at the expense of a sister writer. So Joyce's praise was often paid in the coin of Woolfian "snobbishness." Lionel Trilling refers to T. S. Eliot's "trying to convince his hostess [Woolf] that *Ulysses* was not to be dismissed as the work of one or another kind of 'underbred' person."[5] Woolf, of course, used the phrase in a private diary, not in a published work.

What frame of reference can comprehend both Joyce and Woolf, allowing us to see both writers in relation to some larger whole? To call Joyce's method "masculine," and Woolf's "feminine," is wildly to oversimplify: it is also to suggest. It is, we may notice, no accident that the aggressively masculine worlds of American novelists and American academics have followed Joyce and ignored Woolf who, until the recent revival of feminism, they have misread or scorned. The English have more evenhandedly divided their attention.

For this reason it is particularly helpful to see T. S. Eliot delightfully cast as the mediating figure between Woolf and Joyce's "pivotal" work. We need hardly remind ourselves that it was Eliot who saw the modern sensibility as requiring a refutation of Milton's vision—a vision Kenner properly identifies as pivotal in the same way *Ulysses* is pivotal. It was almost always in connection with Eliot that Woolf, in her diary, mentions Joyce, nor is this accidental: for she saw in *Ulysses,* as Eliot in Milton, the major vision which needed to be not so much refuted as avoided. Like *Paradise Lost, Ulysses* looks back to an old cosmology and an old faith; it is the result of genius looking backward in a world where the new science has put all in doubt. Arguing about *Ulysses* with Eliot, Woolf was the Donne or Marvel to Joyce's Milton.

True, Eliot announced to Woolf that Joyce's work had "destroyed the whole of the 19th century." Trilling quotes this remark[6] and goes on to demonstrate how, in contradiction to Eliot, Joyce was in fact entirely "a man of the century into which he was born."[7] With Victorian patriarchs as with thieves, it takes one to know one. What Eliot meant, of course, was that Joyce had written a new kind of novel, the only kind which could make sense of modern life: a novel which used as its scaffolding an ancient text and a familiar story. Eliot in his plays was to do somewhat the same thing; Milton likewise in *Paradise Lost*. In any case, almost every time Woolf mentions *Ulysses* in her diary, she does so in the presence, so to speak, of T. S. Eliot, of his admiration and her distrust of Joyce, a distrust not only of what she called "underbred," but also of what she found egotistical, narrow, restricting. It is important that it was Eliot against whom this distrust was debated.

Eliot's stiff, puritanical ways had bemused the Woolfs when he was staying with them in the country, before *Ulysses* was published as a book. With difficulty Woolf, who had not yet finished *Jacob's Room*, kept herself successfully, as she wrote in her diary, "from being submerged, though feeling the waters rise once or twice. I mean by this that [Eliot] completely neglected my claims to be a writer, and had I been meek, I suppose I should have gone under." Woolf saw Eliot as "a consistent specimen of his type, which is opposed to ours. Unfortunately, the living writers he admires are Wyndham Lewis & Pound—Joyce, too, but there's more to be said on this head."[8] It was, of course, Eliot and not Woolf who was to be influenced by Joyce; it was Eliot's poetry upon which Joyce made a profound impression.[9] But Eliot, in speaking of Joyce to Woolf, made her fear that "what I'm doing is probably being better done by Mr. Joyce." This was not true, but reflects that female diffidence, that lack of confidence which male writers do not experience that has led her critics, and Joyce's admirers, to take her at her word. No doubt she at times wished to be what she conceived Joyce to be: "self-centered and perfectly self-assured."[10]

In 1922, when Woolf finally read *Ulysses* as she was "laboriously dredging my mind for Mrs. Dalloway," she found herself "amused, stimulated, charmed interested by the first 2 or 3 chapters—to the end

of the Cemetery scene; & then puzzled, bored, irritated, & disillu-
sioned as by a queasy undergraduate scratching his pimples. And Tom,
great Tom, thinks this on a par with War & Peace! . . . But I think
if you are anaemic, as Tom is, there is a glory in blood." The phrases
she then used, which have always made her admirers writhe and her
detractors gloat—"An illiterate, underbred book it seems to me: the
book of a self-taught working man, & we all know how distressing
they are, how egotistic, insistent, raw, striking & ultimately nauseat-
ing"—are distressing, no doubt; but what is she really saying? Why is
she so angry? Particularly since she will record in her diary a week
later: "I shall now rock myself into literature by reading Ulysses!" She
knows that *Ulysses* is "genius," however disturbing to her, and the final
diary entry of that year on *Ulysses* is again in a dialogue with "Tom."
"I said [Joyce] was virile—a he-goat; but didn't expect Tom to agree."[11]
Woolf is here, almost certainly, echoing Keats on Milton: "Life to him
would be death to me."[12]

We must notice, first, that Woolf's oft-quoted tirade against *Ulysses*
as the book of a self-taught working man, etc., is written in close con-
junction with her judgment of Eliot as "anaemic, and glorying in blood."
(She recognizes the honesty of Joyce's work and does not, as Lawrence
did, accuse Joyce of "deliberate, journalistic dirty-mindedness.")[13] She
had good reason to know of Eliot's inhibitions, of which this account
from Leonard Woolf's autobiography gives an idea:

> [Eliot] was walking with Virginia and me across the fields down to the
> river. I suddenly wanted to make water and fell behind to do so. Neither
> of my companions saw what I was doing, but I suppose it was very
> obvious what I was doing. Anyhow, when I caught them up again, I
> felt that Tom was uncomfortable, even shocked. I asked him whether
> he was and he said yes, and we then had what gradually became a per-
> fectly frank conversation about conventions and formality. Tom said he
> not only could not possibly have done what I did, that he would never
> dream of shaving in the presence even of his wife.[14]

It is necessary only to juxtapose this story against Joyce's letters to
Nora in which he is trying sexually to arouse himself and her[15] to see
how Woolf (though she could not of course have known of Joyce's
letters) must have sensed herself to be in a no-man's (no-woman's)
land between the two: Joyce and Eliot.

The fear she feels before *Ulysses* after the cemetery scene ("I may
revise this later. I do not compromise my critical sagacity. I plant a

stick in the ground to mark page 200.")[16] is not really snobbery, although her words form themselves that way. What she feels is terror
before the raw masculinity, the male sexual fantasies that confront her—
and all that such male fantasies imply for women. Stephen the intellectual and Bloom the lost, gentle man give way after the cemetery
scene to the wholly masculine worlds of the newspaper office and the
eating houses. We must remind ourselves that Woolf read this novel
fresh and felt its impact; she did not construe it with the aid of decades
of criticism. (Trilling was to write of Joyce's letters to Nora, which
perhaps affect us as *Ulysses* affected Woolf: "No one, I think, will be
so armored in objectivity as not to be taken aback by the letters. But
their shocking interest fades as we become habituated to them.")[17] To
her, not yet habituated, Bloom must have seemed, after the cemetery
scene, to pass from the world of women and compassion to the world
of men and brutality. Woolf saw herself as excluded and threatened
by this world, as Eliot was attracted by it.

In addition, Woolf was at this time working on *Mrs. Dalloway*. (The
idea that it was an "imitation" of *Ulysses* is superficial; I shall return
to it.) She had only found her own voice at the age of forty with *Jacob's
Room*; Joyce had, of course, produced his masterpiece, *Ulysses*, at the
age of forty. How could she have failed to perceive *Ulysses*, with its
arrant masculinity and seaminess, with its drinking and swearing and
eating and fornicating, but as a direct attack on her own aims for *Mrs.
Dalloway*, whose central character, a society lady, Woolf already feared
would be too "tinselly," too "feminine?" Was Mrs. Dalloway, her world
far removed from the world of Blazes Boylan and his confreres, to
seem unreal? Was it a failure? Feeling thus assaulted by *Ulysses*, she
spoke of it thoughtlessly and brutally in her diary, using the sort of
epithets—racial, sexual, physically descriptive—that come to us when
we are afraid, and angry, and not engaged in public discourse.

For Woolf, Milton was the bogey, past which women must look.[18]
"He was the first of the masculinists," she had written of him in 1918:
"He deals in horror & immensity & squalor & sublimity, but never
in the passions of the human heart. Has any great poem ever let in so
little light upon one's own joys & sorrows? I get no help in judging
life; I scarcely feel that Milton lived or knew men & women . . ."[19]
If Milton was the first of the masculinists, Joyce in 1922 must have
seemed the latest. That she recognized his greatness, how close he was
to the central modernist revolution in literature, only made the threat

more compelling. When Kenner says that *Ulysses* is the pivotal book of its time, as Milton's was of his, he repeats what Woolf sensed: that these are the two writers beyond whose visions she must look for "the passions of the human heart."

It is therefore all the more ironic that for many years Woolf critics have had to defend her from allegations of having imitated *Ulysses* in writing *Mrs. Dalloway*. Far from imitating Joyce's work, Woolf must have feared that its masculinist vision would make her own fictive world unacceptable to readers.

Six years after Woolf's death, when her reputation was at its nadir, William York Tindall, one of the earliest of the academic Joyce scholars, proclaimed *Mrs. Dalloway* an imitation of *Ulysses*: "*Mrs. Dalloway*, her first important work, is indebted primarily to Joyce. His three complementary characters, Bloom, Mrs. Bloom, and Stephen, are matched by her Septimus and Mrs. Dalloway. His episode of the Wandering Rocks, in which several minds are linked by the passage through Dublin of the viceregal cavalcade, is matched by the scene in the park in which she links several minds by a sky-writing airplane."[20] In a book on Joyce published three years later, Tindall achieved this extraordinary judgment: "Almost alone among women, Virginia Woolf, her eye perhaps on Mrs. Bloom, created an essential woman." The "essential woman" "copied" from Mrs. Bloom is, of course, Mrs. Ramsay. Several pages later we learn that "Virginia Woolf's stream of consciousness flows from Joyce and Bergson."[21] Tindall could not anticipate the concept of the anxiety of influence; neither did he evade the full masculinist temper of his time.

A few years later, Woolf critics would begin to counter this nonsense. From 1954 to 1980, they suggested, with growing emphasis, the unlikeliness of Tindall's animadversions on her originality. The first of these critics, James Hafley, was sharp: "If Joyce used the single day as a unity, Virginia Woolf used it as a diversity. Joyce attempted to show all that a single day can hold; Virginia Woolf, to show that there is no such thing as a single day. Joyce exhausted a day; Virginia Woolf destroyed a day. This is not to say that one was right and one wrong, but only that each was doing a different thing and so employing unity of time for a different reason. . . . *Mrs. Dalloway* does not employ the stream-of-consciousness technique. . . . actually, she never did use stream of consciousness—here or elsewhere—mainly because it was completely out of accord with her 'vision.' "[22]

Here is Jean Guiguet, in 1962: "It is quite evident . . . that the two novelists were temperamentally incompatible and impermeable to one another's influence. . . . If *Mrs. Dalloway* is in any way indebted to *Ulysses* it is not for those features which are usually considered points of resemblance, but rather for the points wherein they differ. Far from borrowing anything whatever from Joyce, Virginia Woolf has striven to avoid what she considers as his weaknesses, faults, or mistakes. It may be added furthermore that the parallel nature of their attempts and the similarity between their objectives only enhanced and sharpened the antagonism between their personalities. There exists a family feud between them which is in some way sharper than a conflict between strangers, such as, for instance, that waged by both of them against the Edwardians."[23]

And James Naremore in 1973: "The impression we get from Virginia Woolf's handling of consciousness is quite different from the impression we sometimes get in Joyce, where every atom is accounted for as it falls. This is chiefly because it is characteristic of Virginia Woolf to interpret the mental life of a character rather than transcribe it."[24] Finally, Maria DiBattista in 1980: "Where Woolf departs from Joyce is in her thorough skepticism about the structures (Joyce's micro- and macrocosms) western culture has constructed on the 'void incertitude' and in her radical inquiry into the grounds and legitimacy of the authority commanded by the phantom power of history, society, and religion over life itself."[25] One must conclude from these and other critics that Woolf's work awaited the invention of feminist criticism to deal with her fiction: feminist in the sense of recognizing the many ways in which she sought to overthrow Joyce's method, his authorities, and his conscious effort to account for every atom as it falls, criticism written by men as well as women but developing only slowly after 1970.

Joyce and Woolf, as we have seen, were far from equal at forty. *Ulysses,* as Ellmann recounts, was published on Joyce's fortieth birthday: "Miss Beach, an American woman, timidly offered, in April 1921, to publish *Ulysses* herself under the imprint of her Paris bookshop, Shakespeare and Company. Joyce at one consented. . . . He was greatly agitated by the publication and determined that publication in Paris should not retard the acceptance of his book in England and the United States. . . . The greatness of *Ulysses* would have established itself, but

Joyce felt compelled to accelerate its recognition whenever, wherever, he could."[26] (Probably the only reason that Joyce had heard of Woolf at all, or acquired her first novel, was because the Woolfs had hoped to publish *Ulysses* at the Hogarth Press. They would, however, have had to hire an outside printer for so long a book, and no printer would undertake what would certainly be judged an obscene manuscript. In England, the printer as well as the publisher can be prosecuted for publishing works adjudged obscene.)

Since in the same year in which *Ulysses* was published, Woolf had, as she wryly noted in her diary, "found out how to begin (at 40) to say something in my own voice; & that interests me so that I feel I can go ahead without praise," it is particularly ironic that the "something in my own voice" which is *Mrs. Dalloway*, should have been heard as Joyce's voice. It is doubly ironic because Woolf's voice was the only one Joyce had never heard and never could catch: the voice of a woman passionately intellectual. For her, meanwhile, the triumph of finding her own voice was to be followed by the fear evoked by J. Middleton Murry, when he said "there's no way of going on after *Jacob's Room*."[27]

By the time they were both fifty, however, the woman, slower in finding her voice, had spoken up more assuredly. By 1932, when they had both turned fifty, Woolf had published, in addition to *Mrs. Dalloway*, *To the Lighthouse, The Waves, Orlando, A Room of One's Own*, and two volumes of *The Common Reader*. Joyce had continued, as he would continue, to work on *Finnegans Wake*. Both scarcely noticed their birthdays in the shock of death: Joyce, his father's; Woolf, Lytton Strachey's. Both declined that year what must have seemed the ultimate academic accolades their cultures could offer: Woolf, the Clark lectureship at Cambridge University; Joyce, membership in the Academy of Irish Letters which Yeats was founding. A comparison of their letters written in that year is emblematic; I shall return to it.

What is, however, most important to compare about their work and lives as they passed their fiftieth years is that he had continued, for the third time, to recreate the old cosmology, while she had struggled to invent, or reinvent, a new one. *Ulysses* recreated, reworked one of the great epics: it reflected, in the mirror of a new technique, an old and long-known text. But however modern Joyce's technique, his art was profoundly conservative. Moreover, his characters were unaware of the ancient text against which they spoke: Bloom is not conscious of the classical forebears in whose steps he treads. Bloom does not know he is Odysseus.[28] The ancient text lies behind the book to indicate the unchanging essence of the human (male) experience.

Woolf's characters, on the contrary, are aware of all the texts which preceded them—including those which were, like the female authors who probably wrote them, anonymous and little known. Aware of the entire western culture behind them, Woolf's characters are also aware it is not for them: it does not serve their lives. They try, and often fail, to invent fictions which will explain their hopes and lives. It was, of course, inevitable that while Eliot praised the scaffolding that Joyce had employed for the writing of *Ulysses*, the use of an ancient text which alone made the novel possible in modern times,[29] he scarcely noticed the equally arduous labors of the woman who was his friend: to write without scaffolding, knowing that none of the ancient texts would serve as one tried to net "that fin in the waste of water."[30]

Joyce was received as the literary giant of the age almost upon the first appearance of *Ulysses*; he offered the old cosmology with such novel, intricate, and dazzling technique that seemingly endless analysis was necessary to expound it. Academics could exercise upon him all their ingenuity and talent without having their central conventions or perceptions disturbed. As one critic, admiring *Ulysses* but tired of all these technical interpretations, was to write: "He has nothing especially new to say about social or ethical or religious values; in many ways he seems old-fashioned."[31] Joyce's wish that scholars might devote their lives to unravelling his work was granted. Meanwhile, as late as 1966, the *Times Literary Supplement* in its lead article, would, in praising Tolstoy, refer to "relatively minor writers like Virginia Woolf or Ford Madox Ford."[32] Nor did those critics who wrote on Woolf understand her very well. Only the 1970s would bring us the first of perceptive studies and (the sure sign of being a "major" writer) the attentions of the princes of the critical world.[33] The new art of deconstruction at last provided a critical method that could serve Woolf's art.

We can now see that Joyce was Daedalus, who had constructed a labyrinth and a machine where, in Auden's words, a woman "got laid by a sacred beast."[34] Yet in all Joyce's evocation of Daedalus, only Ariadne was forgotten. Even Homer had remembered that Daedalus had designed a dance floor for her, but Joyce forgot Ariadne as Theseus had forgotten her, as Stephen Dedalus would forget her. Woolf's task was to remember Ariadne.

IN 1900, Arthur Evans discovered the ancient palace of Minos; in uncovering the royal palace at Knossos, Evans recognized that he had also uncovered what the ancient world had called the labyrinth of Daedalus. "The excavations," Diane Fortuna has written in an article on the labyrinth as controlling image in Joyce's *Portrait*, "supported details of the myth. Daedalus's reputed invention of the ax had probably arisen as an explanation of the palace emblem, the sacral double ax, found on marking and reliefs throughout the building. The palace apartments were strewn with frescos of bulls and artifacts describing bull-headed figures, thus accounting for the growth of the Minotaur legend."[35]

In 1904, Joyce published his first stories under the pseudonym of Daedalus.[36] Fortuna has demonstrated that Joyce must have known all about Evans' discoveries: indeed, everyone must have known. The University of Dublin gave Evans an honorary degree while Joyce was at University College. In London, but not at a university, Woolf too must have heard of these extraordinary discoveries. Different as they were, Joyce and Woolf were the same age in the same part of the world at the same time; both had studied Greek and the classical world. For Woolf, there was a further connection to the myth of Daedalus. Jane Harrison had, in 1903, forcefully established, as Fortuna puts it, "that Hellenic initiations had originated in Crete, the mother of mysteries."[37]

Jane Harrison, whom Woolf was to invoke as "the Great Scholar" in *A Room of One's Own,* was one of those closely connected with the Stephens' world. Harrison became a Research Fellow at Newnham in 1898, and remained there while Woolf's first cousin, Katharine Stephen, was principal. (The principal from 1923–41 was Lytton Strachey's sister.) Jane Harrison's work, together with that of Frazer, Cornford, and Murray, established that "behind the legend of Pasiphae, made monstrous by the misunderstanding of immigrant conquerors, it can scarcely be doubted that there lurks some sacred mystical ceremony of ritual wedlock with a bullheaded deity."[38] Behind the beginnings of Orphic ceremonies lay the drama of Dionysus.

We ought, perhaps, at this point to recall the story of the labyrinth, beginning with the arrival of Theseus at Crete. All the standard mythologies tell the same story in slightly different ways. Fortuna's version is this:

> Minos, son of Zeus and Europa, refused to sacrifice a white bull which Poseidon had sent to him for that purpose. Poseidon punished the king for this act of simony by causing Pasiphae, the wife of Minos, to lust after the white bull. She begged Daedalus, the court artisan, to help her. In deference to the queen, Daedalus created a hollow wooden cow within which Pasiphae consummated her passion with the bull. To hide her shame, Minos concealed the offspring of this union, the Minotaur, within the labyrinth built by Daedalus. A monster with the body of a man and the head of a bull, the Minotaur became the bovine god of Crete to whom, every eight years, seven Athenian youths and seven Athenian maidens were sacrificed.
>
> Daedalus had designed the labyrinth so that no ordinary person, having once entered and proceeded to the center where the Minotaur was kept, could find his way out. . . . Only two persons ever escaped from the labyrinth, Daedalus himself, and the Athenian prince hostage, Theseus. Shortly after his arrival in Crete, Minos's daughter, Ariadne, fell in love with Theseus; fearing that he would end as the sacrificial victim of the Minotaur, she gave Theseus a skein of thread. Winding his way to the center of the maze, Theseus confronted the Minotaur and slew him, managing to escape from the maze by rewinding the ball of thread. (pp. 120–121)

Fortuna, interested in the legend as it served Joyce, halts in the telling here. Having served Theseus' purposes, Ariadne need no longer be considered or accounted for. (Fortuna suggests that the "bird-girl" in the *Portrait* is Ariadne; Ariadne is associated with the crane. But, Fortuna adds, Aquinas, rather than Ariadne, will provide the guiding thread—p. 157.) In short, neither Joyce nor Stephen Dedalus, nor anyone who has studied or interpreted classical myths before Jane Harrison, looked upon Ariadne as important. Here is the way the Oxford Classical Dictionary tells the story of Ariadne:

> When Theseus (q.v.) came to Crete, she fell in love with him and gave him a clue of thread by which he found his way out of the labyrinth after killing the Minotaur. He then fled, taking her with him, but (magically?) forgot and left her on Naxos (Dia). It is generally said that Dionysus found her there and married her; but Plutarch preserves a curious local legend and custom. Theseus left her there pregnant, and she died in childbirth. In commemoration of this, every year at Amathus a young man imitated a woman in childbed in honor of Ariadne Aphrodite. It is probable that Ariadne was originally a goddess, Minoan in origin, but with a Greek name meaning "very holy."

Fortuna's thesis is that the labyrinth is the controlling image of Joyce's *Portrait*, in which Stephen moves through "the labyrinth of the world into the paradise of the heart" (p. 136). Clearly, it is far from Joyce's concern to ask: what of Ariadne? Woolf did not ask the question either, not in so many words, perhaps not even consciously. It is nonetheless possible to see the two exact contemporaries as concerned, one with the labyrinth of the world, the other with the forgotten Ariadne. If we assume Joyce's eyes upon Evans receiving his honorary degree in Dublin, as Fortuna reasonably does, we may with equal probability assume Woolf's eyes upon Jane Harrison. Harrison was, indeed, an Ariadne: she provided the thread through the labyrinth of Greek myth to her fellow scholars, Frazer, Murray, Cornford, and others. As Ackerman notes, "Although each man had independently been attracted to the thenographic approach to the classics, she was able to broaden all of them by introducing them to material to which they were largely strangers." To students of Woolf, Harrison's life resembles not only Ariadne's, but Lily Briscoe's. "By what miracle I escaped marriage," Harrison wrote, "I do not know—on to friendship and learning." In later years, Harrison observed "though I am an oldish woman and fairly lonely I have never repented." Jane Harrison connected the sensuous process of learning with sex, and Ackerman goes on to say of her, "her scholarly work and her personal life were inextricably interwoven in a way that is rare for most intellectuals. And I have no doubt that she later embraced initiation and rebirth as enthusiastically as she did because her own experience must have given her the subjective feeling of rightness that she apparently needed before making an idea completely her own." Like Lily Briscoe, Harrison lived out a rather unhappy youth in London, groping toward the central idea of her life.[39] In her forties, her life began when she went to Newnham, as Lily Briscoe's life begins when she is forty-four and has her vision. Woolf was forty-four when she wrote *To the Lighthouse*.

But it was what Harrison taught Woolf of the "marriage" of Dionysus and Ariadne that was more important. "With Dionysus," Harrison wrote, "god of plants and trees as well as human life, there came a return to nature, a breaking of bonds, of crystallization, a desire for the life rather of the emotions than of the reason, a recrudescence it may be of animal passion." Only a mystic, Harrison suggested—at any event, not a doctrinaire scholar or writer—could penetrate the secret of Dionysus' mysticism.[40] The world which Woolf would try to create,

then, was beyond the labyrinth; Ariadne had the secret to that, but
could not use if for herself. Woolf's eyes turned, albeit metaphorically,
to Ariadne, and the life she might make outside of the labyrinth-palace.
While Joyce's characters remained in the ancient labyrinth, the world
of the old cosmology, led more and more magically, with more and
more Daedalean skill and artistry, through the mazes and passages of
the old life, Woolf searched for Ariadne and, looking back through
Ariadne to her mother, for the passion of Pasiphae, a daughter of the
sun, who began, perhaps, a new cosmology subsequently lost in the
triumph of the patriarchal culture founded by Theseus after his return
to Athens. Theseus betrayed Ariadne, leaving her to the world of female myth and female possibility. It was that world into which Woolf
would follow Ariadne.

Nowhere do Joyce and Woolf divide so sharply as in their portrayal
of women and the destinies of women. It is perhaps too harsh to say
of Joyce that, having accepted the male version of the Pasiphae story,
he constructed his literary universe on the basis of male fantasies such
as the notion of Pasiphae lusting after a bull. Had Joyce written of
Pasiphae's passion, how would he have imagined her thoughts? We
know at least how he imagined Molly Bloom's thoughts as she contemplates her afternoon with Blazes Boylan. Woman for Joyce, beyond
her sexual hungers, is nature, earth, as man is culture and civilization.
She is what continues as man goes about his human concerns. As
Goldberg wrote, women for Joyce were not people but biological
symbols.[41]

True to the patriarchy, Joyce used as his central and manly theme
the search for the father, and the father's for a son and heir. Molly
does not especially care for Milly or any other women, and Leopold,
though fond of Milly, thinks most of his lost son and seeks a new one
in Stephen. Woolf writes, on the other hand, of the woman's search
for the mother. Her theme is a maternal theme. It involves, inevitably,
the freeing of oneself from the mother, the mourning of her, the rebirth of the individual woman as herself.[42] Inevitably, the father's heritage is accepted to some degree. Woolf knew herself to be her father's
daughter even as she knew his weight upon her, had he not died,
would have been fatal to her art. The paternal heritage, the male text,
is there for the reading. But the female text, lost (as Harrison and her
colleagues revealed) deep in myth and the unconscious, needed to be

written for the first time. Woolf set out to create a new and female text.

By a process we might well call "feminine," might at any rate see as opposed to the male tendency to account for the atoms as they fall, Woolf discovered the female text by a process she recognized as unconscious. During the writing of *Mrs. Dalloway,* she became aware of her methods: "I should say a good deal about *Mrs. Dalloway,* & my discovery; how I dig out beautiful caves behind my characters; I think that gives exactly what I want; humanity, humour, depth. The idea is that the caves shall connect, & each comes to daylight at the present moment." Later she wrote: "It took me a year's groping to discover what I call my tunnelling process, by which I tell the past by installments, as I have need of it. This is my prime discovery so far; & the fact that I have been so long finding it, proves, I think, how false Percy Lubbock's doctrine is—that you do this sort of thing consciously. One feels about in a state of misery . . . and then one touches the hidden spring."[43] Whether or not the method of "tunnelling" discovered by Woolf and the conscious intentionality of Joyce's method are as opposed as they appear may be questionable. But there seems little enough doubt that Joyce's art was one of consciousness marvelously heightened: nothing can be found in a Joyce text that Joyce did not consciously put there. The process Woolf recognized as hers differs sharply; Woolf knows it to be unconscious, a hidden spring. In defining these two processes, which we may, for convenience, call the search for the father and the search for the mother, we have defined the watershed in modern literature. Joyce's was the pivotal book, the book that women would write against, as they wrote against Milton. Woolf's was the subversive, the innovative text, not only in its language and technique, but in its subject.

At the same time we must remember that both Joyce and Woolf saw the patriarchal culture, centuries after it had abandoned Ariadne and forgotten her, as embodying, in Trilling's words, "the will in entropy, in its movement through ambiguity and paralysis to extinction." In revealing this entropy, Trilling recognized, Joyce set against the world "an indomitable egoism that is itself an emptiness."[44] Woolf set against it a language that Joyce, like his admirers, might have found "feminine," and "frivolous" and distant from the reality of life. Joyce and Woolf were as opposed in their answers to that paralyzed and loveless world as they were in their private lives and in their personalities.

At fifty, when they had much work behind them, had suffered deaths and family sorrows, and turned with scorn from the academic world, they faced the world in different ways reflective of their art. To read their letters, starting in early 1932, is to understand their conditions and the pain unique to each. As Trilling was to write of Joyce's later letters, "there are scarcely any indications of an interplay between the self and the life around it, the existence of which is recognized only as the world rejects or accepts Joyce's art." "*Only disconnect,*" Trilling continues, "had long been an avowed principle of his life, but until now it had not been put fully in force."[45] One must always bear in mind Joyce's trouble with his eyes, and his profound unhappiness over his daughter Lucia's madness. Yet how relentlessly each letter devotes itself to his suffering, his needs. To turn from these letters[46] to Woolf's is to turn to a way of life Joyce could never imagine, and never tried to. Although Woolf was to write "when a person's thick to the lips in finishing a book . . . it's no use pretending that they have bodies and souls as far as the rest of the world is concerned,"[47] her letters are full of that intimacy, that delighted sharing which in our time has been perceived as particularly feminine.[48] Her words are written with delight, and to delight the recipient. Thus to Vita Sackville-West she writes at the end of a long letter, "Well, I think, delightful as this letter is, I must go and put my pie in the oven; then we have ice cream to follow—you know we have a frigidaire—with fresh raspberries. Then we turn on the loudspeaker—Bach tonight—then I watch my baby owls learning to fly on the Church tower—then I read Lord Kilbracken—what a good book—then I think what about bed—on which note, as I chastely put it, I end." And lest it be objected that that is a letter to a lover, here is Woolf at the end of a letter to a deaf old lady from whom she could expect nothing: "I liked the boy who thinks I know about school life. I seem to be a well known authority upon Eton and Roedean. A cutting has just come which says that ignorant as Mrs. W. is about everything else, she is an admitted expert on girls' schools—nobody knows them so intimately. And I've only had the tip of my nose in one once, taking Nessa's child there. Aren't reviewers—well, well, it's a hot day, and I'm to keep cool. So I won't launch out; and I remember too, how we used to review books together, 100 years ago, for that long faced old lantern jawed man, who kept Charlotte Bronte's socks in a glass case in his drawing room"[49]

One can find nothing in Joyce's letters of this quality. They are all business, or the strict enactment of courtesies, or arrangements for himself and his family.

What can such a difference mark? Inevitably it must mark the value placed upon the lives of women, and their function in the world; it marks whether the destiny of women is to serve man as inspiration and comfort, or if it is to create themselves and new, joyful female lives. In a famous letter to Frank Budgen, written when he was finishing *Ulysses,* Joyce described the Molly Bloom chapter: "*Penelope* is the *clou* of the book. The first sentence contains 2500 words. There are eight sentences in the episode. It begins and ends with the female word *yes.* It turns like the huge earth ball slowly surely and evenly round and round spinning, its four cardinal points being the female breasts, arse, womb and cunt expressed by the words *because, bottom* (in all senses bottom button, bottom of the class, bottom of the sea, bottom of his heart), *woman, yes.*" The letter ends with a German phrase, "Woman. I am the flesh that always affirms," which Ellmann translates.[50] Here is the patriarchal view of women, presented in its quintessential form.

In 1977, Phillippe Sollers wrote that "Not enough attention has been given to the fact that throughout his life Joyce wrote with money provided by women."[51] Indeed, the conventional relation of women to men is almost personified by Joyce as he turned fifty. As Janet Flanner was to describe it, Sylvia Beach had determined to publish *Ulysses*; to accomplish this feat

> she became Joyce's secretary, editor, impresario, and banker, and had to hire outsiders to run her shop. She organized international and local subscription lists for the book to help finance its printing. . . . *Ulysses* was the paying investment of his lifetime after years of penury, Sylvia said, while hardly acknowledging the fact that the publishing costs almost wiped out her Shakespeare and Company. The peak of his prosperity came in 1932 with the news of his sale of the book to Random House in New York for a forty-five-thousand-dollar advance, which, she confessed he failed to announce to her and of which, as was later known, he never even offered her a penny. "I understood from the first that, working with or for Mr. Joyce, the pleasure was mine—an infinite pleasure: the profits were for him.[52]

As Sollers goes on to observe, "The last word of *Ulysses* is *yes.* It is supposed to be said by a woman. The most curious part of the whole affair is that people believe a woman says it because a man writes it.

. . . No one seems to have thought of having it spoken on a stage by a man. Moreover, why stage it? If not in order to screen what *it* stages?"[53]

If Joyce's view of women never changed, Woolf's did; after her fiftieth birthday she became less timid about accepting with grace the "yes" men had put into the mouths of women. Although for many years critics were to find her work in the thirties a falling-off, it was a new beginning. She came into touch with her anger about the text men had written for women, and about the world women were required to affirm but not affect. In fact, her work in the thirties is what her friend Tom Eliot was to call a raid on the inarticulate, "because one has only learnt to get the better words for the thing one no longer has to say, or the way in which one is no longer disposed to say it."[54] Woolf in her work after fifty raided the inarticulate because she had found new things to say; Joyce, in the same years, wanted a new way to say the same things, being no longer disposed to say them in the old way. Joycean critics agree that his three novels are the same pattern recreated. Woolf had to adventure into a new land, not only of language but of reality itself. If, as Trilling wrote of Joyce, "his alienation from so many of the modes and conditions of human existence is sometimes chilling,"[55] Woolf's alienation from the expected views and subjects was sometimes threatening.

In the end, these two lives, synchronic, can scarcely fail to strike us as prophetic and fated, in a way the Greeks would have understood. Each willed death in 1941, Woolf by suicide, and Joyce by ignoring an ulcer until it was too late. Their tasks were done. Joyce had written, in the new and ultimate language, the old cosmology, elegantly configured. Woolf had suggested how a new cosmology might be created. Woolf went in search of Ariadne, and Joyce threaded again the old labyrinth. Between them lay all the literary possibilities of the next age.

1982

ENDNOTES

1. Maria DiBattista, *Virginia Woolf's Major Novels: The Fables of Anon* (New Haven: Yale University Press, 1980), p. 2. But see the quotation from Jean Guiguet, a French critic, below, p. 245.

2. Richard Ellmann, *The Consciousness of Joyce* (New York: Oxford University Press, 1977), p. 133. Ellmann has listed in an appendix the books in Joyce's library in 1920.

3. *Virginia Woolf: A Writer's Diary*, Leonard Woolf, ed. (New York: Harcourt Brace, 1954), p. 349.

4. Hugh Kenner, *Joyce's Voices* (Berkeley: University of California Press, 1978), p. xii.

5. Lionel Trilling, "James Joyce in His Letters," in *The Last Decade: Essays and Reviews, 1965–75*, Diana Trilling, ed. (New York: Harcourt Brace Jovanovich, 1979), p. 22.

6. Lionel Trilling, "A Novel of the Thirties," *ibid.*, p. 22.

7. Lionel Trilling, "James Joyce in His Letters," p. 33.

8. *The Diary of Virginia Woolf*, vol. 2, *1920–1924*, Anne Olivier Bell, ed. (New York: Harcourt Brace Jovanovich, 1978), p. 67.

9. See Herbert Howarth, *Notes on some Figures Behind T. S. Eliot* (London: Chatto & Windus, 1965), pp. 243–244, for a discussion of the influence of *Ulysses* on "The Wasteland."

10. *The Diary of Virginia Woolf*, 2:69, 68.

11. *Ibid.*, pp. 188–189, 193, 199, and 202.

12. Harold Bloom has written, in *The Anxiety of Influence*: "the motto to English poetry since Milton was stated by Keats: 'Life to him would be death to me.'" Sandra Gilbert in "Reflections on Milton's Bogey," *PMLA*, 93(3):370, quotes Bloom's line as "even more appropriate to women." See this whole essay and Sandra Gilbert and Susan Gubar, *The Madwoman in the Attic* (New Haven: Yale University Press, 1979).

13. Quoted in William York Tindall, *A Reader's Guide to James Joyce* (New York: Noonday Press, 1959), p. 125n. Tindall judges Virginia Woolf's objections to be "social," Lawrence's to be "moral."

14. Leonard Woolf, *Downhill All the Way* (London: Hogarth Press, 1967), pp. 108–109.

15. See Richard Ellmann, ed., *Selected Joyce Letters* (New York: Viking Press, 1975), pp. 166 passim, and pp. xxiii–xxv for Ellmann's comments on these letters.

16. *Diary of Virginia Woolf*, 2:189.

17. Lionel Trilling, "James Joyce in His Letters," p. 52.

18. See note 12.

19. *The Diary of Virginia Woolf*, vol. 1: *1915–1919*, Anne Olivier Bell, ed. (New York: Harcourt Brace Jovanovich, 1977), p. 193.

20. W. Y. Tindall, *Forces in Modern British Literature, 1885–1946* (New York: Knopf, 1947), pp. 304–305. Tindall called *Between the Acts* "confused and unreadable" (p. 308).

21. W. Y. Tindall, *James Joyce: His Way of Interpreting the Modern World* (New York: Scribner's, 1950), pp. 38, 42.

22. James Hafley, *The Glass Roof: Virginia Woolf as Novelist* (1954; rpt., New York: Russell & Russell, 1963), p. 73.

23. Jean Guiquet, *Virginia Woolf and Her Work* (New York: Harcourt Brace & World, 1965), p. 245. The original French version was published in 1962.

24. James Naremore, *The World without a Self: Virginia Woolf and the Novel* (New Haven: Yale University Press, 1973), p. 78.

25. DiBattista, *Woolf's Major Novels*, pp. 29–30.

26. Ellmann, *Selected Joyce Letters*, pp. 259–260.

27. *The Diary of Virginia Woolf*, 2:186, 308.

28. Many critics have noticed this, e.g., S. L. Goldberg, *The Classical Temper: A Study of James Joyce's Ulysses* (London: Chatto & Windus, 1961), p. 151.

29. For T. S. Eliot on *Ulysses* see Carol H. Smith, *T. S. Eliot's Dramatic Theory and Practice* (Princeton: Princeton University Press, 1963), p. 39. Eliot's essay "Ulysses, Order, and Myth" originally appeared in *Dial*, November 1923.

30. Virginia Woolf, *A Writer's Diary*, p. 165. For an important article on Woolf's enormous task in writing *The Waves*, see J. W. Graham, "Point of View in *The Waves*," *University of Toronto Quarterly*, April 1, 1970, pp. 193–211.

31. Goldberg, *The Classical Temper*, p. 35.

32. *Times Literary Supplement*, "Samodovolnost," Anon., December 8, 1966, p. 1137.

33. For example, J. Hillis Miller, "Virginia Woolf's All Souls' Day: The Omniscient Narrator in *Mrs. Dalloway*," in *The Shaker Realist: Essays in Modern Literature in Honor of F. J. Hoffman*, O. B. Hardison, ed. (Baton Rouge: University of Louisiana Press, 1970), pp. 100–127.

34. W. H. Auden, "Thanksgiving for a Habitat."

35. Diane Fortuna, "The Labyrinth as Controlling Image in Joyce's *A Portrait of the Artist as a Young Man*," *Bulletin of the New York Public Library* (1972), 76:120–180, p. 124. As will be evident, I have relied heavily on Fortuna's excellent retelling of the myths surrounding Daedalus.

36. *Ibid.*, p. 122

37. *Ibid.*, p. 129. Woolf was, of course, Virginia Stephen before 1912. For simplicity's sake, however, I call her "Woolf" throughout this essay.

38. Jane Harrison, *Prolegomena*; quoted in Fortuna, p. 129. In writing of Jane Harrison I have relied on two works: Robert Ackerman, "Jane Ellen Harrison: The Early Work," in *Greek, Roman, and Byzantine Studies* (Summer 1972), pp. 209–230; Jessie G. Stewart, *Jane Ellen Harrison: A Portrait from Letters* (London: Merlin Press, 1959). See also Jane Marcus, in *Bulletin of the New York Public Library* (Winter 1977), pp. 278 ff.

39. Ackerman, pp. 211, 213, 215, 225, 229.

40. Harrison, *Prolegomena*. Quoted in Stewart, p. 25.

41. Goldberg, p. 159.

42. See, for example, Jane Lilienfeld, "The Deceptiveness of Beauty: Mother Love and Mother Halo in *To The Lighthouse*," *Twentieth Century Literature* (October 1977), 23(3):345–376.

43. *The Diary of Virginia Woolf*, 2:263, 272.

44. Trilling, "James Joyce in His Letters," pp. 31, 27.

45. *Ibid.*, pp. 35, 36.

46. For Joyce's letters in 1932 and after, see *Letters of James Joyce*, vol. 1, Stuart Gilbert, ed. (New York: Viking Press, 1957), and vol. 3, Richard Ellmann, ed., 1966.

47. Virginia Woolf to Ethel Smyth, February 9, 1935. Used as epigraph to *The Letters of Virginia Woolf,* vol. 5, *1932–35,* Nigel Nicolson and Joanne Trautmann, eds. (New York: Harcourt Brace Jovanovich, 1979).

48. See, for example, Minda Bikman, "A Talk with Doris Lessing," *New York Times Book Review,* March 30, 1980, p. 24. See also Lessing's novel, *The Marriages Between Zones Three, Four, and Five,* 1980.

49. *Letters of Virginia Woolf,* 5:88, 95–96.

50. *Selected Joyce Letters,* p. 285.

51. Phillippe Sollers, "Joyce & Co.," *Triquarterly* (Winter 1977), p. 109. I am grateful to Nancy Nystul for bringing this article to my attention.

52. Janet Flanner, *Paris Was Yesterday,* Irving Drutman, ed. (New York: Penguin Books, 1979), p. xi.

53. Sollers, p. 114.

54. T. S. Eliot, "East Coker," *Four Quartets.*

55. Trilling, "James Joyce in His Letters," p. 26.

7

Virginia Woolf in Her Fifties

INSOFAR AS that is possible, Virginia Woolf became another person in her fifties. At fifty (more or less) one is either reborn or moribund. Looking back—as one tends to do at fifty, though not too much if one is busy living—Woolf must have felt that her accomplishment was notable. But she also knew she was beginning again. She writes in her diary, after rereading *The Years,* "For my own guidance, I have never suffered, since *The Voyage Out,* such acute despair on rereading, as this time. On Saturday, for instance: there I was, faced with complete failure."[1] She knew that *The Years* was, in a certain sense, a first novel.

Her fifties were not the time of her first awakening; there are more awakenings than births in a life. Endowed with genius, a writer awakens to its possibilities, if she is fortunate, after she has learned her craft. So it was with Woolf. Her love affair with Vita Sackville-West awakened her to her love for women, and to the possibilities embodied in *Mrs. Dalloway*.[2] In discovering this love, Woolf chanced upon the necessary release—as one might turn the dial on a safe, vaguely remembering the combination, hitting on it at last. From the publication of *Mrs. Dalloway* until 1932, Woolf was in what Olivier Bell, editor of the diaries, has called "perhaps the most fruitful and satisfying years of her life."[3] Then she had to learn a new art, to begin again.

If Vita's was the love that awakened Woolf to her major phase, Ethel Smyth's was the friendship that encouraged her new art.[4] The place of the two women in Woolf's life is reflected in their attitudes toward *Three Guineas*. Woolf expected both to dislike it, but Ethel Smyth replied "Your book is so splendid that it makes me hot." Vita, on the other hand, accused Virginia of "misleading arguments," which Virginia greatly resented. She didn't mind if Vita didn't agree with her, but she wanted to have it out "with swords or fisticuffs" if Vita did not realize *Three Guineas* was an honest book. "I took more pains to get up the facts and state them plainly than I ever took with anything in my life." "Oh Lord," she continued, "how sick I get of this talk about 'lovely prose' and charm when all I wanted was to state a very intricate case as plainly and readably as I could."[5] Woolf had been transformed into a different woman writer than the one Vita had loved.

If Vita's love awakened Woolf to *Mrs. Dalloway*, the writing of *To the Lighthouse* made possible the books that immediately followed it. This transformation was not as profound as the one Woolf underwent in her fifties, but it was essential to it. With the accomplishment of *To the Lighthouse*, Woolf not only was enabled to recognize the fullest possible extent of her genius in *The Waves*, but also freed her submerged gaiety, liberating herself to write *Orlando* and *A Room of One's Own*. Once her struggle with her mother was laid to rest, as Sara Ruddick has pointed out,[6] Woolf was free to write of women and the possibilities inherent in their relationships. *Orlando* was a marvelous jeu d'esprit, a love letter to Vita, restoring to her, as Nigel Nicholson has said, Knole, the inheritance that her birth as a girl had deprived her of.[7] Woolf would have liked, one guesses, to have restored to all women what their talents deserved and their sex denied them. John Graham has written that the second half of *Orlando*, after the change of sex, fails in its use of comedy: the serious elements dominate *Orlando's* "later chapters to its detriments as a work of art." Woolf has, in her own words, failed "to keep the realities at bay."[8] Had she been

able to read this comment by one of the best and most sensitive of
her critics, she would have recognized it as characteristic of the threat
she faced in her fifties. The moment one begins to criticize the destinies of women, even in a less than wholly serious way, the patriarchy
(by no means composed entirely of men) feels that art is betrayed.
Adrienne Rich was the first, as far as I know, to comment on a note
"of dogged tentativeness" in *A Room of One's Own*. "It is the tone of
a woman almost in touch with her anger, who is determined not to
appear angry, who is *willing* herself to be calm, detached, and even
charming in a roomful of men where things have been said which are
attacks on her very integrity." Woolf, Rich sensed, while addressing
women, was acutely conscious of being overheard by men.[9] But in
Woolf's fifties, with great work behind her, she would no longer fear
either the expression of her anger or its effects on the men who overheard her.

   Significantly, Leonard Woolf shared—indeed, to some extent
encouraged—the accepted view of the work Woolf did in her fifties,
the work that did not fear to offend the patriarchy. Leonard Woolf
writes: "Four times in her life she forced herself to write a book against
her artistic and psychological grain; four times the result was bad for
the book and twice it was bad for herself."[10] The four books Leonard
Woolf had in mind are: *Night and Day* (1919), *The Years* (1937), *Three
Guineas* (1938), and *Roger Fry* (1940). Three were written in Woolf's
fifties. I shall not discuss *Night and Day* here, since it does not belong
to the period I am exploring and represents a somewhat different
problem (but only somewhat). I believe that *Night and Day* was an
early and premature attempt to grapple with the "assigned script" of
women's lives. In any case, the other three books were written after
what I have called her transformation. They seemed to Leonard, and
to many others, "against her artistic grain" because this is precisely
what they were: a new start, "a raid on the inarticulate." Such an attempt must, of course, be against the grain in the sense Eliot conveyed
in the *Four Quartets*. Leonard has further muddied the waters by suggesting that in writing *The Years* Virginia was responding to the accusations of critics that "she could not create real characters or the
reality of everyday life."[11] Such an idea is simply nonsense: nothing in
her history suggests she had such a reason for writing. It must also be
noticed that only *The Years* caused her this terrible anguish, both in
revision and, especially, after publication. She cared little about the

public response to *Three Guineas* or *Roger Fry,* a point to which I shall return.

But I must digress to say a word about Leonard. His relationship with Virginia was never an easy one, even in the context of what David Daiches has called a marriage between a man of great talent and a woman of genius.[12] The past years have seen harsh criticism of Leonard, some of it—given the complexities of human life—deserved. I think he was wrong in the judgment of her work I have quoted. Further, one cannot but feel that to go behind her back to doctors, to impose upon her a regimen she dreaded, was to decide too readily that he knew more about her needs than she knew or could understand. I even believe that Leonard, in failing to understand, as he seemed uniquely qualified to do, the connection between the subjection of women and the misuse of authority epitomized in fascism, failed in an important intellectual way. But one knows, even today, sympathetic and supportive men who fail thus. It is not easy to forgive Leonard any of these things, but it is well to remember that he was backed up in his thought by all the medical knowledge of his day as well as by Vanessa; and that he was there coping, not advising from a safe distance, and without the benefit of hindsight. I believe, furthermore, as I shall argue, that Virginia's death was not due to the treatment she received, but to a decision she had taken about life itself, and to the desperate strain of the times. Many have also criticized Leonard for not taking her to Freud or someone among his followers. To be honest about my own bias, let me say that I think, had he done so, Woolf would never have written her novels (she might have written criticism) and would not have lived to undergo the transformation of which I write.[13]

Virginia Woolf, then, began *The Years* with a sense of breaking with the past. She found herself, as she was to write of Roger Fry, "at the beginning of life, not in the middle, and nowhere in sight of the end."[14] By "nowhere in sight of the end," she meant not that there were an indefinite number of years ahead (she was to write later: "I'm 56; and think that Gibbon had allowed himself 12 years, and died instantly", but rather that hers was not the condition of old age where one waits and accumulates years. Neither she nor Roger ever faced that. But, picturing death by a bomb, she thinks: "Oh, I wanted another ten years".[15] Nowhere in sight of the end means that one waits not for death, but for the next achievement, the next daring.

I believe Woolf's next achievement was uniquely female. To allow oneself at fifty the expression of one's feminism ("the awful daring of a moment's surrender") is an experience for which there is no male counterpart, at least not for white men in the Western world. If a man is to break out into revolt against the system he has, perhaps for his parents' sake, pretended to honor, he will do so earlier, at a much younger age. The pattern of men's lives suggests that at fifty they are likelier to reveal their egoism than their hidden ideals or revolutionary hopes. I mention this to emphasize what has been so little understood by Woolf's biographers, editors, and, apparently, by Leonard himself: the nature of what happened to her in her fifties.

In Woolf's decision to express her sense of society's deprivation of women, she had two major obstacles to fear. The first, outside herself, was the ridicule, misery, and anxiety the patriarchy holds in store for women who express their anger about the enforced destiny of women. That not even Leonard could understand this condemns not Leonard, but the extensive influence of the system that has served men so well. Even today, after a decade or more of feminism, young women shy away from an emphatic statement of their sense of self. Perhaps only women who have played the patriarchal game and won a self despite it can find the courage to consider facing the pain that the outright expression of feminism inevitably entails. It is worth noting that, against feminist attitudes, writers and critics who would modulate their language in other contexts feel free to indulge in tirades. Woolf knew what she had to fear, but at fifty she thought she had found the courage to bear it.

The second obstacle was within herself: her own sense of the importance to literature of separating art and propaganda (to put it in its harshest terms, which she never failed to do); she saw art and discursiveness as opposed, and the presentation of "fact" inimical to art. Her sense of art, which had with the force of a religious principle forbidden "propaganda," was the hardest obstacle to overcome. Profoundly felt principles are often the bedrock on which the structure of our sanity rests.

It was this second obstacle, of course, that Leonard spoke of when he said she was writing against the grain. Or, as Quentin Bell put it, *The Years* "was a step back, or at least a step in another direction. It could easily be a wrong direction."[16] In no sense was it a step back, but it was a step in the direction marked for her by the work of Huxley and D. H. Lawrence, whose writing she recognized as the kind from which, all her life, she had shied away. She wrote about Lawrence:

> But it's the preaching that rasps me. Like a person delivering judgment when only half the facts are there: and clinging to the rails and beating the cushion. Come out and see what's up here—I want to say. I mean it's so barren: so easy: giving advice on a system. The moral is, if you want to help, never systematise—not till you're 70: and have been supple and sympathetic and creative and tried out all your nerves and scopes. He died though at 45. And why does Aldous say he was an "artist"? Art is being rid of all preaching: things in themselves: the sentence in itself beautiful. (*WD*, pp. 182–183)

This entry, written a few months before Woolf's fifty-first birthday, must be read in context. She recalls what she had always objected to in Lawrence, what in a way would threaten her own sense of herself as an artist should she imitate it. But after all, if not seventy, she was over fifty and had certainly been "creative and tried out all her nerves and scopes" in the earlier novels.

Then, just after her fifty-first birthday, she read *Point Counterpoint*. "Not a good novel. All raw, uncooked, protesting . . . interest in ideas; makes people into ideas" (*WD*, p. 230). But in a sense perception frees her: Huxley, younger and less tried than Lawrence, had taken to ideas before taking to art. This, at least, she could never be guilty of.

It is significant that, when Leonard Woolf edited *A Writer's Diary,* publishing only those sections that revealed Woolf as a writer, more than half the selections were written after Woolf had turned fifty. The first 172 pages cover the years 1918 through 1931. The rest of the book, through page 351, covers the remaining ten years, with only three months of the last year. One might have expected that in the earlier period, the years of her great "artistic" achievements, she would have been exploring her art. In fact, the most interesting introspection about herself as a writer came in the last period, when she underwent an inner debate between her ideas about art and her feminism.

The greatest turmoil surrounded two books: *The Years* and *Roger Fry.* The reasons for this turmoil become clearer if we realize that *Three Guineas,* the book that has most directly annoyed her male editors and, according to Nigel Nicolson, most of her male correspondents,[17] did not cause her any noticeable anguish. For Woolf herself, the battle was over by the time she published *Three Guineas.* Having fought through to the new courage that marked *The Years,* she was free in what she called her "pamphlet" to assume a tone that is far from ladylike, wholly unconciliatory, beyond the charm of *A Room of One's Own*: she was able to indulge the glorious release of letting her anger rip. She reacted with emotion only to Vita's accusation that she had been dishonest. She knew from her hard work on *The Years* that "facts" were difficult to encompass in a novel; soon she would discover that they are some-times recalcitrant in biography;[18] but in her "pamphlet" she could sim-ply shout them from the rooftops and be glad.

Still, the tone of *Three Guineas*, and its accusation of the connection between the making of war and the treatment of women, *was* angry: Woolf, like all women, had to fight a deep fear of anger in herself. For many years I was made uncomfortable by *Three Guineas*, prefer-ring the "nicer" *Room*, where Woolf never presses against the bounds of proper female behavior—where, it could seem, her art prevailed. I say this to my shame. What prevailed was not her art alone, but her fear (and mine) of arousing the patriarchy to disgust, of acting wholly apart from the "script" assigned to women. For as read in the 1930s *The Years* was easier to live with than *Three Guineas*; for Woolf herself it was otherwise; she struggled with *The Years* and, as her diaries and letters testify, found, in her ability in *Three Guineas* to say the unac-ceptable, an extraordinary release. She, who had worried so about re-views, did not even bother to read Queenie Leavis through.[19] From first to last, *Three Guineas* was a romp.

"Sunk once more in the happy tumultuous dream," she wrote in her diary; "began *Three Guineas* this morning and can't stop thinking it." And a bit later: "Spiritual temperature went up with a rush: why I don't know, save that I'm having a good gallop at *Three Guineas*." Was *Three Guineas*, she wondered, the achievement of her fifty-five years? She did not mean, I think, the achievement of a lifetime, sur-passing *The Waves* or any earlier work. She meant the achievement of being fifty-five, and of finding the courage and relief to utter the for-bidden words. The achievement of fifty-five is different, and in its way harder: "But I wanted—how violently—how persistently, pressingly, compulsorily I can't say—to write this book: and have a quiet com-posed feeling: as if I had said my say: take it or leave it: I'm quit of that: free for fresh adventure—at the age of 56." She had cleared her decks, said what she had always wanted to say, shifted the burden: "now I feel entirely free. Why? Have committed myself, am afraid of nothing. Can do anything I like. No longer famous, no longer on a pedestal: no longer hawked in by societies: on my own, forever."[20] This is the account of a woman who has transformed herself in her fifties.

The transformation had begun with *Flush,* a mock biography of a dog. Perhaps she had in mind a loving parody of Lytton Strachey, whom just then she found newly charming and saw too seldom. She had not liked the mixture of fact and fiction in his *Elizabeth and Essex,* but she was thinking of him with new affection.[21] And we can hardly doubt that, in working on her biography of a spaniel, she found most tempting the conflict between the doggy fact and doggy fiction or between desire and the demands of an imperious world. She had skirted the issue in *Orlando,* her other lighthearted work: where one's hero changes sex, what other "facts" can one brood upon? But here was a chance to play out the conflict in a canine sphere where few would argue or greatly care. In writing about a dog, she risked being called a silly but not a lout: above all, she would not be feared. She was practicing her scales.

When she had turned fifty in January 1932, Woolf still had before her the task of getting into print the *Second Common Reader*—the memorial volume to the old Virginia Woolf. Bell tells us that she did virtually nothing else for the first nine months of 1932.[22] The *Second Common Reader* ends with her essay "How to Read a Book," which closely resembles an essay by her father, also delivered before a school audience.[23] It may have seemed to her, as it surely seems to us, a fitting conclusion to her career as an old-fashioned critic, as her father's literary heir. Once the *Second Common Reader* was finished, she went back to "A Letter to a Young Poet," begun earlier. Here she brought sharply into focus, clarifying it for herself, her sense of isolation, not only from her generation, but, what is harder, from the young. There is a no-woman's-land discovered by those who expound their feminism late in life. Occupied neither by the friends of their youth, who disdained the fight, nor by the youth of the day, who have not yet taken it up, this land is a lonely place. In her "Letter to a Young Poet," Woolf, in enunciating her separation from the young men of her nephew's generation, expressed her own sense of isolation.[24] Responding to John Lehmann, who had written, "it has never been so hard to write poetry as it is today" (*CE,* 2:185), she must have seen their situation as in some ways analogous to her own. Young poets, she felt, had turned from the world to write wholly of themselves; surely they (like her?) should turn their eyes outward. She easily understood how they felt: "You are rasped, jarred, thoroughly out of temper. And if I am to guess the reason, it is, I should say, that the rhythm which was opening and shutting with a force that sent shocks of excitement from your head to your heels has encountered some hard and hostile object upon which it has smashed itself to pieces. Something has worked in which cannot be made into poetry; some foreign body, angular, sharp-edged, gritty, has refused to join in the dance" (*CE*, 2:185–86). This is an accurate account of what happens to the woman writer when she meets the hard and hostile fact of feminism. Woolf, as she knew, had been fortunate in that the world had allowed her to have her poetry first, but she understood the process young poets struggled with now: "The poet as I guess," she continued to Lehmann, "has strained him-self to include an emotion that is not domesticated and acclimatized to poetry; the effort has thrown him off his balance; he rights himself . . . by a violent recourse to the poetical" (*CE*, 2:187). It was not a recourse she would choose.

She did, however, have advice for the young poet, advice similar to what her friend Tom Eliot had written years before. "All you need," Woolf wrote now, "is to stand at the window and let your rhythmical sense open and shut, open and shut, boldly and freely, until one thing melts in another, until the taxis are dancing with the daffodils, until a whole has been made from these separate fragments" (*CE*, 2:191). Perceiving this, Woolf perhaps felt closer in her fifties to Eliot; perhaps she had discovered an affinity with him.[25] She wrote to Vanessa in 1936: "I had a visit, long long ago from Tom Eliot, whom I love, or could have loved, had we both been in the prime and not in the sere; how necessary do you think copulation is to friendship?" (*Letters*, 6:59). These questions that seemed to cluster around Eliot were the ones she was trying to master in *The Years*, spun out, as she wrote to Lehmann, "in the novelist's way."

Finally, in writing "A Letter to a Young Poet," Woolf faced the fame she had won, which she knew would be the price of her fem-inism. The great poets cared nothing for fame, she wrote. Just look at famous people, she admonished Lehmann and herself, how the waters of dullness spread around them (*CE*, 2:194). In seeming to advise on a situation utterly different from her own, Woolf enumerated the costs of not doing what the world expects of you. Meanwhile, she played with facts a bit by pretending to be a dog—the dog, moreover, of a woman whose life was a byword for patriarchal imprisonment.

Woolf began to write *The Years* at the end of her fiftieth year. As is by now well known, the novel began to go with great ease, as had *To the Lighthouse.* She was writing of long-buried feelings, of passions conceived in youth, now a joy to express at last. The problems began with the revision, and with her decision to eliminate the feminist "propaganda" from her work. I shall not here retell the whole story of her painful creation of this extraordinary novel. Suffice it to recognize that an understanding of it awaited feminist criticism, a discipline as derided, and as undeservedly so, as *The Years* itself. Analysis of what Woolf had set out to do, and what she ultimately accomplished, became clearer when the manuscripts were consulted. In reviewing here some of the problems Woolf faced in this revision, I am garnering facts and insights from the work of recent scholars and critics.[26] My aim is to suggest, in the light of my own experience of being in one's fifties, how it was that in middle age Woolf found herself uniquely urged toward an artistic act of great courage. Those professional women of my generation who became frank feminists in their fifties are few enough, and they had the support of a growing women's movement. This meant practically that, though they would be derided, they would not be altogether isolated. Woolf had no women's movement to encourage or support her; her energies were fired by the growing fascist menace in Germany and Italy. What most impelled her, I believe, was precisely that conviction most derided by her editors: the connection between totalitarianism and the subjection of women. She was worrying about the rights of women when, Bell felt, she should have been worrying about the rights of nations. In choosing to demonstrate the deprivation of the girls in her generation, Woolf emphasized the connections between fascism and the patriarchal family. This connection, together with the presentation of patriarchal family life, was what *The Years* was to embody. Her terrible struggles with the novel came after the first free writings, in a revision in which she tried to shape the fiction without the support of the essay. The result, *The Years,* has been widely misunderstood because its effect was, after all, a negative: the failure of communication, of solution. Not even the opening of the professions from which women have been barred —Peggy is a doctor at the end of *The Years*—offers a solution. Woolf understood the fascination "radiated by women who seem to have cut through the constraints and eluded the strictures of the private house."[27] But she knew that this was a delusion. To change the condition of women, and the condition of the world, one had to change the whole structure, beginning with marriage—the institution conservatives are always most eager to retain. The immense courage behind *The Years* lies here: in the demonstration that there is no solution to the human dilemma, least of all marriage, that traditional haven for one sex conditioned upon the self-mutilation of the other. Woolf looked at marriage, furthermore, with scorn, the only weapon suitable to it; and "scorn is deliberately offensive." She added that offensive behavior is judged heroic only "when carried out on a large scale by men with machine-guns."[28]

It has been suggested by Victoria Middleton that *The Years* is "antivisionary," aimed at the very heart of "literary creation itself."[29] This is true only if we are prepared to call "The Waste Land" antiliterary and antivisionary. What *The Years* is, I think, is counter to the visions that had already made Woolf justly famous. When the same critic observes, like Leonard Woolf, that in *The Years* Woolf "chose to work in a mode contrary to her deepest creative instincts,"[30] we recognize how extraordinary it is, in one's fifties, to search out a new creative vein, to allow one's anger to drive one to the discovery of new forms. This measures the terrible daring of Woolf's, and all the best, feminist writing: by its nature it opposes what we have learned from the great art of the patriarchy—that anger is inimical to creation.

All her life Woolf had written against such anger, had, indeed, castigated Charlotte Brontë for this very fault.[31] To discover in one's fifties the courage to go against this conviction is as painful as it is rare. Given the shock of this reversal, it is not surprising that admirers of Woolf's earlier works accuse American critics of overestimating her feminism. As James Naremore has pointed out, Woolf was alone among great modern British novelists in abandoning "nostalgia for the old, predemocratic order of things."[32] She also began to wonder if private values, embodied in women, might not be translated into public values, enacted by men and women.[33] She knew, in any case, that in having given the private values over to women to keep, men had in effect abandoned them. She revealed this in *The Years* and stated it boldly in *Three Guineas*. Her courage was matched only by her relief.

According to Leonard Woolf, Virginia was persuaded against her better judgment to write the biography of Roger Fry. So, at least, it appeared to Leonard and, perhaps at first, to her. But I believe that her assumption of that task was in keeping with the training of the new artist and writer she sought to become. I guess at three reasons why she took on this biographical task, but they are only guesses; perhaps not even she understood them.[34] Above all was the chance to deal with facts, to re-create a life where interpretation must be reconciled with hard evidence: the conflict between vision and fact that she had, in a sense, worked out novelistically in, for example, Lily Briscoe's ideas about painting had now to be confronted in nonfiction as well. Second was the sheer appeal of biography, a form she had always loved, and to which her father, in a sense, had devoted his life. In this biography, moreover, she was writing about a man she had greatly admired, for whom she had felt profound affection. His particular talents and gifts were precisely those she liked to espy in the lives of the "obscure," those who did not fit easily or at all into established institutions. Quentin Bell makes a point of how much she had to suppress, because of pressures from Fry's family, but more important was what she need not fear to unearth. She must have seen the task as a fair challenge. A too-little-mentioned threat to the biographer is that aspect of the subject that is not admirable: the biographer either suppresses it or feels violated by it. The subject of a biography is not like a living friend whom one loves in spite of his or her sinister tendencies: one does not spend one's working hours unremittingly with such a friend.

The third appeal of this task for Woolf must have been the chance to write about a painter, a worker in the visual arts, not in literature (despite Fry's admiration for Mallarmé and its influence on Woolf). Not only was Woolf absolved from recounting painful struggles with literary ideals; she was now enabled to explore her sister's art, which she had previously viewed only as a mirror of her own talents. Bell suggests that Woolf flattered Fry in praising his paintings. Perhaps so. But the writer feels differently toward the painter; ignoring technicalities, she is able to appreciate a kind of vision hidden from, or overlooked by, the art critic. "I could trace so many adventures and discoveries in your pictures," Woolf wrote to Roger Fry. "How you have managed to carry on this warfare, always striding ahead, never giving up or lying down & becoming inert & torpid & commonplace like other people, I can't imagine."[35] This seems to me less flattery than notice of something Woolf had learned to admire, to try to emulate: "the perpetual adventure of your mind from one end of the room to the other."

I may as well declare that I do not denigrate *Roger Fry* as others do. It tells us much about Fry, his family (which resembled Woolf's in many ways), his times, his hopes, his achievement. Compared with Frances Spalding's recent biography of Fry, Woolf's seems remarkably perceptive and well written, despite her need to avoid certain facts.[36] Indeed, those who wish a short course in the art of biography could do worse than to study both books. Furthermore, Woolf's biography tells us a great deal about Woolf herself, as is the way with fine biographies: Roger Fry, who—as Kenneth Clark has told us—changed the taste of England,[37] had in doing so left behind him much of the old England that Woolf fought against and would soon recall in "A Sketch of the Past." In allowing her to come to terms both with her past and with what she saw as the inexorable demands of the future, the biography of Fry served to crystallize her new attitudes.[38]

Woolf died shortly after her fifty-ninth birthday. If one is to understand why she ended her life as she did, it is necessary to set down the events of her last year. After she finished *Roger Fry,* Woolf was ill in bed until March 28, almost exactly a year before her death.[39] In that remaining year Germany invaded Norway, Denmark, Holland, and Belgium; France fell; Italy came into the war on Germany's side. The fear of the invasion of England was real, and the Woolfs, sensibly fearing Hitler's armies, acquired against their advent a lethal dose of morphia from Virginia's brother Adrian. During this year Woolf twice delivered public lectures, always a difficult feat for her, but worse in this time of stress. The Battle of Britain began, with daily air raids and planes fighting over Sussex. Within a month the Woolfs' newly acquired house in Mecklenburgh Square and their old house in Tavistock Square were bombed, the latter left in ruins. Such belongings as they could rescue were moved to Monks House; the Hogarth Press moved to Herefordshire. There was one small, ironic event. Forster, who had so angered Woolf in earlier years by failing to suggest her for the Committee of the London Library (because women were impossible, Leslie Stephen had agreed), now did so: she refused the offer.

Despite the peril and strain of the Battle of Britain, Woolf continued to work on *Between the Acts* and to live in Monks House—largely, compared with her accustomed life in London, in isolation. Between times she wrote "A Sketch of the Past," more detailed by far than any of her previous childhood memoirs, and she began "Anon," her new nonfiction book. In war and middle age, she looked back, trying to organize the past in a new way. In "Anon" the past was history, literature, and the sense of their connections to those whom she had always called the "obscure." She did not wish to write another *Common Reader,* but she was concerned, as Brenda Silver points out, with the battle of the creative instinct's power against "darkness and disruption."[40] Shakespeare and bombs seemed to her at this time, following the advice she had given the "Young Poet," to be part of the same sentence, the same theme. Yet both the memoir and the nonfiction work were left unfinished. She survived only a month after she completed her novel *Between the Acts.* Why did she kill herself? Why did she lack the strength to survive?

I have already mentioned Leonard's misguided act in going behind her back to consult a doctor; added to this was Vanessa's brutal letter to Virginia—"What shall we do when we're invaded if you are a helpless invalid"—the words of a vigorous person trying to "snap" another out of her despair. These factors were important—coming from the two people she loved most, how could they not have been? But I believe the balance was already tipping away from life.[41]

Woolf *was* in her fifties, a time when one either determines to live as long as possible or begins to count the cost of continued life. I believe she began to reckon as one who has long since determined that life is not worth prolonging at any price. Because Woolf had tried to kill herself before, it has been assumed that her suicide was a symptom of her madness. The excellent article by Susan M. Kenney on this subject, and Nigel Nicolson's introduction to volume 6 of Woolf's letters, should serve to dispel that idea.[42] Woolf's suicide was a free act, a choice; I believe Kenney is right in suggesting that the final choice on the side of life in *Between the Acts* was Woolf's ultimate rendering of the balance of the world, her commitment to the possibility of affirmation. As Kenney well puts it, writing of all Woolf's novels, "She made up for her lack of an integrated, meaningful, and above all comforting vision by literally making it up, creating it not out of conviction or even theory, but out of sheer will and imagination, and she gave it to all her characters. . . . [I]n doing so she was both exerting power over the imagined life, and giving the vision to herself as she existed in her characters."[43]

In the case of Woolf's feelings at the end of *Between the Acts,* however, I do not believe that Kenney's description, perfect for all the other novels, is exact. Woolf's affirmation in *Between the Acts,* as I see it, is an affirmation on the side of life, but, unlike the conclusions of the other novels, it is not a vision of life as she might have lived it. The dichotomy Kenney suggests between Woolf and her characters exists, I believe, up to this last novel: Mrs. Dalloway through Bernard in *The Waves* affirm life in a way Woolf herself could conceive of affirming it, had she had the psychic strength to do so. Her characters did, as Kenney asserts, act for her in ways she might have acted but for the pain. I agree with Kenney that this is what writers do. But I think the vision in *Between the Acts* is a different one: Woolf believed that life would begin again, but not that she would ever be a part of it, even in her imagination. She did not wish to be a part of it, and her characters could not act for her. Thus *Between the Acts* ends with the possibility of a childbirth she had not risked, an act unconnected with herself at that time.

She felt this separation, I believe, because of the state of the world, because of her conviction that civilization was done for, and because her feminism had come too late; she felt it above all because of her isolation, her distance from the London she had loved and from its life. Only those who love large cities and die a bit away from them (though they may cherish country vacations and travel for a month at a time) can know the slow depression that follows exile from a loved city. And when that exile is enforced because one no longer has a home there, because the very city is being destroyed, the country isolation becomes an even greater burden.

Other life might begin again, at the beginning of a new civilization, but not hers. She must have thought with great logic about suicide. Women, of course, can approach suicide with greater freedom from guilt than can men. A man will find another woman easily enough (and Leonard indeed found the companionship of Trekki Parsons), but a man who deserts an aging woman will have abandoned her to loneliness, sadness, and an autonomy she may not be prepared to undertake. This is, perhaps, an odd advantage of womanhood, and one that will, if feminism succeeds, not long prevail. But Woolf might well have thought of it and considered the easier life Leonard might find with another woman. Then, she did not find within herself great powers of renewal. They rarely are present in one's fifties, and they were less so for her now; she had, in any case, never thought of more than ten more years of life—that is the longest extensions she ever imagines or contemplates in her letters or diaries. And the battle with what she thought of as "the horrible side of the universe, the forces of madness," seemed to her likely to be lost. As Bell suggests, for her only the feminine as opposed to "the beastly masculine" might have held off the nightmare.[44] She had done all she could on that behalf, but it must have seemed to her, despite her personal relief in taking up the fight, that it was too late: "masculine" behavior, extreme to the point of madness, had taken over the world. She chose to end her life before the chance to make that decision for herself could be taken from her.

In 1939 she had recorded in her diary that her friend Margaret Llewelyn Davies "lives too carefully of life." "Why," Woolf asks, "drag on, always measuring and testing one's little bit of strength and setting it easy tasks so as to accumulate years?" Though Woolf grappled with new ideas, to give her "brain a wider scope," the thought of death was never far away. She found herself quoting Arnold on old age:

The foot less prompt to meet the morning dew
The heart less bounding at emotion new.
And hope, once crush'd, less quick to spring again.[45]

Later she wrote: "The house is damp. The house is untidy. But there is no alternative. Also days will lengthen. What I need is the old spurt" (*WD*, 350). It is the voice of Madame de Staël, exiled by Napoleon from Paris. But friends might visit Madame de Staël: Paris was not under bombardment. Woolf tried to cheer herself up, in letters to friends, about the "snatches of divine loneliness" and her love for Leonard: "and my heart stood still with pride that he had ever married me" (*Letters*, 6:286). She tried to think of the future for her friends, telling Ethel Smyth that there had never been a woman's autobiography: "I should like an analysis of your sex life," Woolf wrote, reminding Smyth that no woman had yet told the truth. But she knew that even if such an analysis ever came (as it has in our time) she would not be a part of it, not in the flesh. Having totted up the score, she decided that death was the way for her. True, she said in her last note to Leonard that she feared madness again. There had been madness in her past, but madness now was, I suspect, not the heart of the matter; it was simply the easiest way to describe despair, or the clear decision that life in her sixties, given the conditions of her world, was simply not worth the terrible effort it would have cost. She had not, after all, petered out. She had done something wholly new in her fifties—embodied her woman's anger and found a new way to speak about the past—and if the effort exhausted her, she had left behind an affirmation that would last, as her earlier novels would last, long after her life and those terrible times were over.

1981

ENDNOTES

1. *Virginia Woolf: A Writer's Diary*, Leonard Woolf, ed. (New York: Harcourt Brace, 1954), p. 257. Hereafter referred to as *WD*.

2. Although many critics have noticed a change in Woolf embodied in *Mrs. Dalloway*, I am chiefly indebted here to the master's essay of Julie Abraham (Columbia University, spring 1980) on the full implications for *Mrs. Dalloway* of Woolf's discovery of lesbian love.

3. *The Diary of Virginia Woolf*, Olivier Bell, ed. (New York: Harcourt Brace Jovanovich, 1980), 3:vii.

4. See also Jane Marcus, "One's Own Trumpet," *Chicago Magazine*, June 1979, pp. 201–203.

5. *The Letters of Virginia Woolf* (New York: Harcourt Brace Jovanovich, 1980), 6:232, 240, 243.

6. Sara Ruddick, unpublished paper.

7. Nigel Nicolson, *Portrait of a Marriage* (New York: Atheneum, 1973), p. 208.

8. John Graham, "The 'Caricature Value' of Parody and Fantasy in *Orlando*," in *Virginia Woolf: A Collection of Critical Essays*, Claire Sprague ed. (Englewood Cliffs, N.J.: Prentice-Hall, 1971), pp. 102, 103.

9. Adrienne Rich, "When We Dead Awaken," in *Adrienne Rich's Poetry*, Barbara Charlesworth Gelpi and Albert Gelpi, eds., (New York: Norton, 1975), p. 92.

10. Leonard Woolf, *The Journey Not the Arrival Matters* (London: Hogarth Press, 1969), p. 40.

11. *Ibid.*, p. 41. See also Virginia Woolf's letter on *The Years* to Stephen Spender, *Letters*, 6:122.

12. David Daiches, *Virginia Woolf* (Norfolk, Conn.: New Directions, 1942), p. 6. Daiches adds that such a marriage "ought by all the laws to have ended in a mess."

13. See also Alix Strachey's essay in *Recollections of Virginia Woolf by Her Contemporaries*, Joan Russell Noble, ed. (London: Peter Owens, 1972), pp. 111–118. I base my view on the lives of many women I have known, some highly talented if none a genius of Woolf's kind, whose lives were destroyed, or impaired, by doctrinaire phallocentric Freudian analyses in the 1940s, 1950s, and 1960s.

14. *Roger Fry: A Biography* (New York: Harcourt Brace, 1980), p. 162.

15. *WD*, pp. 289, 340.

16. Quentin Bell, *Virginia Woolf: A Biography* (New York: Harcourt Brace Jovanovich, 1972) 2:195.

17. *Letters*, 6:240.

18. In an essay from those years, "The Art of Biography," Woolf discussed the difficulty of combining fiction and fact in that genre. *Collected Essays* (New York: Harcourt Brace Jovanovich, 1966–67), 4:221–228. Hereafter referred to as *CE*.

19. Queenie Leavis, the Midge Decter of her day, spoke exactly for the patriarchy, as some women have always found it easier to do. The men who edited the Virginia Woolf volume of *The Critical Heritage* still affirm Queenie Leavis, as does Elaine Showalter in *A Literature of Their Own*. Queenie Leavis' criticism is particularly sad because she attacks Woolf on the grounds of class and of Woolf's childlessness, two issues that, above all, should not divide women.

20. *WD*, pp. 265, 267, 271, 278, 281.

21. See Virginia Woolf's reference to Strachey's *Elizabeth and Essex* in "The Art of Biography"; and Bell, *Biography* 2:162.

22. Bell, *Biography,* 2:171.

23. I am indebted here to Katherine Hill, "Virginia Woolf and Leslie Stephen," Ph.D. diss., Columbia University, 1979.

24. Her nephew, Julian Bell, died in Spain on July 18, 1937. Had he died before *The Years* was finished, it is questionable whether Woolf would have found the courage to transform herself. After his death she finished *Three Guineas* and worked on *Between the Acts*.

25. See T. S. Eliot, "The Metaphysical Poets," in *Selected Essays, 1917–1932* (New York: Harcourt, Brace, 1932), p. 247. If at this time Woolf found herself closer to Eliot, she also found herself further from G. E. Moore and all the sweet principles of his ethics and her youth. When Moore visited Woolf in the thirties, she wondered how she could have revered this man. She was struck by "Moore's lack of what she could only call *mass*." She could no longer capture the sense of Moore's *force*. Paul Levy, *Moore: G. E. Moore and the Cambridge Apostles* (New York: Holt, Rinehart and Winston, 1979), pp. 296–297.

26. Important criticism and scholarship on *The Years* can be found in *Bulletin of the New York Public Library* (winter 1977), vol. 80, no. 2. All the articles are important. The article by Grace Radin, "Two Enormous Chunks: Episodes Excluded during the Final Revisions of *The Years,*" is essential to anyone studying *The Years* or the history of its composition and publication. See also Grace Radin's earlier "'I Am Not a Hero': Virginia Woolf and the First Version of *The Years,*" *Massachusetts Review* (winter 1975), pp. 195–208. Also essential is Virginia Woolf, *The Pargiters: The Novel-Essay Portion of "The Years,"* Mitchell A. Leaska, ed. and intro. (New York: New York Public Library and Readex Books, 1977). See also James Naremore, "Nature and History in *The Years,*" in *Virginia Woolf: Revaluation and Commentary,* Ralph Freedman, ed. (Berkeley: University of California Press, 1980), pp. 241–262. For rare early critical

praise of *The Years*, see references in the works cited; also Herbert Marder, "Beyond the Lighthouse: *The Years*," *Bucknell Review* (1967), pp. 61–70; and "Virginia Woolf's 'System That Did Not Shut Out,'" *Papers on Language and Literature* (winter 1968), pp. 106–111.

27. Sallie Sears, "Notes on Sexuality: *The Years* and *Three Guineas*," *Bulletin of the New York Public Library,* (winter 1977), 80(2):220.

28. Beverly Ann Schlack, "Virginia Woolf's Strategy of Scorn in *The Years* and *Three Guineas*," *Bulletin of the New York Public Library* (winter 1977), 80(2):146, 150.

29. Victoria S. Middleton, "*The Years*: 'A Deliberate Failure,'" *Bulletin of the New York Public Library* (winter 1977), 80(2):158.

30. Ibid., p. 162.

31. Michelle Barrett, ed., *Virginia Woolf: Women and Writing* (New York: Harcourt Brace Jovanovich, 1979), pp. 18–19.

32. Naremore, "Nature and History in *The Years*," p. 243. See essay 6 on James Joyce and Virginia Woolf.

33. See, in this connection, Valerie Saiving, "The Human Situation: A Feminine View," *Journal of Religion* (April 1960), 40:100–112, and Judith Plaskow, *Sex: Sin and Grace* (Washington, D.C.: University Press of America, 1980). Both authors discuss with brilliance (Plaskow in relation to the theologies of Tillich and Niebuhr) how the Christian ideals are in fact left to women to enact; sins therefore are by definition only male sins, since women already suffer from too much self-abnegation, not too little.

34. Here, and at certain other points, I take issue with Quentin Bell in his interpretation of the facts of Woolf's life. It is important, therefore, to state my belief that he has given the facts fairly and that, where he has prejudices, he has stated them. He has given us materials no one else could give, or give as gracefully, and if we reinterpret them (and he may find our reinterpretations foolish or wrongheaded) we can do so only because of his enabling work.

35. Bell, *Biography,* 2:181.

36. Frances Spalding, *Roger Fry* (London: Granada Publishing, 1980). Spalding has presented us with many important new facts about Fry. Her writing, however, is unfortunate; she seems oddly drawn to the dangling modifier: for example, "Working so closely together, their drawings became almost indistinguishable" (p. 20).

37. "His influence on taste and on the theory of art had spread to quarters where his name was barely known. . . . In so far as taste can be changed by one man, it was changed by Roger Fry." Kenneth Clark, "Introduction," Roger Fry, *Last Lectures* (Boston: Beacon Press, 1962), p. ix.

38. See in this connection Virginia Woolf's letters to Benedict Nicolson about her and Roger Fry's world, *Letters,* 6:413–414, 419–422.

39. The facts in this paragraph are mostly from Bell, *Biography,* 2:251–252.

40. Brenda Silver, "'Anon' and 'The Reader': Virginia Woolf's Last Essays," *Twentieth Century Literature* (fall/winter 1979), 25(3/4):358.

41. *Letters,* 6:485. Vanessa added: "you must accept the fact that Leonard and I can judge better than you."

42. Susan M. Kenney, "Two Endings: Virginia Woolf's Suicide and *Between the Acts*," *University of Toronto Quarterly* (summer 1975), p. 275. The whole article (pp. 265–289) is extremeley valuable.

43. *Ibid.*

44. Bell, *Biography,* 2:187.

45. *WD.* 301, 309, 346.

III

LITERATURE

AND

WOMEN

Introductory Note

"WHAT WAS Penelope Unweaving" was a keynote address given at the South Atlantic Modern Language Association. I could not see the Southern gentleman scholar on the platform behind me, but I was later told that if looks could kill I would have dropped dead on the spot. Since I was by then fairly innured to having my words bounce angrily back at me off the breasts of offended male academics, I was not overwhelmed by the general lack of enthusiasm for this speech. I hope it seems less frightening today, even in the South. Of course, many of the women and a few of the younger men applauded the talk even then, but they and I were in a noticeable minority.

"Marriage Perceived" was written for a volume edited by Marlene Springer entitled *What Manner of Woman*. I would certainly change a good deal in this article today, as well as bringing it up to date, but

I have decided not to let a woman a dozen years older rewrite the
words of her junior. I try to remember that this is a historical collection, and that I have decided not to rewrite the past, or at least that
part of it that appeared in print.

The essay on mother and daughter in *To The Lighthouse* was delivered for an annual event (now happily terminated) at the MLA Convention called "Celebrated Teachers, Celebrated Texts." I still think
that the relation between mothers and daughters is the least explored
and understood among all human relationships, and that until we understand it we will not understand something profound about women
and female sexuality. But that is an essay I have not yet written, indeed,
it is probably one that will have to be written by someone younger
and braver than I. I wish only to suggest to the writer of this future
essay that no woman believes she has been sufficiently loved by her
mother. Why is this?

"Alcott's *Little Women*" was written at the request of Kate Stimpson who was running a conference at Rutgers in 1977 on women writers in Paris in the twenties. (Nothing was old hat in those fervent
days.) When she asked me to be part of the conference, I told her I
knew little or nothing about the women in Paris in the twenties. (That
has changed too.) So she, being a woman of infinite resource, suggested that I talk on Alcott; I can't remember why, and I doubt that
she can either. It seemed a good idea at the time, and, oddly, still does.

The two essays on May Sarton were written, one as an introduction
to *Mrs. Stevens Hears the Mermaids Singing,* the other as a contribution
to a book of essays on Sarton edited by Constance Hunting, entitled
May Sarton: Woman and Poet. I have been a friend of May's for many
years now, and have rejoiced in the great fame and recognition of her
important work offered her in recent years. Success well beyond youth
and even middle-age is one of the greatest gifts the gods can bestow.
Unfortunately, it is a gift little appreciated in this country, where we
like to rush things, where we want it *now,* that is, young.

8

What Was Penelope Unweaving?

IN THE old myths, weaving was women's speech, women's language, women's story. Of all human accomplishment, Freud granted woman only the invention of weaving: an art, he conjectured, they had devised to conceal their genital deficiencies. But the old stories confirm that women wove, not to conceal, but to reveal, to engage, to counter male violence. For this they are punished, but not before "the voice of the shuttle" had been heard, if only to be silenced again. Women's weaving was women's answer to their enforced silence about their own condition, their own mutilation.

Here is the story of Arachne, who not only wove better even than Athene, but in a weaving contest dared to illustrate crimes the gods had committed against women. As Ovid tells it:

Neither Minerva, no, nor even Envy
Could find a flaw in the work; the fair-haired goddess
Was angry now, indeed, and tore the web
That showed the crimes of the gods, and with her shuttle

Struck at Arachne's head, and kept on striking,
Until the daughter of Idmon could not bear it,
Noosed her own neck, and hung herself.

Where upon, as we all know, Athena, or Minerva, turned Arachne into a spider, who might weave forever, but who could not testify against male violence.

Then there is Philomela. Tereus, her brother-in-law, had raped her and cut out her tongue to prevent her giving evidence against him. But Philomela weaves the story of her violation into a tapestry, and has it conveyed to her sister Procne. So silenced women find a "voice."

Ariadne did not speak. She provided Theseus with a thread, that with which one weaves, to lead him out of the labyrinth. He rewarded her by abandoning her; her story remains unfinished, or told in different versions. It is notable that Joyce, interested only in the labyrinth of male questing, did not stop to wonder about Ariadne, did not even mention her.

And then there is Penelope. She is perhaps the most famous weaver of all, but only, we have all thought, in a limited way, more notorious, perhaps, as an unweaver. She is the true wife weaving her father-in-law's shroud and unweaving it in the night, as Helen weaves a tapestry of the heroics in the war fought over her. Between them, Helen and Penelope represent what might be called the legitimate weavers, those who weave while men make war, and stop weaving when the violence ends. Arachne and Philomela represent the defiant woman weaver, the one who will not be silenced in her only art though it costs her her life. What I want to suggest is that there is another way to look at Penelope's weaving.

What do we know of Penelope? As W. B. Stanford writes: "The conventions of successive romantic eras in European literature . . . have been heard on faithful Penelope. It would take a whole volume to free her from the accumulated disparagements of centuries." She is no longer young and, as Stanford writes:

For the first ten years, while Odysseus was still with the Achaean chieftains on the Trojan campaign, Penelope had simply to contend with her loneliness and the normal problems of a household whose master is absent. But when, after the sack of Troy, Odysseus failed to return in due time, her difficulties became much more severe. Then she had to cope with the obstreperous attentions of over a hundred lusty suitors insolently frequenting her house and devouring its substance; she had to manage disloyal servants; she had to control a vigorous and rather unsympathetic son in the uncertainties of his approaching manhood. It is hardly surprising, then, that when Odysseus returns in the twentieth year of her ordeal he finds her nerves frayed and her heart almost frozen with despair.

(I would like to suggest here that Penelope's situation, betwixt and between, is paradigmatic of woman's situation in many cases today, allowances being made for the change in time and mores. She is, shall we say, a single parent? But I shall leave that point for a moment. I have not yet done with the historical Penelope.) Let me recall for you (in Lattimore's translation) how we learn of Penelope's weaving and unweaving: One of the suitors speaks:

> . . . you have no cause to blame the Achaian suitors,
> but it is your own dear mother, and she is greatly resourceful. . . .
> She set up a great loom in her palace, and set to weaving
> a web of threads long and fine. Then she said to us:
> "Young men, my suitors now that the great Odysseus has perished
> wait, though you are eager to marry me, until I finish
> this web, so that my weaving will not be useless and wasted.
> This is a shroud for the hero Laertes . . .
> So she spoke, and the proud heart in us was persuaded.
> but in the night she would have torches set by, and undo it.
> So for three years she was secret in her design, convincing the Achaians,
>   but when the fourth year came with the seasons returning,
> one of her women, who knew the whole of the story, told us,
> and we found her in the act of undoing her glorious weaving.
> So, against her will and by force, she had to finish it.
>
> (Book 2:88–105)

Twice in the Odyssey, Telemachos sends his mother out of the circle of men and back to her weaving. Once, when she is saddened by songs "of the Achaians' bitter homecoming" and asks the singer for other songs, Telemachos disallows her right to an opinion in the matter, and sends her to her room with these words:

> Go therefore back in the house, and take up your own work,
> the loom and the distaff, and see to it that your handmaidens

ply their work also; but the men must see to discussion,
all men, but I most of all. For mine is the power in the household.

(Book 1:356–359)

Telemachos will use almost the identical words in Book 21 (ll. 350–353) when he sends away his mother who is discussing the contest with the bow; a contest, we will recall, that is her idea. In this case, we recognize that Homer had to get Penelope off the scene of slaughter; yet here again, woman is dismissed to her weaving, far from violence, and the world of men and power and reverberating public events.

What, apart from the facts I have just reviewed, do we know of Penelope? Until recently, she can hardly be said to have gripped the imagination of either post-Homeric writers on the Ulysses theme or classicists. Joyce took the father-son theme from the Odyssey, and developed it, deepening the psychological interest of Telemachos. As for Penelope, Joyce was content to again present her, in Stanford's words, as "the faithless adulteress of the post-Homeric legend," to which is added what Stanford called, "sordid eroticism." I would call it rather male eroticism: Joyce's Molly is a male fantasy of female sexuality. But recently, all this has changed.

Many classicists have, in recent years, begun writing of Penelope, the scenes of her reconciliation with, and recognition of Odysseus, and particularly of what Stanford has called Homer's "high tribute to a woman's intelligence." There are three major points I wish to extract from all these discussions in order to suggest that Penelope's reasons for unweaving were not as obvious as they have been taken to be.

Let us recognize, first of all, that Penelope in the *Odyssey* is in a unique position for a woman of that culture: she has a choice. Marriage to one of the suitors would have been a socially acceptable choice for Penelope. She is, in Marilyn Arthur's words, "in a state of sociopolitical suspended animation. Thus, she has a freedom of choice open to her which would under normal circumstances be closed; and her decision to remain faithful to Odysseus takes on the character of a freely chosen and therefore morally significant action." Her husband is absent; her son is not yet grown; she is in a rare position of autonomy and choice.

Second, classicists have recently argued with great vigor and persuasiveness that Penelope recognizes Odysseus long before she expresses that recognition in the text. Whether her recognition is unconscious, subliminal, intuitive, or whether she consciously manipulates all events from the moment of the return of Odysseus in disguise does not affect my point. We do not see Penelope between the end of Book 4, when Telemachos is gone, the suitors are harrowing Penelope, and Athene sends her a dream of her sister, reassuring her, and Book 16, when both Odysseus and Telemachos have returned to Ithaca.

Penelope's dream at the end of Book 4 reminds her of her youth. We might mention here, in passing, the loneliness of women, far from their places of birth, and distant from their sisters: it was Procne's wish to see her sister which sent Tereus in search of Philomela. The appearance of Penelope's sister in a dream reminds us of Penelope's youth, about which there is a curious story. Her father Ikarios had given Penelope to Odysseus to marry, but he could not bear to part with her. When she set out for Ithaca, he followed her in a chariot beseeching her. Odysseus told Penelope that it was her choice: she could come with him of her own free will, or return to her father and her home. Penelope thus, in Arthur's words, chose her husband freely, just as she chooses freely to remain faithful to him. Penelope, like Odysseus, is characterized "by independence of mind and spirit." Because Penelope's choice has been the one we might call conservative, we have, I think, failed to see how extraordinary Penelope is. What she must do is to live her life without a story to guide her: no woman before has been in this position.

I have mentioned that we do not see Penelope between Books 4 and 16. What is happening to her in that time is that she is writing her own story, one that has never been written before. During the years between the end of the Trojan War and the suitors' discovery of her unweaving, Penelope has been trying out stories on her loom. She unravels each night what she has woven that day, not only for delay, but also, metaphorically, because unlike the other weavers, she is not writing a story of male violence, but the story of woman's free choice, and there is no narrative to guide her. When Odysseus has returned, it is she who will test him, she who will devise the contest with the bow, she who will be sure enough of his identity to say: the moment has come when I shall choose a new husband, She knows the old husband has returned but that, in any case, the time of her decision is at hand.

In the words of Froma Zeitlin, Penelope's future depends upon her "choice of one of the two possible roles which the two stories offer her—that of the faithful who receives the beggar in disguise and welcomes him or that of the woman who, surrounded by [suitors], practices the wiles of seduction, although another man's wife. Penelope is no teller of stories—quite the contrary. She is worn out with hearing the false tales of Odysseus which travelers have brought to her over the years and with meeting the false imposters of Odysseus himself, and she has become skilled at testing the fictions of another's words which have not power to seduce her. Yet she is the mistress of one fiction—and that to preserve her 'true' self for Odysseus—one 'story' which she tells again and again and never finishes, weaving and un-weaving the fabric of Laertes' shroud."

Zeitlin's is a totally accurate description. But, I would like to suggest, Penelope is faced, not with one story, or even two, but with an as-yet-unwritten story: how a woman may manage her own destiny when she has no plot, no narrative, no tale to guide her. Imagining, inventing, she weaves and unweaves and knows, when the stranger appears, that the time for the enacting of her new story has come.

Why do I say Penelope is without a story. Because all women, having been restricted to only one plot, are without story. In literature and out, through all recorded history, women have lived by a script they did not write. Their destiny was to be married, circulated; to be given by one man, the father, to another, the husband; to become the mothers of men. Theirs has been the marriage plot, the erotic plot, the courtship plot, but never, as for men, the quest plot. Women have been tempted into romantic thralldom, and then married, like the heroines of our great novels of the eighteenth and nineteenth centuries, or like the heroines of Harlequin romances. Their story was over.

Within the quest plot, men might do anything: literature tells us all they have done. Within the marriage plot women might only wait to be desired, to be wed, to be forgotten: as Tennyson more or less puts it, to be perhaps, after the first passion is over, nearer to a man than his horse and dog, but not much nearer. The question women must all ask is how to be freed from the marriage plot and initiated into the quest plot. How may women today find a script, a narrative, a story to live by?

It is, of course, ironic that Freud's annoying question of what do women want must still haunt us. It is not a question we can answer, because we cannot tell stories we have never heard. We women today who have entered the public sphere exist there in a state of intermittent anxiety and pain. Nor is it possible to foretell the source of the pain or the pattern it will follow. When women have had their stories written for them, played out their destinies toward marriage or death, they knew the pain that might follow: the first penetration; childbirth; rejection; aging; the suffering of one's children; the diverted attention of one's husband; the rending away from women whose place, like one's own, changed at the behest of male relatives. Pain is not easier for having been suffered before in the same way, but it is more bearable for having been narrated. That, indeed, is the chief source of patriarchal power: that it is embodied in unquestioned narratives. But for women today in new places and new jobs, there is no story to explain the pain, which is as unexpected as it is acute. We had been told, if we were kind and loving, we would be loved in return. In the public sphere, this is not true, and it must be learned on the pulses. Even when we have grown tough and knowledgeable, the power of the phallocracy is appalling. We invent as we go along, support one another, and recognize, as we must, that our choice is, as Florence Nightingale long ago told us, between pain and paralysis.

One cannot make up stories: one can only retell in new ways the stories one has already heard. Let us agree on this: that we live our lives through texts. These may be read, or chanted, or experienced electronically, or come to us, like the murmurings of our mothers, telling us of what conventions demand. Whatever their form or medium, these stories are what have formed us all, they are what we must use to make our new fictions. Since it is these stories—let me call them tales as a general term encompassing everything from Greek myths through Genesis, Snow White, General Hospital, and Pac Man—from which we shall form the new fictions of our lives, we must ask what tales seem to be available to us today out of which to make women's fictions that are not based upon Derrida's male/female opposition, where male is always dominant. We cannot yet make wholly new fictions; we can only transform old tales, and recognize how women have transformed old tales in the past. Out of old tales, we must make new lives.

What exactly do I mean when I say that we must make up new lives and new fictions? It becomes important, I think, to distinguish carefully between "fiction" and "myth." Not "myth" as in the stories of the Greek gods and heroes, but "myth" in the sense of the sustaining narratives of an ideology. Myth, Frank Kermode tells us "operates within

the diagrams of ritual, which presupposes total and adequate expla-
nations of things as they are, and were: it is a sequence of radically
unchangeable gestures." Myths are agents of stability and call for absolute assent. Fictions, on the other hand, "are for finding things out,
and they change as the needs of sense-making change." An English
writer, Angela Carter, has put it another way: "Myth deals in false
universals, to dull the pain of particular circumstances." A fair definition of myth is consolatory nonsense. It tells us how society says we
must live, rather than teaching us how we might learn to live.

You will understand, then, what I mean when I say women must
make new fictions of their lives, forsaking the myths they have for
milleniums been taught. Roethke has written: "I learn by going where
I have to go," and that is what we all find ourselves doing. The old
female plot provides security, social sanction, and, at the time it matters most, the tremendous ego satisfaction of becoming the object of
male desire. But to become the subject of one's own life is not only
harder, it has all the qualities of that nightmare condition: finding
oneself upon a stage, required to play the violin, an instrument one
has not previously personally encountered. As Avram Fleishman, one
of our more phallocentric literary critics recently said, discussing the
whole field of autobiography: "A man does not sit down to write his
autobiography in cold blood, without a language somewhere at hand
for the enterprise. The need to shape a story will lead the writer to
the story types that prevail in his culture." Exactly. Since the male
plots, unchanged, will not do for women, and since there are so few
female plots, how are we to make the new fictions that will sustain
us? Can we combine the female erotic plot and the male quest plot,
evolving for ourselves a new tale of female achievement? Is our only
choice between being Snow White, waiting for the prince's kiss to
awaken us to the only life appropriate to women, or being the step-
mother, planning her life, making plots, called a monster and forced
to dance herself to death in her red shoes. Is our only choice Penelope's:
to fend off the wiles of seduction, or to succumb?

Women, Virginia Woolf has told us, must "piece together fragments of beliefs, unsolved and separable, lacking the unity of phrases
fashioned by the old believers." And women have begun to do so.
Many of us find ourselves, like Penelope, no longer weaving a shroud
for the old ways of life, but needing to finish it, needing finally to
weave upon it the new stories we shall, in wonder and terror, begin

to live. In our own time, those who have written the new stories for us are, for the most part, poets, and they have often looked back, rewriting and reclaiming the Greek epics and stories to provide new narratives for lives. So the poet Kate Ellis has dreamed of the new woman; we wait:

Until she rises as though from the sea
not on the half-shell this time
nothing to laugh at
and not as delicate as he imagined her:
a woman big-hipped, beautiful, and fierce.

What I like best to remember, however, was Samuel Butler's inclusion among his arguments, most of them misogynistic, for why the *Odyssey* had been written by a woman. "When Ulysses and Penelope are in bed," he wrote, "and are telling their stories to one another, Penelope tells hers first. I believe a male writer would have made Ulysses's story come first, and Penelope's second." But of course, we know the answer is not that the *Odyssey* was written by a woman, but that we have already heard Odysseus' story, between Books 4 and 16. We know it, it is one of the narratives on which we have been nurtured. But Penelope's is a new story, a story of a woman's choice, her anxiety and her terror, and it must be heard now by the man who, despite all temptations, returned to her, and to the decisions he could trust her to make. He who had traveled far and seen many marvelous things, listened first to the new story of the woman who, staying home, had traveled to a new place of experience, had created a new narrative, who had been able, finally, to stop unweaving and to invent a new story.

1985

9

Marriage Perceived: English Literature
1873–1944

"WEDDING IS destiny, and hanging likewise," Heywood wrote over 400 years ago. It appears that novelists, until the modern period, agreed with the proverb in all its implications: weddings, like hangings, marked the end of experience. The novelist averted his eyes from married life as from the grave: perhaps he suspected a resemblance between them. If married people reappeared in the fictional world, it was to take part in social arrangements—perhaps the weddings of their children—but not to reveal aught of marriage. No select society ever demanded stronger oaths of secrecy, or commanded silence with greater success. Odysseus and Aeneas, among others, have visited the dead and heard accounts of that state; when, in literature, we have heard an account of marriage, it has not been dissimilar. Achilles, having chosen glory and a short life, said, when dead, that to have the gift of life again he would be the lowliest peasant. "Oh, when I was single, my pockets did jingle," conveys the same emotion less elegantly. In Dante's Hell, one goes on doing what one is doing; in marriage, apparently, it is the same.

Courtship has been another matter. On the road to marriage, as on a voyage to discovery, the journey not the arrival matters. Whether because the earth must be peopled, which was Benedick's excuse, or because of all the economic factors that marriage alone rationalized, each journey was for a land unreported upon. Had the voyagers been eaten by savages, forced into obscene rites, or lost all memory of their homeland? Marriage, like death, seemed a bourn from which no traveler returned, not, at least, as more than a ghost of his former self.

Recently, however, we have heard from a returned voyager. He is a Victorian—what Steven Marcus, who has edited his report, calls an "other" Victorian. Here is his view of marriage, smuggled out of the uncharted land:

> I tried to like, to love her. It was impossible. Hateful in day, she was loathesome to me in bed. Long I strove to do my duty, and be faithful, yet to such a pitch did my disgust at length go, that laying by her side, I had wet dreams nightly, sooner than relieve myself in her. I have frigged myself in the streets before entering my house, sooner than fuck her. I loving women . . . ready to be kind and loving to her, was driven to avoid her as I would a corpse. . . . My health began to give way; sleepless nights, weary days made me contemplate suicide.[1]

He remains married because, as he tells a friend, he would be all but a pauper without her money. His hate for his wife grows:

> Fear of the pox kept me awake some time. Then the scene I had passed through excited me so violently, that my prick stook like steel. I could not dismiss it from my mind. I was violently in rut. I thought of frigging, but an irrepressible desire for cunt, cunt, and nothing but it made me forget my fear, my dislike to my wife, our quarrel, and everything else—and jumping out of bed I went into her room.
>
> "I shan't let you,—what do you wake me for, and come to me in such a hurry after you have not been near me for a couple of months, —I shan't—you shan't,—I dare say you know where to go."
>
> But I jumped into bed, and forcing her on to her back, drove my prick up her. It must have been stiff, and I violent, for she cried out that I hurt her. "Don't do it so hard,—what are you about!" But I felt I could murder her with my prick, and drove, and drove, and spent up her cursing. While I fucked her I hated her,—she was my spunk-emp-

tier. "Get off, you've done it,—and your language is most revolting." Off I went into my bedroom for the night.[2]

A bit extreme, perhaps? Vulgar language, an obvious case of satyriasis, and the man is a brute. Let us, therefore, replace his obscenities with the discreet tones of Jane Austen:

> Had Elizabeth's opinion been all drawn from her own family, she could not have formed a very pleasing picture of conjugal felicity or domestic comfort. Her father captivated by youth and beauty, and that appearance of good humour, which youth and beauty generally give, had married a woman whose weak understanding and illiberal mind, had very early in their marriage put an end to all real affection for her. Respect, esteem, and confidence, had vanished for ever; and all his views of domestic happiness were overthrown. But Mr. Bennet was not of a disposition to seek comfort for the disappointment which his own imprudence had brought on, in any of those pleasures which too often console the unfortunate for their folly or their vice. He was fond of the country and of books; and from these tastes had arisen his principal enjoyments. To his wife he was very little otherwise indebted, than as her ignorance and folly had contributed to his amusement. This is not the sort of happiness which a man would in general wish to own to his wife.[3]

Let us add to this paragraph the fact, carefully provided by Austen, that the Bennets have five children and were for many years in expectation of a sixth. How carefully we avert our eyes from what we like to think Austen has failed to tell us, failed, even, to observe.

Novelists, from the eighteenth century until late in the nineteenth, paid to marriage the tribute Chaucer paid to the Roman Catholic Church: while little about it approached the ideal, no alternative was conceivable. For the novelist from the beginning, marriage, like money, class, property, and sex, with all of which it was, of course, intimately connected, was part of the landscape, part of that reality which Henry James defines for us as that we "cannot possibly *not* know." But, as James has elsewhere pointed out, "There is a traditional difference between that which people know and that which they agree to admit that they know, that which they feel to be a part of life and that which they allow to enter into literature."[4] It is my contention that marriage was not allowed to enter into literature, except as a condition universally acknowledged, but either unobserved, or glimpsed so occasionally that little was discovered beyond casual misery or boredom or both.

It is shocking at first to realize that all our tender ideas about marriage in literature are derived, not from marriage at all, but from court-ship. Marriage as a subject for literature has been avoided with an assiduousness that would be astonishing if we had not always taken the presence of marriage so for granted that we have failed to notice its absence.

Why was the married state itself so little examined in premodern fiction? In the first place, marriage is quotidian. It takes an Arnold Bennett to seek to give us what he was to call a tragedy in a million acts: an ordinary life. In the second place, happy marriages, we are fond of saying, are not news. There has been, then, a sense in the novel, as in life, not that marriage might be happy, but that those within it might, with luck, survive. Shaw, as always, astonished us by announcing what we had not known we knew:

> . . . sensible people make the best of one another. Send me to the gal-leys and chain me to the felon whose number happens to be next before mine; and I must accept the inevitable and make the best of the com-panionship. Many such companionships, they tell me, are touchingly affectionate; and most are at least tolerably friendly. But that does not make a chain a desirable ornament nor the galleys an abode of bliss. Those who talk most about the blessing of marriage and the constancy of its vows are the very people who declare that if the chain were broken and the prisoners left free to choose, the whole social fabric would fly assunder. You cannot have the argument both ways. If the prisoner is happy, why lock him in? If he is not, why pretend that he is?[5]

Before the twentieth century brought with it the cold Shavian shower of truth, we all assumed that marriage as a rewarding institution had been continually confirmed by novelists. As Forster said, speaking of the end of courtship novels, which is to say of most novels, "Any strong emotion brings with it the illusion of permanence, and the novelists have seized upon this. They usually end their books with marriage, and we do not object because we lend them our dreams."[6] The appeal of courtship over marriage as a literary subject is obvious: there is built in like the equipment in modern kitchens, suspense, danger, thwarted hopes, and a clearly understood reward—what, in earlier ages, they called the guerdon. The princess has been rescued, the dragon (money, averse parents, initial misunderstandings, competition) slain, the re-ward claimed. It begins "Once upon a time," and ends "they lived happily ever after." We all know this last phrase to be a fantasy, part of the fairy tale we tell only to our youngest children. Marriage, the

true ending of comedy, amounts to integration into the society. As
T. S. Eliot puts it:

> The association of man and woman
> In daunsinge, signifying matrimonie—
> A dignified and commodious sacrament.[7]

That is the past. When, in the twentieth century, Eliot searched the
wasteland, he founds its essence to be in marriage: in "A Game of
Chess," the two monologues signify matrimony as an undignified and
sterile perversion.

If, surveying nineteenth-century literature, we look beyond England
for a presentation of marriage as a viable relationship, Tolstoy is the
first writer to come to mind, "All happy families are happy in the same
way," he has told us in that famous first sentence. The way is soon
made clear: Dolly struggles with the ironing board and convinces herself that her life is acceptable because it is more serene than Anna's,
Kitty is moving the bedroom furniture when Levin wants to discuss
his soul, Anna has been so revolted she has fled out of society altogether. A man might settle to be Levin or Oblonsky—so might a
woman—but what human being able to read Tolstoy's novel with intelligence would settle for being Dolly or Kitty? One would rather be
Anna, and be dead, unless one yearned for life as unreservedly as did
Achilles.

If, still surveying the nineteenth century, we consider life, as we did
with the "other" Victorian, is there any marriage known to us we can
point to as "alive"? (The difficulty even of finding an adjective with
which to describe a "good" marriage is a clue to the problem: "successful" sounds like a business, or a machine; "happy," unreal, like a
fairy tale, without complex human tensions; "good" connotes class
achievement, as in "she made a good marriage.") The most obvious
and best example has the misfortune of not being, legally, a marriage
at all: nonetheless, the union of George Eliot and George Henry Lewes
was, by any standard, a "good" marriage. I shall not restate here the
account of how these two found each other, nor of how each did his
best work while their "marriage" lasted. What is remarkable, however,
is that George Eliot allows none of her heroines such a union, nor
any destiny like her own. Gail Godwin has written of Eliot's heroines,
"Each had intelligence, imagination, passion, and a keen desire to use
her life to the fullest. Yet each fails or languishes through a mistaken

sense of duty, or through death, before the book is done."[8] The question is a wide one. Graham Hough has noted that "George Eliot passed her personal life among the philosophic radicals, yet became the great novelist of the traditional sanctities of pastoral England."[9]

The traditional sanctities of pastoral England included, of course, marriage as the principal nexus of socioeconomic organization. Apart from all its connections with money and property, marriage was the only destiny possible to women who were trained for nothing else. We are all familiar with Charlotte Lucas' reply to Elizabeth when Elizabeth is horrified at her friend's decision to marry Mr. Collins. "When you have had time to think it over," Charlotte tells Elizabeth, "I hope you will be satisifed with what I have done. I am not romantic you know. I never was. I ask only a comfortable home; and considering Mr. Collins's character, connections, and situation in life, I am convinced that my chance of happiness with him is as fair, as most people can boast on entering the marriage state."[10] Who will wonder at Elizabeth's horror? Who can dispute the clear-sightedness of Charlotte, twenty-seven, not pretty, forced to choose between nonexistence and the possibility of a place, however inadequate, in society, and with no illusions about marriage. Four decades later, a Charlotte Brontë heroine would cry out, "I have to live, perhaps, till seventy years. As far as I know, I have good health; half a century of existence may lie before me. How am I to occupy it? What am I to do to fill the interval of time which spreads between me and the grave? . . . Probably I shall be an old maid . . . I shall never marry. What was I created for, I wonder? Where is my place in the world?"[11]

So Edward Carpenter (1844–1929), one of the most perceptive and least acknowledged commentators of the period, watched the slow torture of his six sisters:

> For indeed the life, and with it the character, of the ordinary "young lady" of that period, and of the sixties generally, was tragic in its emptiness. The little household duties for women, encouraged in an earlier and simpler age, had now gone out of date, while the modern idea of work in the great world was not so much as thought of. In a place like Brighton there were hundreds, perhaps, of households, in which girls were growing up with but one idea in life, that of taking their "proper place in society." A few meagre accomplishments—plentiful balls and dinner-parties, theatres and concerts—and to loaf up and down the parade, criticizing each other, were the means to bring about this desirable result! There was absolutely nothing else to do or live for. It is

curious—but it shows the state of public opinion of that time—to think that my father, who was certainly quite advanced in his ideas, never for a moment contemplated that any of his daughters should learn professional work with a view to their living—and in consequence he more than once drove himself quite ill with worry. Occasionally it happened that, after a restless night of anxiety over some failure among his investments, and of dread lest he should not be able at his death to leave the girls a competent income, he would come down to breakfast looking a picture of misery. After a time he would break out. "Ruin impended over the family," securities were falling, dividends disappearing; there was only one conclusion—"the girls would have to go out as governesses." Then silence and gloom would descend on the household. It was true, that was the only resource. There was only one profession possible for a middle-class woman—to be a governess—and to adopt that was to become a *pariah*. But in a little time affairs would brighten up again. Stocks were up, the domestic panic subsided; and dinner-parties and balls were resumed as usual.

As time went by, and I gradually got to know what life really meant, and to realize the situation, it used to make me intensely miserable to return home and see what was going on there. My parents of course were fully occupied, but for the rest there were six or seven servants in the house, and my six sisters had absolutely nothing to do except dabble in paints and music as aforesaid, and wander aimlessly from room to room to see if by any chance "anything was going on." Dusting, cooking, sewing, darning—all light household duties were already forestalled; there was no private garden, and if there had been it would have been "unladylike" to do anything in it; *every* girl could not find an absorbing interest in sol-fa or watercolours; athletics were not invented; every aspiration and outlet, except in the direction of dress and dancing, was blocked; and marriage, with the growing scarcity of men, was becoming everyday less likely, or easy to compass. More than once girls of whom I least expected it told me that their lives were miserable "with nothing on earth to do." Multiply this picture by thousands and hundreds of thousands all over the country, and it is easy to see how, when the causes of the misery were understood, it led to the powerful growth of the modern "Women's Movement."[12]

In *Love's Coming of Age,* Carpenter had earlier characterized the marriages resulting from the female situation: "The man needs an outlet for his passion; the girl is looking for a 'home' and a proprietor. A glamor of illusion descends upon the two, and drives them into each other's arms."[13] By the eighteenth century, the unmarried woman had already ceased to be an economic asset[14] so that spinsters of some achievement were granted the courtesy title of "Mrs.," the mark of a woman who had achieved an adult role.[15] Spinsters were not written of, though Henry James wished that George Eliot had left Dinah "to the enjoyment of that distinguished celibacy for which she was so well suited";[16] no one would write of them until Gissing's *The Odd Women* (1893), a novel whose title refers to the superfluity of women in an England where they could not possibly all find husbands and would not, probably, find any alternate destiny.

By the last two decades of the nineteenth century, then, the literary state of marriage was this: marriage was not really presented, but was accepted, like death, as one of the unavoidable conditions of life. Where we do see it in literature, marriage appears to be a situation like war, as Auden tells us, calling for "patience, foresight, manoeuvre."[17] Only occasionally is there a glimpse of a marriage which seems to hold the promise of life. In these marriages (there are examples in *Bleak House* and in *Persuasion,* with that uniquely happily married couple in all Austen, the Crofts), the woman is noted for being unusually competent, for sharing to a rare degree her husband's life, decisions, and adventures, and for being openly admired by him. What we notice here, of course, is that these marriages, like that of Eliot and Lewes, bear the marks of friendship. We shall return to this.

Oddly enough, the only extended view of a marriage in literature which can be said to be a union, not of equals but of comrades, is between men: Holmes and Watson. If we observe them in their adventures and their domestic life, we discover their relationship to be in accord with tradition to the extent that the husband, Holmes, is the unquestioned leader in all their doings; but at least Watson is a companion rather than an appendage or a domestic convenience. Commentators have often noted Watson's almost archetypal necessity to the detective story, but few have found his functions also to be in the domestic comforts he offers Holmes—comforts, furthermore, which do not entail a large family and chintz on all the furniture. Rex Stout also identified Watson as a woman and Holmes' wife in an article designed to appear a shade more outrageous than it was.[18]

By the times Holmes came along, we were well into the so-called "modern" period. Nothing so well marks that period as its refusal to take marriage for granted or to be content only to hint at its defects. Courtship, while not abandoned, is now handled with more awareness of its ramifications. The economic and social confidence in marriage, not quite eroded, is being worn away by irony, sometimes by satire. Here is Wilde in 1895. Gwendolen, you will remember, has informed her mother that she is engaged to Mr. Worthing. Lady Bracknell's response is properly immortal: "Pardon me, you are not engaged to anyone. When you do become engaged to some one, I, or your father, should his health permit him, will inform you of that fact. An engagement should come on a young girl as a surprise, pleasant or unpleasant, as the case may be. It is hardly a matter that she could be allowed to arrange for herself."[19] The impeccable defenses of marriage have, for the most part, been breached. If not a union of equals, marriage has become at least a contract between two recognized parties acting on their own behalf. Childbirth does not necessarily result from marriage, and sexuality does not necessarily require it. For many modern novelists, indeed, it appears that marriage is necessary to the discovery of identity. Even in novels of courtship, the courtship is not a separate exercise, but the playing out of the marriage roles. There are no longer novels and plays of courtship; the subject now is marriage.

CHARLES TANSLEY sits at the dinner party, in *To the Lighthouse,* wanting someone to give him a chance to exert himself. Sitting opposite him, Lily Briscoe, the artist, understands this:

> There is a code of behaviour, she knew, whose seventh article (it may be) says that on occasions of this sort it behoves the woman, whatever her own occupation may be, to go to the help of the young man opposite so that he may expose and relieve the thigh bones, the ribs, of his vanity, of his urgent desire to assert himself; as indeed it is their duty, she reflected, in her old maidenly fairness, to help us, suppose the Tube were to burst into flames. Then, she thought, I should certainly expect Mr. Tansley to get me out. But how would it be, she thought, if neither of us did either of these things?[20]

It is this question, among others, the modern novel and the modern play begin to ask.

Writing in 1880 his second novel which, like his first, "nobody would publish," Shaw not only dubbed marriage "the irrational knot," but portrayed it for what it was: a matter of woman-purchase.[21] Susanna refuses to marry the man with whom she is living:

> "I can support myself, and may shew Bob a clean pair of heels to-morrow if I choose. . . . I confess I shouldn't like to make a regular legal bargain of going to live with a man. I don't care to make love a matter of money; it gives it a taste of the harem, or even worse. Poor Bob,

meaning to be honorable, offered to buy me in the regular way at St. George's, Hanover Square, before we came to live here; but, of course, I refused, as any decent woman in my circumstances would."[22]

Shaw was ahead of his time, but not by much. In his 1908 play, *Getting Married*, the bride-to-be reads the marriage service, is shocked, and almost refuses to go through with the ceremony. In 1918, when Robert Graves married a young woman who was kept in a continuous state of anger by the attitude of the Huntingdon farmers to their wives and daughters, nature followed art: "Nancy had read the marriage service for the first time that morning, and been so disgusted that she all but refused to go through with the wedding, though I had arranged for the ceremony to be modified and reduced to the shortest possible form."[23]

Because the major critics between 1939 and 1969 have been men for whom marriage was still seen as the central fact of the social universe, the degree to which modern literature had come to question marriage in all its ramifications has for a long time gone unnoticed. Lionel Trilling, one of the most brilliant and influential of these critics, can speak for all of them when he reads *The Bostonians* as a novel written in praise of its hero and in fear of destruction of the old marital balance: James' novel, Trilling wrote, "is a story of the parental house divided against itself, of the keystone falling from the arch, of the sacred mothers refusing their commission and the sacred fathers endangered."[24] Trilling, like most of his peers, attributes to the novelists his own convictions about the immutability, the inevitability of the patriarchal structure, in whose arch marriage was certainly the keystone.

But the overwhelming fact which we must confront is that the modern novel is extravagantly marked, not only by its technical innovations and its "imagination of disaster," but also by its changed attitude toward marriage. We may still have novels like Conrad's which almost ignore marriage altogether; we may still have the occasional novel of courtship. Yet that strange double vision which accepts marriage as the proper end to a story, but cannot render marriage either real or vital or threatened as an institution, is gone. Perhaps coincidentally, marriage ceases to be an absolute economic necessity at the same time that it ceases to be taken as an inevitable stage in human development, like death. We can now see that James, in *The Bostonians*, was suggesting not only the utter misery to be expected from Verena's married

life with Ransom—the end of the novel makes that quite clear, if the
rest of the novel has not—but the agonizing difficulty of considering
any other alternative for women. Indeed, from the beginning, James
questioned marriage. The heroine of his first novel returns, in *The
Princess Casamassima,* to try to compensate for the terrible folly of her
"economic" marriage to the Prince. We are left in no doubt in *The
Portrait of a Lady* about Isabel's marriage, nor about her need to come
to terms with the consequences of her having been married wholly for
"economic" reasons. It is extraordinary that critics saw James in support of the old idea of marriage, but such is the simple fact.

If we think back upon the shocking passages from the "Other" Victorian, we are sharply reminded that the deep flaws in marriage might
have been seen earlier if people had been able to be outspoken about
sex and the marriage bed. There can be no question that marriage
would have been a different institution had women been free to talk
openly about their sexual experiences, and had their sense of their own
sexuality been revealed. Yet, oddly enough, marriage began to be questioned in novels, by Hardy, James, and Meredith, for example, long
before the strictures on writing about sex had been lifted. Furthermore, despite our present age's enormous emphasis upon sex, we did
not begin to understand the reason for marriage's growing failure until
we began to see what marriage ought to have in common with friendship, with companionship. Openness about sex was not sufficient to
enlighten our views on marriage, nor was idealization of sexual relations sufficient to save it.

D. H. Lawrence, the novelist who most influenced the influential
critics of our time, rejected the idea of marriage as combining passion
and companionship. Friendship was rejected as the model for the Lau-
rentian marriage. Searching always for an ideal of marriage and sexuality which might replace the shattered social institutions he observed
about him, Lawrence, insisting upon the polarization of the sexes, looked
more to the dark "phallic" knowledge of sex than to the gentler possibility of comradeship. This view, while giving us magnificent novels,
led his followers sadly astray in their hopes for marriage. No wonder
that Birkin, having achieved his sexual polarizations with Ursula, returns to the idea of a love-friendship with a man. The question is one
of the human need for intense relationships which may include, but
which cannot be solely sustained by, sex. Martin Green, one of Lawrence's greatest admirers, has written of Lawrence's twentieth-century

hypocrisy, "the erotic movement hypocrisy, of sexual heroics in a drama of fulfillment. It seems likely that in those late years when he was most publicly the prophet of sexual fulfilment, Lawrence himself was sexually passive. He got himself into the position of having to claim more sexual prowess, more masculine desire, than he had."[25]

Forster, in certain ways more revolutionary than Lawrence in ideas, though not in technique, asks of Helen in *Howards End*: "Had she ever loved in the noblest way, where man and woman, having lost themselves in sex, desire to lose sex itself in comradeship?"[26] Woman's desire for comradeship runs like a leitmotif through Forster's earlier *A Room with a View*, but in *Howards End* is seen connected to another idea. The desire for work, Margaret Schlegel says, "is a new desire. It goes with a great deal that's bad, but in itself it's good, and I hope that for women, too, 'not to work' will soon become as shocking as 'not to marry' was a hundred years ago."[27] If we put beside these comments Ansell's Byronic complaint in *The Longest Journey* that "man wants to love mankind, women wants to love one man,"[28] and the sad observance that nature wants dutiful sons, loving husbands, responsible fathers, "and if we are friends it must be in our spare time,"[29] we begin to see that Forster understood that deep human need for something more than Eros, for which society provided no possibility. Men and women in Forster's novels might eschew marriage for friendship, but in so doing they placed themselves outside of the central social situation. In Lawrence's novels, as we have seen, men might look to profound sexuality for the redemption of marriage. Other modern authors, however, came to see that the lack of friendship in marriage doomed not only marriage, but women. As long as she was only Kurtz's "Intended," the woman to whom Marlow lies at the end of *Heart of Darkness* is incapable of entering the realm of adult reality. Marlow has already told his audience that women do not live in the real world. Even Conrad, then, whose fictional world almost excluded women, was aware that in promising themselves in marriage women declared themselves prepared only for lies.

C. S. Lewis, a devoted and lifelong masculinist, saw Eros and Friendship as distinct if not opposed kinds of love. Yet he conceived also of the coexistence of Eros and Friendship:

> Suppose you are fortunate enough to have "fallen in love" and married your Friend. And now suppose it possible that you were offered the

choice of two futures: "*Either* you will cease to be lovers but remain forever joint seekers of the same God, the same beauty, the same truth, or *else,* losing all that, you will retain as long as you live, the raptures and ardours, all the wonder and the wild desire of Eros. Choose which you please." Which should we choose? Which choice should we not regret after we had made it?[30]

Lewis notices that in most societies friendships are between men and men, women and women, for "where men are educated and women not, where one sex works and the other is idle, or where they do totally different work, they will usually have nothing to be Friends about."[31] In marriage, as society and novelists before the modern period conceived it, husband and wife have "nothing to be friends about." Auden, who mentions marriage more than once in his essays, defined the securest foundation for a happy marriage as a "healthy mixture of physical desire and *philia,* a mutual personal liking based on common interests and values," where "the dominant feeling is of mutual respect between equals."[32] Novelists seem rarely to have had this view of the matter; nor is it frequently encountered even among essayists.

If we return to *Pride and Prejudice* with these definitions of marriage in mind, we see that the horror of Charlotte Lucas' marriage to Mr. Collins was not mainly the inevitable fumblings of their sex life, but the impossibility of their ever having between them anything resembling friendship. We anticipate that Darcy and Elizabeth will have a lovely time in bed, but we have hopes for the marriage primarily because each has chosen it (one in despite of economic and class concerns), and because we conceive the two as equal in their claims upon society and human relations. We trust there will continue to be dialogue between them. In short, they can become friends. It is barely possible that *Pride and Prejudice* has remained Austen's most popular novel, while not technically her highest achievement, not because it is "romantic," but because at its end the married pair are most nearly capable of what Auden calls "a mutual respect between equals."

A recent critic of the modern novel, looking at marriage as the old, established institution, inevitable, necessary, and unchanging as death, has distinguished between Meredith and James by observing that Meredith's young women move as inevitably toward marriage, and the ability to love, as James' heroines move away from it.[33] This distinction is less vital than at first appears. Meredith was essentially a comic, James a tragic writer: the end of comedy is integration into society, the end of tragedy is isolation. Meredith and James, however, are more alike than different in that both understand marriage to be doomed where all of a woman's human qualities are not exercised within it. That Clara Middleton in *The Egoist* avoids marriage to Willoughby Patterne and is handed to Vernon Whitford, while Isabel Archer in *The Portrait of a Lady* perceives too late the disaster of marriage to Osmond is less important than that both women, one before the wedding and one after, learn what it is to be considered by one's husband merely an extension of his being.

The similarity of marriage and death ought to be looked at more closely. For the women before modern times marriage is, except in rare instances, a kind of death. It is the death of her individual identity, the death of her as a person under law, her sexual sacrifice (for she enters into sexual experience ignorant, and without acknowledged desire, whatever may follow), perhaps her literal death in childbirth. In Woolf's first novel, Rachel contemplates marriage and then dies; the similarity of the two experiences is suggested. Ottoline Morrell wrote of her youth, "I didn't think of marrying then, and clung to my solitary liberty. I believe in many women there is a strong intuitive feeling of pride in their solitary life that when marriage really comes it is, to a certain extent, a humiliation."[34] Clarissa, achieving death in Richardson's novel, avoids marriage to the man who rapes her. Of the two states, death or marriage, death is preferable. Novelists before the modern period were as unwilling thoroughly to explore the one state as the other. Both states were too final.

My thesis that marriage for the modern English novelist is a failed institution in which passion is not supported by friendship is substantiated by the work of almost every major novelist writing after, say, 1873, the year in which Hardy published *Far From the Madding Crowd*, and Butler began *The Way of All Flesh*. Hardy's work seems nowhere to have been appreciated for the important marriage novel that it is. James was repelled by its "unpleasantly aggressive heroine."[35] Bathsheba passes through the possible marriage ideals. First there is the sexually exciting man whom every women wants to spend a month with, but whom no women should marry; she is saved from the usual marital fate by his death. Second, there is the man who wishes to make an idol of the woman he desires, bringing disaster upon himself and the woman. Gabriel Oak, the only man with whom marriage is possible, is a long time being appreciated, since he is so far from the socially accepted ideal. Readers have readily assumed Bathsheba to have compromised and Gabriel to be a fool. In fact, Hardy has emphasized the possibility of friendship and mutuality, rather than the glamour of romance. She had to learn that men who do not exploit her are not therefore less manly—most women have still to learn this. He has the wisdom to wait, since it is vitality and originality he admires.

Butler's novel has been more easily praised, since it holds up for condemnation not only marriage but the family, an institution whose glories people were earlier beginning to doubt. Butler, however, both in the marriage of Ernest's parents, and in the decision of the double hero, Ernest and Overton, not to marry, makes clear the bankruptcy of marriage as a personal institution, though it continues to serve the ends of society and business. Escaping from marriage, Ernest, unlike his father, need not victimize his children to revenge himself upon the world for having, through marriage, victimized him.

The definition of marriage as a process of victimization is fully enunciated by the beginning of the eighties. Meredith's Clara Middleton, appearing in 1879, is explicit about what she loathes in Willoughby: his insistence upon envisioning her entirely as an extension of himself. Her father, in his turn, is prepared to trade her for a cellar of fine wine: she is the only payment he has to offer for such indulgences. We watch Clara escape the trap as eagerly as we follow the escape of any hunted creature: it is only comedy and the impossibility of thinking of an alternate career that give Clara to Vernon at the end. We know that Clara, like Willoughby's former fiancée, would marry King Kong himself to escape life at Patterne Hall. In 1881, Isabel Archer, victimized by the money that was to have freed her, is, like a Greek tragic hero, allowed to understand her destiny: women viewing marriage from the other side of the great divide are granted tragic perceptions of how fate has entangled them. By 1885, in his creation of *Diana of the Crossways,* Meredith has joined James in portraying the disasters of marriage after the fact. In 1886, James will write, in *The Bostonians,* his last courtship novel, one in which, as in Meredith's *The Egoist,* his perceptions of martial failure are cast back over the courtship.

By the nineties, the theme of marriage as the most sinister of arrangements begins to dominate the most lasting novels. In *New Grub Street* and *The Odd Women,* Gissing dramatizes the failure of marriage to serve either society or its incumbents. The hollowness of marriage is revealed in Ibsen's plays and in Shaw's rendition of their plots and themes in *The Quintessence of Ibsenism* (1891). By 1895, Wilde's *The Importance of Being Earnest* perfectly spoofs marriage *and* courtship, as we have seen, pausing on the way to notice that the polarization of sexual roles has contributed to this madness: "All women become like their mothers. That is their tragedy. No man does. That's his."[36]

Jude the Obscure, appearing the same year as *The Importance,* repeated in tragic form that play's farcical emphasis on the modern theme of the double. Sue Bridehead and Jude, fatally alike, destined for one another as only doubles can be, are so isolated and forced into their relationship that disaster, dramatized in Sue's refusal of sexual intercourse, is inevitable. Had they been free to choose one another, to choose their experience of passion, and their occupations, theirs would have been a wholly new kind of marriage. As doubles, they are drawn to one another in a situation where, given the society, the death of one, or both, is inevitable. "Marriage" is possible only to Jude and Arabella where, providing the opportunity for nothing but sexuality, it satisfies neither the man nor the woman.

The theme of the double is developed quintessentially by James in *The Wings of the Dove* (1902). James here presented, perhaps for the first time, the double as woman. In doing so, he revealed that it is the disconnection between energy and power for the woman that has doomed marriage. Kate Croy has energy, health, intelligence, the discipline to do what she does not like, and an appreciation of the things of the mind. She is without power. Milly, without Kate's qualities, has power—that is, money—a longing for experience, and an appreciation of the things of the spirit. Inevitably, one must manipulate the other, using as instrument the man each loves. Milly achieves spirituality, Kate money, each at the price of marriage and love. While this great novel may be interpreted in many ways (and has been), its testimony to the cost of female powerlessness has been little noticed. The reason, no doubt, includes the inability of critics to admire energy in a woman (it is always called aggression or manipulation) since they expect and approve woman's passivity and spirituality. Milly's great and final act is not dovelike; on the contrary, it is to give power, money, the least spiritual and "feminine" of forces.

The Edwardian period, famous for its golden afternoons, also deserves fame for relentness consideration of marriage in all its disastrous aspects. The strange double standard of the premodern years has utterly dissolved: courtship no longer evolves toward a marriage shown to be despicable in the society the novel presents. Marriage, for all but Conrad, is, in the modern novel, neither ignored nor denigrated in the comic mode. The Edwardian period brought four of Forster's novels, James' major marriage novel, *The Golden Bowl,* and the works of Wells and Bennett which, whether futuristic or naturalistic, showed forth marriage's failures. In the theater, the subject of marriage is ubiquitous. Of the five plays, for example, reprinted in Gerald Weales' anthology, *Edwardian Plays,* four have marriage as their major theme, the fifth confronts it at least by implication.[37] Hypocrisy about marriage is seen as the marriage trap's chief mechanism.

The Edwardian period can be said to close with the publication of *Dubliners* (1914), *The Good Soldier* (1915), and *The Rainbow* (1915). Within *Dubliners* itself can be seen the modern period's progress toward its final realization of marriage as an analogy for death. What Joyce was to call the paralysis of Dublin life is set forth with marriage and the hope of courtship ("Evelina") and fear of entrapment ("A Painful Case") as chief marks of lifelessness. The final great story, "The Dead," displays among much else, the picture of a marriage in which the woman has never really been *seen.* A symbol to her husband, recognized at a party only by her dress, encountered only through society's protective covering (a heliotrope envelope, a glove), Greta reveals herself, and her husband's spiritual deadness, in one moment when Gabriel's desire is exposed as lust and his tenderness as condescension.

The Good Soldier, whatever is to be believed concerning the narrator's competence, is indisputably a novel about marriage's failure to serve any purpose whatever. Dowell ends by loving the mad Nancy: "I should marry Nancy if her reason were ever sufficiently restored to let her appreciate the meaning of the Anglican marriage service."[38] Perhaps the novel can be said to be critical of all upper-class life, at least in modern times. But marriage is the paradigm of that life for Ford, here and in his great tetralogy, *Parade's End.*

Lawrence's *The Rainbow* could qualify as a disquisition upon the failure of marriage. From this failure there emerges an individual, Ursula. But, once into the twenties and *Women in Love,* Lawrence can see her only as the mate for the proper man; married to him, she disappears from the novel. Lawrence tells us that the marriage succeeded, but even so he does not lie to us. He allows us to see that Ursula is an appendage, and little more. Gudrun, the artist, the woman who will not submit to marriage, has not yet been seen by critics as more than destructive.

Gudrun was prologue; with Virginia Woolf in the twenties came the first full fictional development of the woman as artist. Inevitably, she could not marry. Having presented, in *To the Lighthouse*, the cannibalism of marriage, Woolf ended her final novel, *Between the Acts*, with a marital confrontation stripped of all societal association and returned to its beginnings.

> Left alone for the first time that day, they were silent. Alone, enmity was bared; also love. Before they slept, they must fight; after they had fought, they would embrace. From that embrace another life might be born. But first they must fight, as the dog fox fights with the vixen, in the heart of darkness, in the fields of night.[39]

The figure who perceives this marital scene is La Trobe, the woman artist. Husband and wife are her creations, part of her new play, while she remains single, and, as far as is possible for human beings, autonomous.

Woolf is the only woman writer of the modern period to challenge in a profound way conventional views of marriage. Katherine Mansfield, it is true, looked at marriage and saw that it was bad, but the quality of her insights, not their innovativeness, is notable. Alone in the twenties and thirties, Woolf conceived of marriage as partaking more of friendship than of passion. Unlike George Eliot, she was able to translate into her fiction the marriage she lived. This is how Nigel Nicolson describes it:

> When two people of independent minds marry, they must be able to rely upon each other's tolerance, affection and support. Each must encourage, without jealousy, the full development of the other's gifts, each allow the other privacy, different interests, different friends. But they must share an intellectual and moral base. One of them cannot be philistine if the other is constantly breasting new ideas. They cannot disagree wildly on what is right and wrong. Above all, their love must grow as passion fades . . . particularly if they have no children.[40]

What the Woolfs experienced, and what Virginia Woolf recreated in fiction, was the need of individuality in marriage, of space: "A love affair brings human beings unnaturally together," John Bayley has written, "while marriage keeps them the right and dignified distance apart."[41] In the popular mind, and for many years among the "manly" critics, the ideal of martial passion and "togetherness" has persisted in the face of all evidence that these are the signs of a love affair, not a marriage. As views on marriage begin slowly to alter, Woolf will, I think, be seen in this regard as prescient. Mrs. Dalloway's marriage to Richard in *Mrs. Dalloway* is not ideal, in any romantic sense. Yet her decision that life with Peter Walsh would have forced them always "unnaturally together" is correct; indeed, within the novel, Clarissa can be seen to move from being Mrs. Dalloway to becoming herself, Clarissa. Surely this, rather than development toward a greater dependency, is the proper movement within a marriage. "Taking other people's reality for granted," John Bayley has also said, is "the first requirement of love."[42] But it is the requirement most breached in marriage. We know the Dalloway marriage has served both partners, for Richard brings flowers to express his love, and she herself is recognized, at the end, as triumphantly "there."

Woolf is, of course, feminist in the profoundest sense, insisting upon the autonomy of female, as well as male, persons. Rachel Vinrace, and, even more, Katherine Hilbery perfectly understand this. So, in fact, does Eleanor in *The Years,* though they all think she is sterotypically an "old maid." Whatever the problems of humanity in the twentieth century, marriage, as Austen conceived it, does not hold the solution: that much Woolf makes clear. For all her revolutionary techniques, for all her innovations in the use of time and language and reality, she is nowhere more radical than in her perception that marriage, if it is not companionship, celebrated by the breaking together of bread, is nothing. She had discovered this truth in her own marriage:

> They never experienced jealousy of another person or of a talent unshared. She deeply respected his judgement on what meant most to her, her writing; and he, lacking the flight of searing imagination and recognizing that she possessed it, shielded her, watched her fluctuating health, nurtured her genius, and with instinctive understanding left her alone in a room of her own, while he remained always available in the common room between them.[43]

Today, past the so-called modern period, Doris Lessing is the single British woman writer who questions as profoundly as did Woolf marriage and the patriarchal society it supports. More political than Woolf in her insights, Lessing writes of the connections between marriage and the economic structure of society. It is no accident that Lessing, though she is far from a writer of comedies of manners, has called Meredith "that astonishingly underrated writer."[44] In this perception she celebrates the moment when the novel turned its back upon both patriarchy and the accepted marital conventions, and looked to the new demands women might make now upon the most unexamined of institutions. Modern writers have at least established that the unexamined marriage, like the unexamined life, is not worth living, and that Eros alone will not sustain an institution which has lost, or totally outlived, its social and economic justification.

1977

ENDNOTES

1. Steven Marcus, *The Other Victorians* (New York: Basic Books, 1964), pp. 91–92.

2. *Ibid.,* pp. 93–94.

3. Jane Austen, *Pride and Prejudice* (New York: Norton, 1966), p. 162.

4. Henry James, "The Art of Fiction," in Henry James, *The Future of the Novel,* Leon Edel ed. (New York: Vintage Books, 1956), p. 25.

5. George Bernard Shaw, *Man and Superman,* act 3.

6. E. M. Forster, *Aspects of the Novel* (New York: Harcourt, Brace, 1927), pp. 86–87.

7. T. S. Eliot, "East Coker," *Four Quartets.* T. S. Eliot, *The Complete Poems and Plays* (New York: Harcourt, Brace, 1952), p. 124.

8. Gail Godwin, "Would We Have Heard of Marian Evans?" *Ms,* September 1974, p. 75. Godwin goes on to confess: "As a novelist myself—and one who has, so far, denied my heroines the crucial strengths and options I myself have needed—I am fascinated by this question of why so many of us deny our heroines what we refuse to deny ourselves."

9. Graham Hough, *The Last Romantics* (New York: University Paperbacks, 1961), p. xi.

10. Austen, *Pride and Prejudice,* p. 88.

11. Charlotte Brontë, *The Professor* (1845, 1857), ch. 10.

12. Edward Carpenter, *My Days and Dreams* (London: Allen & Unwin, 1916), pp. 30–32.

13. Edward Carpenter, *Love's Coming of Age* (New York: Modern Library, 1911), p. 80.

14. Ian Watt, *The Rise of the Novel* (Berkeley and Los Angeles: University of California Press, 1959), p. 145.

15. Hazel Mews, *Frail Vessels* (London: Athlone Press, 1969), p. 173.

16. Quoted in *ibid.,* p. 102.

17. W. H. Auben, "Fairground," in *City Without Walls* (London: Faber and Faber, 1969).

18. Rex Stout, "Watson Was a Woman," rpt. in Howard Haycraft, *The Art of the Mystery Story* (New York: Grosset & Dunlap, 1947), pp. 311–318.

19. Oscar Wilde, *The Importance of Being Earnest*, act 1.

20. Virginia Woolf, *To the Lighthouse* (New York: Harcourt, Brace, 1927), p. 137.

21. Mona Caird, in articles in the *Westminster Review* which appeared from 1888 to 1894, found the evils of modern life to have their origin in the patriarchal custom of woman-purchase. Quoted in Amy Cruse, *After the Victorians* (London: Allen & Unwin, 1938), p. 129.

22. Bernard Shaw, *The Irrational Knot* (London: Constable, 1909), p. 220.

23. Robert Graves, *Good-bye to All That* (Garden City, N.Y.: Doubleday Anchor Books, 1957), p. 272. There is no indication that Nancy has heard of the Shaw play.

24. Lionel Trilling, *The Opposing Self* (New York: Viking Press, 1955), p. 117.

25. Martin Green, *The von Richthofen Sisters* (New York: Basic Books, 1974), p. 173. Green goes on in this passage to compare Lawrence to Max Weber, who was involved in the opposite hypocrisy.

26. E. M. Forster, *Howards End* (New York: Vintage Books, 1921), p. 311.

27. *Ibid.,* p. 110.

28. E. M. Forster, *The Longest Journey* (New York: Vintage Books, 1962), p. 88.

29. *Ibid.,* p. 69.

30. C. S. Lewis, *The Four Loves* (London: Fontana Books, 1960), p. 64.

31. *Ibid.,* p. 68.

32. W. H. Auden, *Forewords & Afterwords* (New York: Vintage Books, 1974), p. 64. The same definition is repeated on p. 101.

33. Donald David Stone, *Novelists in a Changing World* (Cambridge: Harvard University Press, 1972), p. 135.

34. *Memoirs of Lady Ottoline Morrell,* Robert Gathorne-Hardy, ed. (New York: Knopf, 1964), p. 72.

35. Stone, *Novelists,* p. 77.

36. Wilde, *Importance of Being Earnest,* act 1.

37. *Edwardian Plays,* Gerald Weales, ed. and intro. (New York: Hill and Wang, 1962). The plays are: Maugham, *Loaves and Fishes;* Hankin, *The Return of the Prodigal;* Shaw, *Getting Married;* Pinero, *Mid-Channel;* Granville-Barker, *The Madras House.*

38. Ford Madox Ford, *The Good Soldier* (New York: Vintage Books, 1951), p. 236.

39. Virginia Woolf, *Between the Acts* (New York: Harcourt, Brace, 1941), p. 219.

40. *The Letters of Virginia Woolf,* vol. 2, 1912–1922, Nigel Nicolson and Joanne Trautman, eds. (New York: Harcourt Brace Javanovich, 1976), p. xiii.

41. John Bayley, *The Characters of Love* (New York: Basic Books, 1960), p. 229.

42. *Ibid.*, p. 273.

43. *Virginia Woolf Letters,* 2:xiv.

44. Doris Lessing, *A Small Personal Voice* (New York: Knopf, 1974), p. 28.

10

To the Lighthouse: The New Story of Mother and Daughter

To the Lighthouse is one of those works that wait, with a patience akin to Mrs. Ramsay's, for us to catch up with them. For many years it was viewed, with varying degrees of adoration and scorn, as a sentimental evocation of a beautiful woman, a model wife and mother. We all, women and men, recognized her seductive appeal and mourned her untimely death. Most of us also, certainly in the years when I first taught *To the Lighthouse,* took Lily Briscoe at her own evaluation, as a skimpy, dried-up old maid; her painting, similarly valued, as likely to be flung under sofas, hidden in attics, forgotten. As to her vision, why should it be worth more than she herself or her art? Lily Briscoe's essence was her love for Mrs. Ramsay and her failure, because of her Chinese eyes, to marry. What we can now begin to discern is that Woolf here created a new plot: the story of mother and daughter, of that ignored couple's progress to disengagement and mutual respect and, for the daughter, of a quest that modifies but does not seek to escape maternal love.

The oedipal drama, certainly since Freud but perhaps ever since property first passed by inheritance from father to son, has been the primary, controlling plot. Sometimes there were whispers of other stories, as in the *Odyssey*. Joyce seized on the father-son drama, allowing it to diminish other themes, particularly those concerning women. *To the Lighthouse*, which requires, like Mrs. Ramsay, fifty pairs of eyes to see round, can now marvelously be read as the untold struggle and love of mother and daughter, that other story of the family romance which did not interest Freud or Joyce, for which they had no room, for which women, before Woolf, had no language.

Mrs. Ramsay has three daughters in this unique drama: Cam, whom Elizabeth Abel has described as "Woolf's Portrait of the Artist as Her Father's Daughter";[1] Prue, who

> sat in the middle between brothers and sisters, always occupied, it seemed, seeing that nothing went wrong so that she scarcely spoke herself. . . . How she drooped under those long silences between [Mr. and Mrs. Ramsay]. Anyhow, her mother now would seem to be making it up to her; assuring her that everything was well; promising her that one of these days that same happiness would be hers. She had enjoyed it for less than a year, however.[2]

And there is Lily, the daughter who demonstrates and overcomes the mother-daughter struggle, the love that threatens, not murder, as between father and son, but engulfment.

Yet only recently have these other two, Cam and Prue, been seen as foils for Lily. Lily's double is James, the son who *will* enact the oedipal struggle, in counterpoint to Lily's adult acceptance of the mother. Patricia Joplin has written that "by making Freud's Oedipal drama manifest so early, Woolf eliminates it as the end of her plot."[3] But Woolf does not so much eliminate the oedipal plot as make it parallel to Lily's; James accepts his father at the same moment that Lily accepts the mother (indeed within two sentences), but for James that acceptance is instantaneous. For Lily, it is the work of a lifetime of forty-four years, it is the achievement of a vision. (And since I have mentioned two of the critics whose work has illuminated for me the mother-daughter drama in *To the Lighthouse*, let me name the others: Rachel Duplessis, Susan Friedman, Jane Lilienfeld.)[4]

We all know about Oedipus—"that story," as Anne Sexton would say. But of the grown mother and daughter we hear little since the story of Demeter and Persephone. Feminists in recent years have evoked the importance of the "preoedipal" years, when the mother is the dominant figure for both sexes. But in contemplating *To the Lighthouse* I refuse the term *preoedipal*, partly because woman's destiny ought not to be described in the leftover term from phallic psychoanalysis but mainly because the drama, as with Oedipus and Laius at the crossroads, must be enacted in adulthood, when identity can be formed and adhered to, when risks are taken and confrontations defy avoidance.

The daughter identifies with the mother; she will also, as Lily does Mrs. Ramsay, idealize her, desire an intimacy that will make her and the mother one (79). And yet, if the woman is to be an artist—so Lily aspires—and if the mother is an ideal earth goddess formed perhaps long ago in a forgotten world of women but preserved by the patriarchy for its own purposes, the questing artist, while loving the mother, must learn to escape the mother's restrictions on her vision. Few women are such adequate earth goddesses as Mrs. Ramsay, as was Woolf's mother, and at that moment when one finds one's own voice (Woolf was 44, Lily's age, when she finished *To the Lighthouse*) it is time to cease being obsessed by her, to stop needing but not loving her. As James will need Mr. Ramsay to recognize himself, so Lily will need Mr. Ramsay to be reminded of that so-called male world where identity and separation are never in question. To stop asking of the mother more than she can give is also to stop being satisfied, as is Cam, with the little men will offer.

How does one know an earth goddess when she has been colonized for exploitation by the patriarchy? She makes of the moment something eternal. She transforms a meal into a consecration. She bears about with her the torch of her beauty. She has the whole of the other sex under her patronage. She has stars in her eyes, and veils in her hair, with cyclamen and wild violets. She steps through fields of flowers and takes to her breast buds that have broken and lambs that have fallen. She loves best her preoedipal son but recognizes in Lily "a thread of something; a flare of something; something her own which Mrs. Ramsay liked very much indeed, but no man would, she feared" (157). And Lily, in not marrying, would miss, the earth goddess insists, the best of life. For she would not be included in Paul's "we," the "we" that springs to his lips when he has asked Minta to marry him, when he has thus paid homage to Mrs. Ramsay.

The daughter must learn to quest without ceasing to love. She need not choose between the loved mother and the worldly father but must instead find another path, beyond the romantic plot, beyond the usual ending of female lives, marriage or death or, as with Prue, both. Locked still in the language that identifies her as a "peevish, ill-tempered, dried-up old maid" (226), Lily will nonetheless convince herself, by repeating her secret truth: that she can plan her painting and need never marry anyone.

For Mrs. Ramsay is impelled to entice all her daughters into the oedipal plot. How else could it remain the central story, if women did not consent to its enactment, to their roles as stock figures in a drama of which they could never be the protagonist? Yet there are moments when even Mrs. Ramsay dreams that she might become "an investigator, elucidating the social problem" (18). She recognizes her daughters' mute questioning "of deference and chivalry, of the Bank of England and the Indian Empire." But she cannot acknowledge "the manliness in their girlish hearts" (14). She persuades them, with her beauty and her love, that it would be wonderful always to have babies in their arms, always to be "trustful, childlike, reverential" (13). She knows that Mr. Ramsay likes to think her not clever, that her part is to be "a lady in a grey cloak, stooping over her flowers" (205).

James, different from the mother, ultimately recognizes that difference, perceives his likeness to his father, and breaks the terrible maternal bond. But for Lily? She is both like and unlike the mother; she recognizes the mother's self-annihilation yet knows it as virtue in the world's eyes. If one does not marry, does not move into the marriage plot, how does one keep one's love for one's mother and for oneself? Freud has said that what women look for in their husbands is their mother, but what of the woman artist who will not accept that unworthy substitute? She must learn, as Lily does, to say "she did not want Mrs. Ramsay now" (290), meaning not that love for Mrs. Ramsay will not always fill her but that Mrs. Ramsay's service to the patriarchy ceases to be, even momentarily, desirable. Lily may recognize also that in becoming an artist, she has lived out a profound desire, however hidden, of the patriarchal mother: to investigate, to change, rather than ameliorate, the social condition. Even the patriarchal mother seeks, in hidden moments, another plot, longs not always to be an attendant lady in someone else's play.

Yet Mrs. Ramsay continues to hide her essence, continues to hug to herself a mystery, some secret, as Joplin writes, unlike the father's, unnameable, only to be guessed at. Lily, of course, though she has reduced mother and son, "objects of universal veneration" (81), to a purple shadow, still paints Mrs. and not Mr. Ramsay; the answer, if one could but find that wedge of darkness which is Mrs. Ramsay, might lead, as even Freud guessed, to the wisdom and wonder of the prepatriarchal Mycenaen age. Lily and her painting ask the new question: "Could loving, as people called it, make her and Mrs. Ramsay one? for it was not knowledge but unity that she desired, not inscriptions on tablets, nothing that could be written in any language known to men, but intimacy itself, which is knowledge" (79). Yet at the same time, Lily desires something of Mr. Ramsay's: "she longed to cherish that loneliness" (39). As she tells us at least seven times, she will move the tree further to the middle of her painting and need never marry anyone.

Before she paints her second picture, Lily realizes that when Charles Tansley repeated "women can't write, women can't paint, it was not so much that he believed it, as that for some odd reason he wished it" (292). That wish, along with Mrs. Ramsay's internalization of it, is what Lily must ignore. The problem is to reject that part of the mother which the patriarchy has claimed and to identify with what is lovable, feminine for its own and not for men's sake, with what reaches out to other women, supports them in their quests. Women like Mrs. Ramsay will always walk, as Lily has seen her, "putting her wreath to her forehead and going unquestioningly with her companion, a shade across fields" (270).

Lily passes through the ten years of the novel's middle section as through a birth canal, through a time of transformation to another life. And that transformation ends as Lily Briscoe, at the conclusion of "Time Passes," stirs in her sleep. "She clutched at her blankets as a faller clutches at the turf on the edge of a cliff. Her eyes opened wide. Here she was again, she thought, sitting bolt upright in bed. Awake" (214).

And in the novel's final section, she will not, like Steven Dedalus, encounter for the millionth time the reality of experience but, like no one before her, seek and find a vision that the mother, living, would have prevented; that the mother, dying, allows; that mothers and daughters, living and dead, must learn to reenact and discover: how the mother may simultaneously keep the love of the daughter and set her free. The mother's secret and the daughter's quest will find a unity beyond knowledge, not written in any language known to men, where the mother ceases to be "a sponge sopped full of human emotions" (51), and the daughter, armed with a maternal blessing, learns to enclose an as yet undiscovered, undefined space. And, Lily asks, "what could be more formidable than that space?" (236). In that space is the untold story of mothers and daughters and the language they learn to speak to one another.

1986

ENDNOTES

1. Elizabeth Abel, " 'Can the Wicked': Woolf's Portrait of the Artist as Her Father's Daughter," *Virginia Woolf and Bloomsbury,* Jane Marcus, ed. (Bloomington: Indiana University Press, 1987), pp. 170–194.

2. Virginia Woolf, *To the Lighthouse* (1927; New York: Harcourt, Brace, 1964), p. 298. Page references hereafter given in text.

3. Patricia Klindienst Joplin, "The Art of Resistance: Authority and Violence in the Work of Virginia Woolf," diss. Stanford University, 1984.

4. Rachel Blau Duplessis, *Writing Beyond the Ending: Narrative Strategies of Twentieth-Century Women Writers* (Bloomington: Indiana University Press, 1985); Susan Stanford Friedman, "Lyric Subversions of Narrative in Women's Writing: Virginia Woolf and the Tyranny of Plot," *Reading Narrative: Form, Ethics, Ideology,* James Phelan, ed. Jane Lilienfeld, " 'The Deceptiveness of Beauty': Mother Love and Mother Hate in *To the Lighthouse,*" *Twentieth Century Literature* (1977), 23:345–376.

11

Alcott's *Little Women*

THE INFLUENCE of *Little Women* upon women artists in Paris between the wars is a matter of faith. As the Bible tells us, faith is the evidence of things not seen. If only Gertrude Stein had written of Jo March, or at least stopped into Sylvia Beach's bookshop and requested *Little Women*. What she requested, I am constrained by truth to report, is *The Trail of the Lonesome Pine* and *A Girl of the Limberlost*.[1] There is a reference to Alcott in Stein's writing, but not to *Little Women*. It is to *Rose in Bloom*, and Stein is reminded of it by the New Englanders' fear of drinking: "I always remembered it in *Rose in Bloom* and how they worried about offering any one a drink and even about communion wine, any one in that way might suddenly find they had a taste for wine."[2]

Sylvia Beach mentions *Little Women* only as the source of a joke on Frank Harris who, rushing to make a train, was in search of something "exciting" to read. Beach asked him if he had read *Little Women* which, rendered into French as *Petites femmes,* connoted something exciting to a man of Harris' tastes. He was resentful of being locked in a train for hours with such an appalling lack of eroticism.[3] Thornton Wilder, who knew Stein and many of the others, evokes *Little Women* in *The Eighth Day,* supposedly not for the first time. But is any of this evidence?

Yet I do not admit that my faith in *Little Women* as an influence consists solely of the substance of things hoped for. Everyone read *Little Women*—there is evidence enough for that; certainly every pre-pubescent female absorbed that book with the air she breathed. My own children—just to show you the extent and persistence of the influence—went to school with four sisters named Meg, Jo, Amy, and Beth. Unfortunately, no one could notice that Jo differed perceptibly from the others. But in the book itself, Jo differed more than perceptibly: Jo was a miracle. She may have been the single female model continuously available after 1868 to girls dreaming beyond the confines of a constricted family destiny to the possibility of autonomy and experience initiated by one's self.

We literary critics welcome complexities which challenge our carefully honed talents and enable us to unravel novels whose profundities can be suspected of escaping the untrained reader. Complex novels and poems are meat and drink to critics, but children are more in the position of the puzzled ice cream manufacturer who asked Wallace Stevens if in "The Emperor of Ice Cream" he was for ice cream or against it. We forget sometimes, though Frank Kermode has reminded us, that "fictions are for finding things out."[4] One of the things they are for finding out is the process of growing from a girl into a woman. Men may ask pretty girls: "Are there any more at home like you?" Most girls may, in the past, have considered that a pretty question. But girls who were going to grow up and go to Paris were more likely to have exclaimed with Jo: "I hate affected, niminy-piminy chits. I hate to think I've got to grow up, and be Miss March, and wear long gowns and look as prim as a China-aster. . . . I can't get over my disappointment in not being a boy." Beth soothes Jo by assuring her she can be a brother to them all, and Jo, to be sure, in her father's absence, recognizes herself as "the man of the family."

Jo's is an identification only possible in those innocent days when one could say what one felt without being accused of nameless, or worse, named Freudian perversions. Jo recognized (along with her readers) that girls such as she, few enough in number, *were* ideally the fathers of their families because there was no other model. Such girls might want to care for their mothers; they certainly did not wish to imitate them. Who in her right mind (which few girls were in those dark days) would want to imitate such a creature? Marmee's vision of a woman's role in marriage is enough to turn the stomach, and the exceptional young reader could declare with Jo: "I wasn't meant for a life like this."

Great books are so identified because they turn out, a century or so later, to have been amazingly prescient. Today, armed with the data and insights of all those social sciences focusing their attention upon achieving women, we recognize that Alcott provided for Jo those conditions likeliest to produce this interesting creature. While Alcott depended upon the facts of her own life, she nonetheless transmuted them into a pattern of female selfhood. Reviewers might attribute the success of *Little Women* to the threefold accomplishment of preserving the family as the foundation of the republic, making female adolescence into a life stage, and picturing loving self-sacrifice according to female dreams[5]—but beyond all this is Alcott's recognition of the opportunity her all-girl family had provided for her own development.

Bronson Alcott, at the birth of his fourth female child, noted that her birth manifested God's will that the Alcotts be content to "rear women for the future world."[6] Whatever God's will, if any, in the matter, girls without brothers are far likelier to end up as true women of the future world, questioning the conventional female destiny. Achieving women are statistically likely to be from all-girl families. Margaret Hennig, for example, examining top-range women managers in business firms, of whom there were not many, discovered that all the women in her sample were only children or from all-girl families —an extraordinary statistical finding. These girls were brotherless and therefore qualified as "sons." Louisa and her older sister were objects of educational experiments by their father: he had no sons on whom to apply them. Not uncommonly, if the unconventional woman is not the only or oldest child, she will be the one among a father's daughters selected by him as his "son." Writer Dorothy Richardson, for example, was "odd girl out" for her father: third among his four daughters, the child with whom he formed a union against a household of "women."[7] Louisa, we know, was Bronson Alcott's "son."[8]

While the tomboy character has long been a staple of life and fiction, most tomboys exist in relation to boys; certainly those of fiction do so, emulating and envying their brothers. These tomboys may be teased as hoydens, but they are not recognized as sons, as the independent ones among weaker women. Maggie Tulliver, for example, in George Eliot's *The Mill on the Floss,* creates herself in emulation and adoration of her brother Tom. Their father may mourn that it is the wench who is the smart one, but it is Tom who will get the education. For Jo, male destiny may be envied, but not in the person of a brother. Similarly, in an all-girl school girls may win the attention of teachers and aspire to positions not automatically considered the property of males: there are no males. Laurie in this eccentric book is made to look with envy on the happy female world.

A word of caution is necessary regarding girls chosen by their fathers as "sons." He does not think of her nor does the girl think of herself as a boy. Penis envy, despite Freud's strictures rigidified with the eager help of his female disciples is not the issue. These young women never doubt their core gender identity. They inhabit female bodies gladly, and dream, not of male anatomy, but of male autonomy. Here Alcott was again both naive and, in the wonderful freedom of that naiveté, prescient. She knew that for women who considered Marmee's destiny, or Meg's, impossible for themselves, the only model was a male model—she adopted it.

Women have been trapped here. The world, wishing to keep them in their place, where the world found it very convenient for them to be, warned them that if they did not accept the female role they would lose their femininity and become, moreover, monsters: imitation men. It followed that in imitating men they were also robbing them of their masculinity. This has to be the most extraordinary double bind in history. Jo could be so clear about her choice between male and female destinies, at least for half the book, because no one had arrived to tell her that she was courting some hideous Freudian disaster. The chosen "son" within the all-girl family, Jo was free to follow the male model, the only acceptable one around.

Jo plays the male part in plays, wears a "gentlemanly" collar and has a gentlemanly manner, thinks of herself as a businessman and cher-

ishes a pet rat. (The pet rat is male and has a son, "proud of his whis-
kers," who accompanies him along the rafters.) Jo finds it easier to
risk her life for a person than to be pleasant when she does not want
to, and she admires the "manly" way of shaking hands. The point is
clear: men's manners speak of freedom, openness, comradery, physical
abandon, the chance to escape passivity. Who would not prefer such
a destiny, except those taught to be afraid?

Strictures against women imitating the male model are universal.
Even today if one recommends the male model for women (shorn of
its machismo and denigration of women), one is likely to startle everyone. But Jo knew that there was no other, and that to search for female
models makes good history but poor consolation. Jo knew that in a
conventional family pattern, where the mother could recommend only
her own confinement, there was no other model than the father. Some
women indeed provided another model. Where did they discover it?
Partly, in a young fictional creature who, as Natalie Barney was to say
of Gertrude Stein, "had such faith in herself as passeth understanding."[9]

In the end, Alcott betrayed Jo. Women have great difficulty imagining autonomous females (even if they have managed to become one)
and sustaining the imaginative creation once they have achieved it. Jo
had to be more or less conventionally "disposed of."[10] Those who hold
to the romantic view of tomboys resent the fact that Jo had to marry
a German twice her age. Alcott could not, apparently, prevent Jo's
marrying, but she could and did prevent her marrying Laurie, despite
the demands of her publisher and public. When Jo's father returns
from the war to this female world, he "compliments" Jo by saying that
he does not see the "son, Jo" whom he left a year hence. "I see a young
lady who . . ." and there follows an account of a young lady's attributes. We feel sold. Alcott will tell us at the end of *Little Women* that
spinsters "have missed the sweetest part of life" (how persistently women
buy that line!) despite the fact that she signed her letters from Europe
in the months following the success of *Little Women* "spinsterhood
forever," and when asked for advice to give girls, told them of "the
sweet independence of the spinster's life."[11] Alcott was confused in her
fictional, if not in her usual mind, but her biographers muddle the
two. The latest, Martha Saxton, writes as though not finding a man
to marry were a failure explicable only by psychological wounds.

Of course, Jo starts a school for boys. Who would want to mess around with silly girls? If you cannot change the destiny of girls, you can at least take on the education of the sex with some chance of freedom and accomplishment outside of domesticity. The feeling is most commonly reflected in the woman's wish for male children, as Adrienne Rich tells us: "When I first became pregnant I set my heart on a son. (In our childish, acting-out games I had always preferred the masculine roles and persuaded or forced my younger sister to act the feminine ones.) I still identified more with men than with women; the men I knew seemed less held back by self-doubt and ambivalence, more choices seemed open to them. I wanted to give birth, at twenty-five, to my unborn self—someone independent, actively willing, original."[12]

Once one has opted to support the male system and put one's ambitions, as Jo does, into the raising of boys, one writes of Meg's twins as though stereotyped destinies for the sexes were among the eternal verities. There may be something more sickening than little Daisy, but where to find it outside the precepts of the Total Woman movement, I do not know. It has been argued, most persuasively by Nina Auerbach in her excellent study of female communities, that in the end Jo becomes "a cosmic mother," the greatest power available in that domestic world.[13] Jo was the girl who embodied the impossible girlhood dreams, and not the young female who became—heaven forbid—a mother.

Jo's readers probably overlooked the conventional ending. Jo wanted to end up, when she knew she could not become free as a man, as a "literary spinster," an apt way to describe the women in Paris between the wars. Jo's youthful experiences may have provided a model for sisterhood, as Nina Auerbach so well demonstrates. The all-girl family in Austen's *Pride and Prejudice,* Auerbach points out, lives in an empty world, awaiting rescue by men.[14] The March world is complete in itself; there women suffice to each other for happiness, and "permanent sisterhood is a felt dream rather than a concrete possibility."[15] Auerbach further suggests that in giving the family the name of a month, Alcott took her mother, whose maiden name was May, as the true progenitor of the family, the source of energy and possibility. To me Alcott's portrayal of sisterhood is too sentimental, too doomed by marital conventions both as to its present and future; yet it is, for all that, a memorable dream of sisterhood, perhaps the one fictional world where young women, complete unto themselves, are watched with envy by a lonely boy.

Alcott's other literary works, with Jo or without her, are certainly of interest, especially *Work,* yet they appeal perhaps more to the feminist historian and critic than to the girl reader. We recognize with pleasure that in *An Old Fashioned Girl* there is a community of women artists, and that in an unpublished fragment of an adult novel Alcott, most enticingly, has a woman say: "Do not look for meaning in marriage, that is too costly an experiment for us. Flee from temptation and do not dream of spoiling your life by any commonplace romance."[16] But these fragments, these interpretations, are what the critics find. For youngsters, reading in search of legends they need not even consciously acknowledge or remember, it is Jo who is immortal.

What must be emphasized is her uniqueness. She is a myth, alone and unchallenged—peerless. For she has the whole business absolutely straight as a child, an adolescent. Maybe Alcott did not know what to do with her when she grew up, but Natalie Barney, Gertrude Stein, and Janet Flanner knew what to do with themselves when they grew up, and I am inclined to give Jo part of the credit. Perhaps remembered only dimly, in children's literature, safe as homes, she nonetheless expressed, as few had, what it felt like to be a girl who was not going to grow up conventionally female and knew it when she was very young. Because there was no fantasy in Jo's end, her beginnings were believable. Romance promised a prince. *Little Women* promised whatever you could make of your life; anyway, not the boy next door. What Stein, Barney, Alice B. Toklas, and Sylvia Beach made of their lives, we know or will learn here. I want to suggest Jo as the daimon, the unique girl who dared to speak as they felt. Alcott, who created her, was not the mother of us all, but Jo was, and not because she became a cosmic mother in fiction. In fiction her children were boys. In life, her true children were girls who grew up and went to Paris and did wonderful things.

1977

ENDNOTES

1. Sylvia Beach, *Shakespeare and Company* (New York: Harcourt, Brace, 1959), p. 28.

2. Gertrude Stein, *Everybody's Autobiography* (New York: Random House, 1937), p. 237.

3. Beach, *Shakespeare,* p. 92.

4. Frank Kermode, *The Sense of an Ending* (New York: Oxford University Press, 1967), p. 39.

5. Sarah Elbert, Introduction to *Work* by Louisa May Alcott (New York: Schocken Books, 1977), p. xviii.

6. *Ibid.,* p. xi.

7. Horace Gregory, *Dorothy Richardson: An Adventure in Discovery* (New York: Holt, Rinehart, & Winston, 1967), p. 19.

8. Martha Saxton, *Louisa May Alcott* (Boston: Houghton Mifflin, 1977), p. 256.

9. Linda Simon, ed., *Gertrude Stein: A Composite Portrait* (New York: Discus Books, 1974), p. 44.

10. Patricia Spacks, *The Female Imagination* (New York: Knopf, 1975), p. 100.

11. Mary Jane Moffat and Charlotte Painter, eds., *Revelations: Diaries of Women* (New York: Random House, 1974), p. 29.

12. Adrienne Rich, *Of Women Born* (New York: Norton, 1976), p. 193.

13. Nina Auerbach, "Austen and Alcott on Matriarchy," Radcliffe Institute Reprint, p. 24. See Nina Auerbach, *Communities of Women: An Idea in Fiction* (Cambridge: Harvard University Press, 1978).

14. Auerbach, "Austen and Alcott," p. 17.

15. *Ibid.,* p. 24.

16. Quoted in *ibid.,* p. 23.

May Sarton's *Mrs. Stevens Hears the Mermaids Singing*

MAY SARTON'S life is a mirror image of the usual American success story. In those wildly famous lives where, Scott Fitzgerald has told us, there are no second acts, the glories and riches soon betray the writer to madness, impotence, alcohol, literary vendettas, and the ashes of despair. For Sarton, perhaps uniquely so, considering the accomplishment, there has been little organized acclaim, no academic attention,[1] indifference on the part of the critical establishment. Yet the inner life has been sustained: Neither alcohol, nor breakdown, nor the sinister satisfaction of personal cruelty has claimed her. Agonizing, in letters and conversation, over life's injustices, she has never ceased to examine with artistry her demons of anger and despair, and her consolations of solitude and love. Her success, at least until now, has been with those who read books from desire rather than compulsion. Today, still ten years younger than Mrs. Stevens, Sarton can say with her, "They haven't got me yet." ("They" are the critics and her own demons.) She has published twenty-seven books and, widely read, is only now beginning to receive the critical attention properly due her. Success that comes late has its special flavor, particularly to a writer still productive, still capable of poetry and amazement.

May Sarton was born an outsider and has remained one. Even her closeness to the town of Nelson, New Hampshire, with which she became identified for fifteen years, had, as in friendship or a love affair, its beginning in suddenness and its end in passionless affection. Exiled many times over, from her native land, Belgium, from Cambridge, Massachusetts, the city of her youth, from any community of poets or artists, from established religion, from family life (the primal exile of the only child), she has sought salvation in exile no less fervently because it was frequently of her own choosing. But her chief place of exile, like Mrs. Stevens was not her choice: that land between the "masculine" world of the critical establishment and the "feminine" world of wife and motherhood. In this between land, she has found a voice in which to express what she calls the intensities of private life, and that voice has continued its declaration that women, and disconnected men, might be explorers. Her readers have been outsiders like herself, primed for discovery, whose bags have been secretly packed for weeks, or for a lifetime.

"Women are afraid of their demon, want to control it, make it sensible like themselves," Mrs. Stevens says. One remembers the lines from Louise Bogan's poem "Women"

> Women have no wilderness in them,
> They are provident instead,
> Content in the tight hot cell of their hearts
> To eat dusty bread.

Wildernesses are not tidy and cannot be explored with elegant skills. Sarton has suffered critically because, improvidently, she has opened the wilderness within and faced it. Mrs. Stevens envies the male interviewer because "he would never be conflicted, rent in two as she was most of the time." Sarton has long recognized and celebrated her doubleness in the wilderness: "I was broken in two/By sheer definition," she writes in the poem "Birthday on the Acropolis."

Between her conventional self which perhaps, like Mrs. Stevens, "would have liked to be a woman, simply and fruitful, a woman with many children, a great husband . . . and no talent," (ellipses are Sarton's) and the talented, seeking self for whom the world has no preordained place, a dialogue of undiminished intensity has been carried on in Sarton's work for thirty-seven years. Its greatest daring, the source of its greatest moral energy, has been openness: to experience, pain, the perils of passion, loneliness, and truthtelling. This has inevitably been the dialogue of an isolated human being, a self-dialogue, recognizable certainly to housewives, desperate in loneliness and devoid of the solitude Sarton has created.

Sarton has not avoided the dangers inherent in such an openness and such a dialogue: the appearance of self-indulgence, self-pity. These dangers might as well be mentioned in their harshest form, together with her other sin: a certain laxity of style, a tendency to seize the first metaphor to hand, rather than search out the one, perfect phrase. In the intensity of her exploration, Sarton has not eschewed the assistance of the familiar metaphor, nor always observed the niceties of point of view. She has, like all writers, the defects of her virtues. But critics, and particularly academics, are understandably prone to admire and overvalue the carefully construed, almost puzzlelike novel, not only for its profundities, but because it provides them, in explication, with their livelihood. We have learned to be very harsh with those who, unlike Flaubert and Joyce, our models, do not endlessly bend language to its ultimate uses; in that harshness, we have often deprived ourselves of literature which, though less abstruse, is not less valuable. Perhaps with the advent of women's studies and the new approaches they make possible, perhaps in weariness at allusion hunting, we shall stop judging literature by its obstinacy in withstanding interpretation. Sarton has not escaped the fate of the readable, to be disdained by the unreadable.

However atypical, May Sarton shares one dominant characteristic with other modern writers: a concern with the life of the artist, and with the artistic rendering of life even by those who, like Woolf's Mrs. Dalloway or Conrad's Marlow, work in the medium of moments of awareness rather than of words or paint. The question of why the artist should be so unequivocally the modern hero is complex and profound. In the fictions of Henry James, for example, each of his protagonists who is not actually an artist is concerned with rendering the stuff of life into artistic form; and it is clear that for James life becomes meaningful only as it is shaped in response to growing awareness. If events

are not actually altered by the artist of life—and frequently they are
—the consciousness of the hero is refined to an extent where life's
rewards lie as much in "awareness" (it was James' favorite word), of
moral complexities as in control of them. To suffer becomes meaningful when one understands the suffering and condones its inevitability. This is almost the moral principle of modern literature, and it
is most readily symbolized in the hero as artist.

For women, this fascination with the role of artist has, however,
held great danger. Virginia Woolf, unlike her readers, was never confused about this. She did not suggest, though for years it was supposed
she had, that Mrs. Ramsay in *To the Lighthouse* was as satisfactory an
artist as Lily Briscoe. James' heroes might be artists of life, but women
with babies in their arms and dinner for twenty to be arranged were
not. Mrs. Ramsay has been mistakenly celebrated as an artist of life
because it satisfied both men and women to think of the wife-mother,
whether as servant or earth-goddess, as fulfilling a role equally important to that of the true artist. But Woolf knew that to be truly an
artist is to retain control of one's own destiny (one may use that "control" for self-destruction, but that does not contradict the point) and
that the women struggling their way to a sense of identity through
the encircling meshes of domesticity were not artists, but victims.

Women have not perceived this and, perhaps, have moved too easily
into the fantasy of being an artist. No doubt they have been influenced
by the apparent autonomy of the artist, the apparent ease with which
art can be fitted in with the domestic life. In fact, however, in seeing
the artist as their own ideal, women have to a large extent betrayed
themselves. They do not understand that unless they are ready to sacrifice all the "feminine" virtues to their art, they have not changed their
relation to their own destiny, which is one of powerlessness and passivity. Art cannot be achieved by those for whom anything else matters
more. Art, like passion, is not a part-time occupation.

May Sarton has not only been an artist—poet, novelist,
memoirist—but, like other modern writers, she has seen her life as
interacting with her art. Experience becomes meaningful, reveals itself,
when it has been transformed into art. She has, furthermore, put artists at the center of many of her novels or, if not artists, teachers or
craftsmen. But she has not failed to make explicit the division between
Mrs. Ramsay and Lily Briscoe: Mrs. Ramsay, who would have liked
always to have a baby in her arms, and Lily Briscoe, who thought

about her painting and realized with relief that she would not have to marry anyone. Hilary Stevens, with her chance at marriage and the passivity of a "feminine" destiny, realizes after the death of her husband that she never wrote a poem to him. For poems are written to, or inspired by muses, and muses, Hilary tells us, are women. This is a very intricate concept which must be looked at more closely, but it is well at the start to realize that if Sarton seems to bow too low to the convention of the proper wifely functions, she does know that the real artist is not the fantasy creature imagined by women trapped in domesticity. The real artist is engaged in a full-time struggle, which is harder for women, among other reasons, because they do not have wives.

At first glance, *Mrs. Stevens Hears the Mermaids Singing* seems conventional in its acceptance of male and female roles. Hilary is responsible for the following: "She had no idea what these two [men] would be like together alone, in their world, the impenetrable masculine world." "The women who have tried to be men have always lacked something." "Women do not thrive in cities." And so on. Yet the novel in its searching dialogue reveals in the end the misconceptions of women who, like Jenny, want to be "whole." "I want to believe that a woman writer must be a whole woman," Jenny says, wanting to marry, have children, the whole bag. But women cannot have the whole bag, and *Mrs. Stevens* is one of the few novels whose attention is centered on this theme. The theme is never made explicit, nor does Sarton allow herself to suggest that Mary's work is holier than Martha's. She does, however, refuse to the woman with a spare hour stolen from the kitchen or nursery the deluding daydream of being an artist. In marriages, at least as we know them at the time of the novel, the woman's role is to be loved, to lie protected in a man's arms, and the artist cannot be the loved one. The artist must be the loving one which is, as Hilary points out, more convenient if someone else is cooking the stew and arranging the flowers. We remind ourselves that of the great women writers, most have been unmarried, and those who have written in the state of wedlock have done so in peaceful kingdoms guarded by devoted husbands. Few have had children. The dream of the girl interviewer, Jenny, is a silly dream though Hilary is too kind to say so. Yet with singularity, Sarton has allowed Martha into the dialogue. Jesus had said that Mary's was the better part, and the world has almost unanimously exalted Martha. Sarton alone has allowed them to converse with one another.

Hilary, like Sarton, knows that poems begin in passion, an emotion hard to retain for him who wears the socks one darns. In any case, passion of this sort does not belong to marriage, which is quite a different state, however fervent its sexual life. Muses are never husbands, and rarely wives.

For Hilary then, as for Sarton, the muses have been women. Must they inevitably be women, even for women writers? The question is premature at this stage of our knowledge. Edna St. Vincent Millay appears to have had male muses, but we know little about her. Emily Dickinson's muse was apparently male, but we know even less about her. For Hilary, in any case, it was women who inspired her to poetry, and that fact must be considered in two ways.

Most obviously, Hilary is homosexual or, more accurately, bisexual; but for her it is the love for another woman that inspires. This, of course, was the shocking element in the novel when Sarton's agent read it and advised against publishing. We are a good deal less inclined to be shocked these days. Sarton revealed, with the publication of this book, her own homosexuality which, like Hilary's, has not been absolute. She was, in her youth, in love with several men, including one she thought of marrying. Sarton knows, and through her I have learned, how many women writers have had homosexual lovers, and I think the matter is not of particular importance here, except to suggest that it is about time we got such matters into better perspective.

It is time also, perhaps, to suggest that when the great homosexual novel, which Noel Annan tells us has not yet been written, appears, it may well be a woman's. "There are many important novels in which homosexual characters and situations appear," Annan writes in reviewing Forster's *Maurice*, "and a number of technical attempts in minor works have been made to explore this or that part of homosexual life. At the moment it appears impossible because, while we may accept that homosexual relations are as normal and as unremarkable as heterosexual relations, the subject with all its history and hysteria and social overtones comes between the writer and his work and between him and the reader. Implicitly he is still explaining as Forster felt bound to explain."[2] But Annan, of course, is thinking of the male homosexual novel with all its social anguish. *Mrs. Stevens* is outstanding because its homosexuality is not seen in its social or shocking aspects at all. It is used, thematically, to discover the source of poetry for the woman artist.

It is in its second or metaphoric sense that Hilary's concept of the muse is important: because, as a lover of women, Hilary cannot possibly assume that women can achieve art through passivity, fecundity, or the avoidance of their own anger. Each time the muse appears to Hilary, it is Hilary who acts, Hilary who loves, Hilary who rages and pursues and writes the poem. Sexuality apart, *Mrs. Stevens* is a novel which unites absolutely the artist and the active principle. We remember Lily Briscoe who refused to solace Mr. Ramsay's soul, and we see why the givers of solace are never painters or poets, and never can be.

What is therefore apparent is that *Mrs. Stevens* is meaningful for women who are not homosexuals, who may indeed have found their inspiration in male lovers they do not or are not called upon to serve. It seems likely that muses, like artists, come in both sexes. One needs above all to remember that neither Sarton nor Hilary has failed to understand the quality of the relationship necessary to a writer, homosexual or not. "I blame myself," Oscar Wilde wrote, "for allowing an unintellectual friendship . . . to entirely dominate my life. An artist, the quality of whose work depends on the intensification of personality, requires the compansionship of ideas."[3] Hilary never made Wilde's mistake; there was no Alfred Douglas in her life. The quality of the relationships, like the active role Hilary played in them, are more important than the sex of her particular muse.

SARTON'S FIRST novel, *The Single Hound,* was about a young man who wanted to be a poet. So probably was Hilary's first novel, but hers, more daringly, was also "about women falling in love with each other." *The Single Hound,* not about this, did present two figures of accomplished women artists. Doro—only slightly an adumbration of Hilary—is an elderly poet who has published a book of poems under a male pseudonym. The young male poet, Mark Taylor, seeks her out because her poems have, literally, inspired him. The moment he sees her he knows she is the poet, although he had expected an old man: Her femininity reveals itself as inevitable. The other woman artist, with whom Mark Taylor becomes infatuated, is Georgia Manning, a painter and, incidentally, a vivid and perhaps unique fictional portrait of Elizabeth Bowen in those years. The novel's title is from a poem by Emily Dickinson which might stand as motto to Sarton's whole accomplishment:

> Adventure most unto itself
> The Soul condemned to be;
> Attended by a Single Hound—
> Its own Identity.

The women artists of *The Single Hound* were not to appear again in Sarton's novels until *Mrs. Stevens,* although she came close to the theme often.[4]

Sarton has said that if she had no readers, she would still write poems, but not novels, which are a continuing exploration of the individual straining against the forces of disintegration in the twentieth century; such an exploration in a novel becomes in part a dialogue with the reader, while in a poem there is the dialogue with the self alone. Partly for this reason, she continued in her novels to present marriages, and marriage became for her the ground upon which the needs of the struggling individual are played out. There was always, perhaps, an undue admiration for marriage as such, an unsearching acceptance of stereotyped sex roles, and a certain lack of daring in the solutions. Perhaps this represents the refusal of an outsider to assault too brutally so long established an institution as marriage. She did present a marriage where the wife was the breadwinner in a business inherited from the mother and passed on to the daughter (*The Bridge of Years*) and, in *Faithful Are the Wounds,* took up a different subject altogether: that of a man, modeled on F. O. Matthiessen, who committed suicide in despair during the McCarthy era. *The Small Room,* set in a women's New England college, includes two older women who are homosexual lovers, and other adult female characters who do not wonder, as does Melanie in *The Bridge of Years,* if "her dreams had been a man's dreams." But again, there is a marriage, this time of a young professor who threatens to "spank" his wife, the wife who speaks of taking her sons away to Italy to grow up into men "who are not threatened by the power of women," and the students who are described as "not cranks or creeps, girls in spectacles, girls who walk with their heads down, . . . [but] frighteningly healthy and natural." It is this sort of conventionality which has, I believe, helped to keep from Sarton the critical attention she deserves. Searching female readers do not welcome stereotypes, and male critics are not interested in conventional women unless they appear in novels by and about men.

Yet many women readers, particularly those who are or who have been teachers, have found *The Small Room* to be important, because it treats of openness, of the pressures inevitable on any campus (but without the usual cruel humor), and of the never easy student-teacher relationship. Hitherto, with the rare exception of a book like *Olivia* by Dorothy Bussy, this relationship has always been depicted as a woman teacher with a male student (*The Corn is Green*), a male teacher with a female student (every fifth American novel), or a male teacher with a male student who is a son or disciple. For all its minor conventional languors, *The Small Room* broke through into the world where women function as individuals.

Oddly enough, after the teacher-student relationship in *The Small Room*, there is no case in Sarton's works of a woman artist passing on to a younger woman her own convictions of the dedicated life; there are no young female heirs. Sarton seems almost to draw back from such a thought, as if to argue for her life as opposed to the normal destiny of a woman were too terrifying a prospect. *Kinds of Love,* her popular novel of a few years ago, again is without an artist figure, except for a young girl who writes poems and whose inspiration ceases when she falls in love or, rather, is fallen in love with. We cannot fail to notice that in *Mrs. Stevens* the woman interviewer is used for one part of the dialogue, but that the more interesting youthful foil is the boy, Mar, someone far closer to Sarton herself, but who is also, of course, an aspect of Hilary. It is only young males like Mar whom Sarton will accept, within the novels, as poets of the future, as those who will dare to confront life.

In her own life, Sarton continued as exile, turning into poems and memoirs her dialogue between solitude and love. *Plant Dreaming Deep* has probably affected more single or lonely lives than any other memoir published in recent years, but the response was in small rooms; again, the masculine critical world was largely uninterested. In this memoir, Sarton attempted to confront, as she had done in *Mrs. Stevens,* the life of the artist and single woman. Her accomplishment was the more impressive in that she had seen what no one else had seen: the outsider as single woman. We all know who are the outsiders of our society: Jews, like Leopold Bloom and his numerous American progeny; blacks; the poor. But though Sarton has always been sympathetically drawn to the persecuted and excluded, she has not made them the embodiment of her own sense of exile, but has kept that where she has lived it, in the woman artist, alone in a house, eschewing social life, in a town of which, when she moved there, she knew nothing.

"We have to make myths of our lives," she wrote in *Plant Dreaming Deep*. "It is the only way to live without despair." This was an extraordinary gift to the women who read her: the idea that their lives, which they had formerly conceived only as an aspect of failure, might be mythologized into achievement. There was a fallacy here: Her readers were rarely artists, and the order she had created of her life seemed, though she had not intended this, more easy of achievement than it was. *The Journal of a Solitude,* published last year, was written in an attempt to let people know of the rages, the assaults from the critics, the despairs. Yet for all that, *Plant Dreaming Deep* did give us for the first time a new myth, that of the single person, and a woman, recovering her identity through work and discipline. Unique as a memoir in American letters, it brought her, not critical notice, but an adoring public given to writing endless letters and turning up on the village green at dawn to survey her house through field glasses.

The two books published in 1973, *The Journal of a Solitude* and *As We Are Now,* although the first was mutilated by enforced excisions and other difficulties, mark a new courage in her work, and a new, more forthright assault upon the barriers between people. Once more she has celebrated that openness which many people now are learning as the necessary prelude to the discovery of identity. To those barriers she has always kicked against has been added now the barrier of age. In *The Small Room* Sarton quoted from an essay by Simone Weil: "Two prisoners in contingent cells, who communicate by blows struck on the wall. The wall is what separates them, but also what permits them to communicate. So it is with us and God. Every separation is a bond." *As We Are Now* is the story of old age confined to the cell where our society relegates the old, separated from life, a cell on whose walls no one knocks. If Sarton has not been a revolutionary against the ingrained ideas of women's destiny and place in marriage, she has recognized the barriers between the sexes and the generations for what they are: walls which, will we but strike them, can carry our communication.

"Is there no compassion?" a friend asked me./"Does it exist in another country?" This question, from the poem "A Hard Death," is not the least of this century's questions: it is one which Sarton has never ceased to ask. Compassion is usually conceived as a malady from which we struggle to recover. It has never been so for her. Her own personal suffering and rage, her own quarrels with the world, have never been muted as her compassion has never been muted. Louise Bogan, in a letter to Ruth Limmer, calls some poems of Sarton's "sentimental,"[5] an easy charge, a palpable danger to any writer not barricaded against revelation. But what appears sentimental to the society Mrs. Stevens envisioned as composed of male critics is an inevitable aspect of the compassion which, in Sarton, has never cowered behind the usual defenses. As a result, life is never absent from her work as it is from, to name a master, the work of Flaubert. And even Bogan must have understood something of this. Writing of Elizabeth Bowen's crystalline and pristine prose, never for a moment lax or sentimental, Bogan observed, "*The Death of the Heart* is too packed, too brilliant, for its own good. What Miss Bowen lacks is a kind of humility."[6]

Sarton has another too little celebrated virtue: She gives pleasure. "Though large sales are not necessarily a proof of aesthetic value," Auden has written, "they are evidence that a book has given pleasure to many readers, and every author, however difficult, would like to give pleasure."[7] Sarton gives pleasure and (notice this in *Mrs. Stevens,* a book in which "nothing happens,") the reader is carried along on a current rather than, as in many more celebrated books, swimming his way upstream like a spawning salmon because it is his duty to do so. E. M. Forster has remarked that one always tends to overpraise a long book because one has got through it, and one wonders if, in the academic world, the same does not also apply to books that make hard reading.

Finally, Sarton and Mrs. Stevens are outsiders not least because, in this machismo age, violence and cruelty have offered them no satisfactions. Whatever Sarton has done, she has never imitated male writers, which may be what Hilary means when she says that women who have imitated men lack something. For to imitate men is not to want a place in the world, autonomy, a chance for self-creation, and the freedom to express anger and aggression. To imitate men is to remain enslaved to those standards men have declared eternal, and to deny one-self, because one is a woman, selfhood. Which is why, though Sarton, with the nostalgic eyes of the only child and the single adult, has looked upon marriage and family life less critically than she might, she has never limited the women of her creation to passivity, nor failed to be, long before the word passed into its current usage, liberated.

The reappearance of *Mrs. Stevens Hears the Mermaids Singing* is an important occasion, is, as Sarton has said in another connection, our "good luck in a dirty time."

1973

ENDNOTES

1. At the meeting of the Modern Language Association in December 1973, a seminar was held on "The Art of May Sarton." Ten papers were presented on many aspects of her work. They were by L. W. Anderson, Jane S. Bakerman, Fredrica Bartz, Melissa Cannon, Sigrid N. Fowler, Charles Frank, Susan Hauser, Kathleen Klein, Paula G. Putney, Henry Taylor. Dawn Holt Anderson, the discussion leader, has herself published an essay, "May Sarton's Women," in Susan Koppelman Cornillon, ed., *Images of Women in Fiction* (Bowling Green, Ohio: Bowling Green University Press, 1972), pp. 243–250. Agnes Sibley, *May Sarton* (New York: Twayne, 1972), is useful for chronology and biography.

2. Noel Annan, "Love Story," *New York Review of Books,* October 21, 1971, pp. 17–18.

3. Oscar Wilde, *De Profundis.* Quoted in the Introduction by Jacques Barzun (New York: Vintage, 1964), p. xi.

4. Joanna in *Joanna and Ulysses* is a painter, but this is one of those Sarton fictions which I prefer to call fables, as Sarton herself sometimes calls them. One would particularly like to recommend all four of them to those who interest themselves in books for youngsters; like the best books for young people, they were written for adults, are wise, and do not condescend or lie. There is nothing else produced in this line lately that is nearly so good as *Joanna and Ulysses, The Fur Person, The Poet and the Donkey,* and *Miss Pickthorne and Mr. Hare.*

5. Ruth Limmer, ed., *What the Woman Lived: Selected Letters of Louise Bogan, 1920–1970* (New York: Harcourt Brace Jovanovich, 1973), p. 325.

6. Louise Bogan, *A Poet's Alphabet,* Ruth Limmer and Robert Phelps, eds. (New York: McGraw-Hill, 1970), p. 64.

7. W. H. Auden, "A Poet of the Actual," *New Yorker,* April 1, 1972, p. 104. (Auden was reviewing a biography of Trollope.)

13

May Sarton's Memoirs

LITTLE HAS so marked contemporary literature as the melding of genres. Once the "certainties" of a steadier time were revealed to rest upon arguable assumptions, the slippage of genre was inevitable. Today biography and fiction are met together; novel and poetry, like righteousness and peace, have kissed each other. Ambiguity dilutes taxonomy. We now read "it" because it is by Lessing or Pynchon, Mailer or Millett, not because we know precisely what "it" is.

Here as in so much else, May Sarton has been unusual. Moving between many genres, occasionally distilling the same offering from life into several distinct artistic forms, she has defended the boundaries of genre: her journals and memoirs, tales and novels, poetry and translations of poetry have retained their claim to form. Her memoirs, therefore, distinguish themselves from her other works and may, with some precision, be defined and analyzed.

The Sarton memoirs are in three volumes, of which two, *I Knew a Phoenix* (1959) and *A World of Light* (1976), are collections of discrete pieces, while the middle volume, *Plant Dreaming Deep* (1968), is a unified narration of a single extended experience. The perfection and originality of *Plant Dreaming Deep*, which I shall explore in a moment, required that accounts of the agony and triumph of those years, thematically and chronologically a part of *Plant Dreaming Deep*, should be exiled to other genres. Thus we have riding postern to *Plant Dreaming Deep, The Poet and the Donkey* (1969), a tale, and *Journal of a Solitude* (1973), written to qualify the serene effect of the memoir. These works were properly exiled, for in *Plant Dreaming Deep* Sarton achieved something close to a new form for female writing: she transformed the genre, even as she reported a new female experience.

But one must begin with an analysis of the earliest memoir, *I Knew a Phoenix*. In this collection of short pieces, Sarton excelled in the use of a form already well established. That most of these memoirs were published in *The New Yorker* confirms this point. *The New Yorker*, certainly at the time these pieces appeared, and for many years before, was the cloister of polished writing. To achieve publication in its pages was not only to have written well: it was also to have acquired fame and money without the price of corruption and sinful success demanded by less exalted journals. *The Atlantic* might offer esteem, The *Ladies' Home Journal* riches; only *The New Yorker* bestowed both. And one of the reasons it attracted so much good writing was that within its pages had been perfected the form, whether a short story or memoir, into which highly talented writers might pour the narrative of their youth.

The New Yorker memoir, therefore, provided Sarton with the form she needed to capture, with a kind of pure grace, the experiences of childhood which may be preserved, as an insect is preserved in amber, bereft of all its whirling complexities and messy dangers. The memoir keeps, as a photograph keeps, some outward form, not dishonest but devoid equally of animation and the indifference of time. Roland Barthes, recalling photographs of his mother, puts it thus: "At the mercy of these photos, I sometimes recognized a part of her face, a certain resemblance of the nose and the forehead, the movement of her arms, of her hands. Except in bits, I never recognized her, which is to say that I lacked her being, and that, consequently, I lacked her entirely. I recognized her differently, not essentially."[1] Which is to say that even the best photographers, like the best memoirists, must fail even as they uniquely succeed. Sarton was among the best, but the form, self-limiting, recognized the past differently, not essentially.

Sarton herself, in the memoir of the Belgian home where she and her parents lived for a few years before the First World War, offers a different metaphor for the memoir: my mother, she writes, "had lifted out of a pile of rubbish a single Venetian glass on a long delicate stem so dirty it had become opaque, but miraculously intact. How had this single object survived to give us courage? It went back with us to Cambridge and it was always there, wherever we lived. And now it is here, in my own house, a visible proof that it is sometimes the most fragile thing that has the power to endure."[2] Her memoirs which, like this fragile object, endure, concern the lives of her parents before her birth; her transplantation to America, her father's profession, her mother's work, less encouraged, more frustrated; the school in Cambridge, Shady Hill, which Sarton attended in its early days when the energy, available to new, idealistic enterprises, had not yet been dissipated or hardened into institutions. Finally, there is the account of the Belgian school Sarton attended in her twelfth year. Not to dwell upon these seven lovely memoirs is merely to acknowledge their perfection.

The remaining five essays, less perfect, but adumbrating the originality of *Plant Dreaming Deep*, did not, significantly, achieve publication in *The New Yorker*. As soon as Sarton wrote of uncertainty and discontent, of adventures disinclined to fossilization, *The New Yorker* memoir form could not contain that force, that confusion. With adolescence and the beginning of experience not imposed by parents and schools, Sarton began to encounter the conflict endemic to the lives of unconventional women. Before she was seventeen, she would move against the consensus of her time, refuse college, and seek a special destiny, though in "the manliness of her girlish heart" the specialness was clearer than the destiny.

Responding to the power of Eva Le Gallienne, the most forceful woman she had yet encountered, Sarton became an actress. In her perhaps unconscious attempt to escape conventional womanhood (her mother's life), she thus chose the conventional female route to unconventionality. An actress is told what to say and do; she imitates, without enacting in her proper self, the destinies of women in dramatic situations. Thus the girl can satisfy the terrible social pressures that forbid her deep originality, and yet mollify her own daemon.

Sarton could not, I suppose, have remained an actress: her dream to play Hilda in Ibsen's *The Master Builder,* while it would have allowed her a grand entrance as a "new woman," would also have forced her to function only as an event in the life of a man, the hero of the play. There is, in any case, no way in which Sarton could have long endured a career devoted to the lives and actions of others: she needed to hold the pen, and be herself the author of the story. Her life in the theater was defeated, indeed, by her attempt to run a company, to direct events. She wished, in short, to act in her own play. As she might have said with Isa in Woolf's *Between the Acts,* "surely it was time someone invented a new plot."

But before this, in the way of the young in those years, she went to Paris. In her memoirs, Sarton looked back on that time as "a period of illness and even insanity"; so youth later appears in the lives of those who will be original. Her description of standing before Paris's museums and libraries "like a cat with one paw raised, unwilling to step into cold water," beautifully captures that time of indecision when one knows one will be called, but not when nor to what vocation. "I did nothing wise or sensible. I simply lived in Paris. I wandered about, ardent and hungry, picking up whatever was accidentally brought to my attention, tasting it and then wandering on, casual and solitary." She had the courage, trancelike as it seemed, to avoid that "network of responsibilities" which catches us all soon enough, and catches soonest those who most fear the risk of originality. She wrote poems, she remembers, as a way of persuading herself that she existed. For most young women, marriage serves that function. Sarton's memoirs of that time in Paris, naked in their confusion, speak of life plans Koestler has described as written in invisible ink, not yet brought into decipherability. Unable to read the text of her own life, Sarton read in the great novels what others had inscribed, so that all she encountered "flowed in and out of the printed page."[3]

The uncertainty of youth, however mildly extended, is rarely described in the lives of women. Even less often are we shown the uncertainties and risks of female middle age. *Plant Dreaming Deep,* extraordinary in many ways, is not least so in being the account of a woman between forty-five and fifty-five; indeed it is unique among what few examples there are. Those women who have published accounts of their middle years have usually written of their lives as wives or mothers (and perhaps as something else as well), or at least, like Simone de Beauvoir, of an existence anchored in another person. Not so Sarton, whose memoir deals with the extraordinary possibilities of solitude. Colette is another rare example of a woman writing the autobiography of her choice of solitude in middle age; yet Colette in life chose not that solitude, but marriage to her young lover. As Nancy Miller has written: "The textualization of a female 'I' means escape from the sphere inhabited by those 'relative beings' (as Beauvoir has characterized women) who experience the world only through the mediation of men. To write is to come out of the wings, and to appear, however briefly, center stage. . . . These autobiographies are the stories of women who succeeded in becoming more than *just* women, and by their own negative definition of that condition."[4]

What makes *Plant Dreaming Deep* unique and uniquely important is that Sarton has written a memoir of the possibilities of the solitary female life, but without negatively defining the condition of those who are *just* women. Indeed, as we shall see, she was naively astonished that married women should read into it that negative meaning. Her friends, too, could not escape the analogy to marriage. "My friends," she has written, "realized that my whole relation to the place was a little like that of an old maid who suddenly gets married."[5] It was in fact, very little like, as one can see, for example, by comparing the life of Mary Wilkins Freeman, an "old maid" who married late: she was later to deny all the passionate assertions of her lonely years. For Sarton it was otherwise: the buying of a house where she would live alone was in Unamuno's words, "the effort of [her] past to transform itself into [her] future."[6] The move from solitude to marriage is an escape from what is perceived as incompleteness. Sarton's move, on the other hand, was an effort to crystallize her female autonomy. Once she had written *Plant Dreaming Deep,* had created thus the account of a woman's making of the solitary life, the need to remain in the house slackened and finally disappeared. Within a few years of publishing the memoir, she would move, retaining the solitude but not the drama of that first, hard assertion of selfhood.

The story Sarton tells in *Plant Dreaming Deep* is this: A woman who for forty-five years has never owned property nor lived alone, decides to become a householder, to buy, renovate, and move into her own house. In a manner characteristic of American culture, she is faced with the possibility of living anywhere: certainly she can pick any spot within a few hours' drive of Boston. But why New Hampshire?

Sarton credits this choice of place to her "guardian angel," a male figure whose guidance is invoked half a dozen times in her memoirs. This guardian angel is related, somehow, to the ancestor whose picture she tells of hanging at the beginning of her memoir. When she puts up the picture of this male ancestor, she is fifty-four years old, has been in the house eight years, and describes herself as "the last of her line." She does not of course consider herself, as we do, the first in a line of women who will, by her memoir, be enabled to make different fictions of their lives. The guardian angel and the ancestor, however, both male non-beings endowed by her with protective powers, offered her support in a world readier to see an old maid marry than a woman artist rejoice in her own solitude in her own place. These gentle male figures reassure her, it seems, rescue her from the marginality of lonely female existence. And in the early stages of the making of this home, the male world supports her: contractor, architect, mover, the tiller of her land, all shape her needs and desires. Later, when she is established, this male world will grow destructive, personified in the ignorant well-diggers, the literary agent who fears the honesty of her lesbian novel, the reviewer of her selected poems. This pattern is never expressly stated: it is merely presented, but confirmed in the celebration of her home's completion: her first guests are a mother figure from Belgium, who was the first to hold the newborn May in her arms; the woman with whom for years Sarton had shared a house; and Louise Bogan, the poet. In this house she will write of the love of women for women, will claim the female Muse for women no less than for men.

Ultimately, what is celebrated in the memoir and indeed created by it, is not the house itself, nor its lonely occupant coping with the harshness of nature, and the inevitable rush of all earthly things toward deterioration; what is celebrated is the survival of the solitary female artist in the face of the inevitable pain of life, and the need to rage alone at that pain. As Sarton makes clear, she survives without the aid of those regular professional activities and commitments through which we can move, when we must, like automatons, and in which we can forget pain and loneliness. As an artist, furthermore, she survived without

the media acclaim available to some established writers and intellectuals through their links to the network of journalists and reviewers.
The New Yorker was gone from Sarton's life. It published no more of
her work and, as she explains in her account of Bogan's column, took
little further notice of her. (One wonders what Bogan might further
have accomplished as a poet had she cut free from *The New Yorker*
column in which she reviewed the work of other poets.) Sarton chose
the way of solitude with all its costs, and heartened others with the
news that this adventure, this terrible daring, might be endured.

Ironically, but not unnaturally, Sarton did not wholly understand
this heartening of others. In *Journal of a Solitude* she agrees that women
devalue their own powers, but goes on to assert that "there is something wrong when solitude such as mine can be 'envied' by a happily
married woman with children."[7] Hers is not, she feels sure, the best
human solution. Is there a best human solution? The point is that the
creation of the narrative about a woman's working solitude is so rare
that, inevitably, it must be envied by a "happily" married woman, or
by any woman less original or less creative than Sarton, who feels less
than herself. If Sarton's is not the "best" human solution, neither is
there a "happily" married woman. There is only the struggle, and the
fiction of that struggle, which we call a memoir, for which Sarton has
given us the form.

What Sarton did was to write a new plot for women, a new script.
In *Journal of a Solitude* she was to speak of her fears that in *Plant
Dreaming Deep* she had not sufficiently rendered her anger, her rage,
her sense of isolation, both physical and artistic, not the agonies of
love. Had she led some woman astray by idealizing her lonely struggle?
The answer is emphatically, "No." Every new text, every adventure, is
full of danger both to oneself and to others. There is a moment in
Sarton's memoir when all seems lost: her job, the publication of her
most courageous novel, even, one guesses, a lover, a moment of drought
when the springs have run dry, and the well-diggers go deeper and
deeper and do not reach water. Then within hours water is reached,
a new job offered, the book to be published after all. It is a woman's
moment, water reached and the house covered with mud, new professional opportunities revealed. It is original and will long inspire.

If one seeks a commentary on *Plant Dreaming Deep,* I would suggest not *Journal of a Solitude* (which should, of course, be read for its
own reasons) but The *Poet and the Donkey.* This tale recounts how a

solitary writer finds her way back to the sanity of poetry. But Sarton tells it as the tale of a male poet (always easier to tell) whose solitude can be claimed and need not be accounted for. The poet has lost his Muse. He needs an activity apart from himself and decides to borrow a donkey and care for it. The donkey is a charming creature, requiring imaginative attention, and in the end rescues the poet from despair. So in fact a donkey rescued Sarton. This tale teaches how attention on a new subject which must be slowly learned can help us to channel our way out of despair.

The three journals which Sarton wrote after *Plant Dreaming Deep* do not come within the purview of this essay; only the first, *Journal of a Solitude,* records Sarton's life in the house in Nelson, ending with the sentence, "Once more the house and I are alone." But even as these words appeared, she was moving away from Nelson, from rugged New Hampshire to a gentler, though no less solitary life by the sea. The journals that record that new life belong to another genre: they catch life on the fly, and for all that Sarton's journals are carefully edited, pruned, and arranged, their very form counters the completeness of the Nelson experience, catching instead something centrifugal and diffused, perhaps characteristic of successful women's lives.

Sarton published one more collection of memoirs, again made up of short pieces, in a companion volume to *I Knew a Phoenix,* covering the years between that novel and *Plant Dreaming Deep. A World of Light* can stand as a work of instruction upon the short memoir form. It is divided into four parts, of which the middle two sections are again memoirs of what is already written in the mind, in some way even already published: she has committed to paper what she has long known the words for. These are accounts of people once vital in Sarton's life, whose power and effect have long since faded; they are mementos, precious perhaps, but reminders only of a dead past. It is the first and fourth parts, rather, that have most to teach us about the memoir form.

In the first part, Sarton attempts to write about her parents, those unique persons from one's past whose terrors are never quite diffused into adult understanding, whose demands upon one's self and each other echo to the end of life. Sarton has tried to see her parents as an outsider might want them revivified, and she has succeeded in this. It is good to have George Sarton returned to our contemplation: he was a man singularly devoted to the new discipline of the History of Science, which he created and nursed into viability. (It saddened me greatly a year or two ago when I was among those interviewing a Harvard candidate in the History of Science for a Mellon Fellowship. I mentioned George Sarton, and she dismissed him and his work with that particular sneer characteristic of youth in its disdain for the achievements of the recent past.) May Sarton allows us to remember George Sarton and his hard and ill-rewarded work. As to Sarton's mother, the great difficulty in writing of her has not been transcended, though the portrait is suggestive enough. My guess is that the key to these two individuals is the marriage between them, the total self-centeredness of the man, the internalized rage, the thwarted talent of the woman. Only a future biographer perhaps may be harsh enough to guess how the marriage between these two created the artist May Sarton, burdening her with rage as well as courage.

Part Four of *A World of Light,* particularly the three portraits of those renowned figures, S. S. Koteliansky, Elizabeth Bowen, and Louise Bogan, illuminates alike the subjects and Sarton's rare gifts as a memoirist. These are the sort of essays without which every future biographer of their subjects would be bereft. More impressive even than their verisimilitude is the energy with which these individuals are imbued by Sarton's love for them, and our sense of how she vibrated to the personalities of these three figures, and was made to suffer with and by them as only those who dare love and friendship can suffer. One truth among the many Sarton teaches us is that, lightly as the words love and friendship are tossed about in connection with the merest lusts and acquaintances, love and friendship are rare experiences whose cost is great. With each of these people Sarton was to feel, as we all inevitably feel if we dare to love, that our gifts are in the end too readily taken, perhaps less generously returned.

Throughout all the memoirs Sarton feels, as who does not feel when they have worked as long and honorably as she, that she has been insufficiently loved and appreciated. I do not speak of a petty person seeking empty reassurance and emptier public acclaim. Hers is the sudden chill of doubt reserved for those who have been unusually courageous, unusually generous, unusually overlooked. Auden was to write of Virginia Woolf that by his own generation, "even in the palmiest days of social consciousness, she was admired and loved more than she realized."[8] I think the same is true of Sarton not only in her own generation, but beyond it to the youngest young woman today (and young man, too, unhappy in the role allotted him) reading of what might be. I suspect that Sarton does not know in these media-centered days how profound her effect has been in the academic world as well as among those who read only for love. Certainly, she has been remarkably unlucky in her reviewers, especially in the powerful *New York Times*. Yet her life and work have had effect far greater than many of those who have been more grandly praised. Every genre she has taken up has contributed to that effect. If I have chosen here to celebrate the memoirs, and especially *Plant Dreaming Deep,* it is because in that profoundly inventive work she has, with rare artistry, claimed for women their chance to be both solitary and triumphant.

1982

ENDNOTES

1. Roland Barthes, *La chambre claire: Note sur la photographie.* Quoted in J. Gerald Kennedy, "Roland Barthes, Autobiography, and the End of Writing," *Georgia Review* (Summer 1981), p. 389.

2. May Sarton, *I Knew a Phoenix* (New York: Norton, 1959), p. 81.

3. The quotations in this paragraph are from *I Knew a Phoenix,* pp. 169, 163, 165, 167, 174.

4. Nancy K. Miller, "Women's Autobiography in France: For a Dialectics of Identification," in *Women and Language in Literature and Society,* Sally McConnell-Ginet, Ruth Borker, Nelly Furman, eds., (New York: Praeger, 1980), p. 266.

5. May Sarton, *Plant Dreaming Deep* (New York: Norton, 1968), p. 39.

6. Miguel de Unamuno, *The Tragic Sense of Life,* quoted in Ian Watt, *Conrad in the Nineteenth Century* (Berkeley: University of California Press, 1979), p. 41.

7. May Sarton, *Journal of a Solitude* (New York: Norton, 1973), p. 123.

8. W. H. Auden, "Consciousness of Reality," in *Forewords and Afterwords,* selected by Edward Mendelson (New York: Vintage Books, 1974), p. 416.

IV

FEMINISM

AND THE

PROFESSION OF

LITERATURE

Introductory Note

THE FIRST two essays in this section were delivered on different occasions under the auspices of the MLA to regional Chairs of English
Departments. They are from the earlier days of feminism, and I hope
evoke to some extent the spirit of that time. In the second of these,
"Women, Men, Theories, and Literature," I mention that I cannot call
long distance from my office phone at Columbia. My concern that
Columbia's parsimony not be exaggerated forces me to say that I can
today make long distance calls from my office phone.

The third essay, "Feminist Criticism in Departments of Literature"
was delivered at a convention of the AAUP. As will by now be clear
to anyone moving right along in this book, I have ever flirted with,
been enamored by, the classics without knowing a word of Greek. I
would like, in this connection, to thank Helene Foley, Professor of

Classics, who alone among the knowledgeable has encouraged me to engage "her" literature even in the face of my ignorance.

The last two essays constitute, collectively and separately, the bravest acts of my professional life. In the first, as President of the MLA, I dared to talk, not as a "we," a genderless member of our profession, but as a woman who had lived her life as a professor of literature. One woman academic of some renown left the hall (so I was later told; the lights prevented my seeing her) noisily, loaded with shopping bags, at the mention of the word "menstruation" in a passage I was quoting from a former President of MLA. Other faculty women of a fundamentalist turn of mind also objected. I didn't hear any complaints from men. By the end of 1984, they were (at least in the northeast) either staying away, or paying little attention or, more rarely, concurring. "The Politics of Mind" was delivered at Columbia as a University Lecture, an occasion of great formality including a dinner before and a reception after, as well as an introduction from a high administrator. Here again, I spoke as a woman in the academy. The gods, clearly male administrators themselves, caused a wild rain storm that continued all day and into the night; many people, understandably, stayed away. That as many came as did on this, for me, very anxious occasion, has always been a happy memory.

14
Bringing the Spirit Back to English Studies

LET US admit that English studies are in the doldrums. What I really believe is that they are in a state it would be meiotic to call parlous, but doldrums will do. As one of my colleagues put it to me, professors of English today must either choose wearily to teach "the same old stuff" or else dig their way into new theories that are concealed in a thicket of language so dense as to be virtually impenetrable. Meanwhile, students arrive unconvinced that literature holds important truths and insufficiently educated in myths and the Bible to catch even the most obvious of civilized echoes.

There is, I believe, hope in the midst of this, a hope whose name is feminist, or women's, studies; but that hope too is imperiled. Those already in the establishment turn away from this solution in horror; those who aspire to the establishment fearfully avert their eyes. Yet, as I shall attempt to argue, feminist criticism offers a vital alternative, recognizable among the old texts, waiting for exploration and enlightenment.

Let us be blunt. Today's youth, whatever the reasons, no longer go to literature and what we used to call "culture" as to the fountain of wisdom and experience. Youth today respond rather to an alternative culture, outside the English classroom, vital, challenging, relevant, and usually electronically transmitted. From this culture they receive vibrations far more intense than those literature, taught in the old way, is able to convey. Furthermore, today's youth are living out experiences only fantasized by previous generations. If students are to see literature as capable of informing them about any of the aspects of life, they must become convinced that literature is as capable of revolutionary exploration as their own lives are.

Against such obstacles, what maneuvers? I am reminded of Robert Graves, returning to Oxford after the horrors of the World War I trenches. The Anglo-Saxon lecturer." Graves wrote, "was candid about his subject: it was, he said, a language of purely linguistic interest. . . . I thought of Beowulf lying wrapped in a blanket among his platoon of drunken thanes in the Gothland billet."[1] Edmund Blunden, his lungs gassed from the war, attended the same lectures and with Graves found Beowulf fascinating as they translated everything into trench-warfare terms. So it is, even more fundamentally, with the women and men who begin to perceive how great is the sexual revolution that now confronts us. The vitality that can be felt in one's pulses as one looks at literature from this new vantage point has often been described to me. The question is: How shall English departments learn not to be afraid of this new way of looking at literature, not to trivialize it, since trivialization is the main expression of that fear?

Nothing so well exemplifies the exclusion of women from the profession of English studies as the Penguin Modern Masters series, edited by Frank Kermode. Kermode proclaims his task thus: "By Modern Masters we mean the men who have changed and are changing the life and thought of our age. The authors of these volumes are themselves masters, and they have written their books in the belief that general discussion of their subjects will henceforth be more informed and more exciting than before." In each volume, on the page preceding these remarks, are listed the masters and those, "themselves masters," who have been chosen to write the books.

Need I say that all, in both lists, are male? Nor is the exclusion of women from either list immediately self-explanatory. The "Masters," beginning with Freud, Marx, Lenin, and Einstein, soon dwindle into figures like Fanon, McLuhan, Orwell, Mailer, Reich. Far be it from me to suggest that Mailer and Orwell do not have their place in the stars. But are there no women to stand beside them? Are there no women who might have written, perhaps even from a different point of view, on Laing, Beckett, Lawrence, or Jung? I, thirty years girl and woman in the field of English studies, wonder anew that among all the changes of "the life and thought of our age," only the feminist approach has been scorned, ignored, fled from, at best reluctantly embraced. Join us if you wish, male stars and drudges alike have said to young women scholars— and indeed, they allow, in their less guarded moments, that women are now a majority of the best students— but do so to study the Masters, male Masters, and learn from us, male masters, in the old way. There is no room for a feminist viewpoint here: that is a fad, an aberration. There is no male or female viewpoint; there is only the human viewpoint, which happens always to have been male. Any other conclusion is inconceivable, not to be thought of. Deconstruction, semiology, Derrida, Foucault may question the very meaning of meaning as we have learned it, but feminism may not do so. Saussure, Jonathan Culler announces (in the Modern Master on Modern Master that happens to lie before me), has taught us "that you cannot hope to attain an absolute or Godlike view of things but must choose a perspective, and that within this perspective objects are defined by their relations to one another."[2] So long, of course, as the perspective chosen is not feminist.

Let us remain calm, manly, objective. Is there not a certain wry humor to be found in the fact that while no one in the profession can agree on what is literature, or meaning, or the metalanguage, everyone can agree on the deplorable state of English studies? As Gerald Graff, in a book devoted to the phenomenon he calls "Literature Against Itself," expresses it, "The loss of belief—or loss of interest—in literature as a means of understanding weakens the educational claims of literature and leaves the literature teacher without a rationale for what he professes."[3] Graff's book makes many debatable points—that is its strength—but probably no one will debate the lack of rationale felt by teachers of literature on every side. That is where we are, and any book or article on the subject will try to explain how we got there.

Let me choose Jonathan Culler once again, this time not speaking as master on master:

> If there is a crisis in literary criticism it is no doubt because few of the many who write about literature have the desire or arguments to defend their activity. . . . The historical scholarship which was once the dominant mode of criticism could at least, whatever its faults, be defended as an attempt to bring supplementary and inaccessible information to bear on the text and thus to assist understanding. But the orthodoxy bequeathed by the "New Criticism," which focuses on "the text itself" . . . is more difficult to defend . . . What then are we to say of criticism? What more can it do?[4]

Et cetera. Culler considers that he has a solution in structuralist poetics. Others offer other debatable, uncertain solutions. The only answer the profession has failed seriously to consider, politically to act on, is feminism. Yet feminism, able to combine structuralism, historical criticism, New Criticism, and deconstructionism, reaches into our past to offer, through fundamental reinterpretation, a new approach to literary studies. Moreover, it offers vitality to counter what threatens us: the exhaustibility of our subject.

Meanwhile, as English professors wait, like Auden, "hoping to twig from what we are not what we might be next," feminist criticism has been victimized by analogy. Either it is called a "fad," like psychoanalytic criticism, a regrettable minority imperative, like black studies, or it is considered a nonacademic dalliance, like the study of popular, nontraditional forms of art. It touches on all these, as do all literary studies, but is not comparable to them. Rather, feminist studies are justified by the centrality they offer, a centrality literary studies enjoyed in the nineteenth century, when, in Ortega y Gasset's words, art was important "on account of its subjects, which dealt with the profoundest problems of humanity, and on account of its own significance as a human pursuit from which the species derived its justification and dignity."[5]

While literary critics are losing their audience both in the classroom and without, the fear of feminism persists, even as the feminist audience grows. Why? There are, I believe, several answers, all of which stem from the belief that women's studies are not mainstream, are not central, are not where the power is. Women and men alike avoid a commitment that promises only marginality. Let me be more explicit.

Men's fears are palpable. Men have long been members of a profession whose masculinity can, particularly in our American society, be questioned. I suspect that the macho attitudes of most English professors, their notable male bonding, can be directly attributed to the fear of female dominance. Now comes the additional threat of the profession's being feminized. More students are women. The pressure for studying women authors and hiring women professors increases. Those in power in departments still safely male-dominated close their ranks. These male fears are profound, and no less so for being largely unconscious. Meanwhile, the old familiar habits of male dominance and scorn of female interests in the profession make these attitudes appear natural and right.

Women students and professors, in a tight market and cruel economic situation, are in no position to fight those who control jobs. While willing to benefit, passively if possible, from affirmative-action programs, they accept the fears induced by their professors and eschew feminism, particularly as an academic study. If to this we add the burden of anxiety borne by all women who confront the male power structure, we have a situation in which there are few inducements to either sex to undertake feminist studies. Why then not ignore the whole thing? Why not let the question gracefully disappear?

The answer, I believe, does not lie in the political rights of women, who are half the students, who earn half the doctorates (or more), and who comprise, in their sex, half the peoples of the world. The answer lies, rather, in the political situation of English studies today, in the threatened state of literature.

Our young teachers still begin eagerly and enthusiastically to teach the literature we have all taught for so long. But the most gifted of them, certainly in modern studies, emphasize far more the latest critical theories and methods than they do the literature itself. Meanwhile, their older colleagues face, whether they admit it or not, an enormous sense of loss, of lack of clarity in the purposes from which they speak; the old Arnoldian pride in literature is gone, and little has arisen to take its place. As philosophy did in the middle of this century, literary studies have begun to ask about methodology and language, have begun to question what in fact we "know" and to suggest that in fact we know little. Only the old-time textual scholars remain apparently content, with fewer and fewer students, but even they whisper, sometimes, of their sense of surviving from a vanished world.

My own experience here is offered as one individual's literary adventure. When I began, first alone and then with a colleague from another department, to teach from a feminist approach the French and English novel (by both male and female authors), a vitality entered the classroom that I had not experienced, I realized, for many years, nor had the students. We had a sense, as we used to have when I was young and the field of modern British literature was relatively unexplored, of being near the center of the life and thought of our age. Novels one was certain had been exhausted by endless analysis now declared themselves to us as full of new possibility, revealing new truths, reconstructing themselves in new ways. If they were indeed self-consuming artifacts, they at least left the students alive at the end of the class, full of hope for new, vital achievement.

One of the outstanding figures in the department in which I teach is a scholar once devoted exclusively to the new methodology. It was from his writings that I first gained some understanding of Derrida, Foucault, and others. For a long time it seemed to me that he and I were at the opposite poles of English studies. Nothing connected us. The body of humanist documents that I had known had vanished to leave behind two newly evolved professors speaking different languages, sharing nothing.

Then this scholar published a book whose subject was the Western world's view of the East, and especially of Islam. My erudite and brilliant colleague had filled the book with references to scholars unknown to me, quoted in languages also unknown. But at the heart of the book was an extraordinary vibrancy. In writing of how the Western world had seen Arabs only as it chose to see them, for its own purposes, and had even imposed that view on the Arabs themselves and on history, my colleague had suggested that we review the literary uses of orientalism to suggest ways in which they had been distorted to serve the needs of the Western culture.

All at once, this formerly incomprehensible colleague had revealed the source of life in humanist studies. I saw that if "women" were substituted for "Arabs," we would begin to understand the way in which the male world had viewed women, and equally, I saw the plea that feminist scholars now might make for a fresh start from a new perspective. I realized, in reading his book, that women had differed from Arabs in one important way: far more than Arabs internalized the Western view, women have internalized the male view of themselves, have accepted it as the "truth," as Arabs rarely accepted—or at least not for so long—the Western view of their ineptitudes and essential inhumanity. Despite this difference, I could learn much from the way my colleague had taken his profound knowledge of Derrida and Foucault, and used it to reveal how long-accepted attitudes can be reconsidered, leaving the texts that had seemed unarguable ready for new interpretations.

There remains the problem of fighting opposition on all sides. I do not know if my colleague would countenance feminist studies. Most of my male colleagues, and some female ones, still feel the most profound disinclination to reconsider texts in the light of feminism, though they may be more easily persuaded in a less threatening atmosphere. Oddly enough, feminism is above all viewed as narrow, confining. By some mysterious fiat, the study of women in literature is narrower, more peripheral, less mainstream than the study of American Indians or minor religious sects in the seventeenth century. Is it perhaps because there is no humanistic or literary study without a feminist aspect that studying such an aspect appears both superfluous and superficial? Have we not all had mothers, and known the fact for years? Who needs to study it? Everything to be said on the subject has been said, and those who say it again are too passionate and intense.

Yet feminist courses continue to attract students wherever they are offered. The National Endowment for the Humanities has found a rapidly growing demand for such courses among its summer seminars for college teachers. Department chairpersons, sometimes reluctantly, must more and more admit the evidence of the popularity, the vitality, of such undertakings. Only when they are earmarked as injurious to the reputation of the student or placed outside the requirements for departmental certification are feminist courses avoided. The blunt fact is that the feminist aspect has been so steadily ignored that almost any period or work will reveal a whole new landscape to those who teach and learn from this point of view. That now rare phenomenon, excitement, reappears in the classroom.

My hope is that eventually the viewpoint of feminism will begin to permeate all courses, whether taught by men or women, as psychoanalysis has done. Even if, like a professor friend of mine, we refer to psychoanalytic studies, endearingly, as "shrink crit," we will never look at literature again as we did before Freud, whether or not we have specifically studied him and his theories. While nothing is drearier than facile psychoanalytic interpretations of literature (or facile Marxist interpretations), we cannot live as though no light had been cast on the world by Freud or Marx, or for that matter, by Einstein and Darwin. Feminism, too, will in time become such a generally enlightening discipline.

My own hopes rest also on sheer economic pressure to assure feminism new life. Scholars have edged away from feminism because it appears faddish, because the media have to some extent embraced and therefore demeaned it. But today, even the soundest of historians dealing with imperialism have allowed new attitudes toward Third World peoples to infuse their work. Teachers of literature can do no less for women.

Of course, all this is problematic. (Gerald Graff says that "the word problematic' is perhaps the one indispensable piece of equipment for anybody wishing to set up shop as a literary critic today."[6] Nevertheless, the discomfort we all feel about feminism, as about other matters, is no reason to avoid the subject. The discomfort of the male establishment, or even of some female members of that establishment, seems insufficient cause.

In 1931, when Willa Cather was the first woman to be granted an honorary degree by Princeton University, Louise Bogan, writing in *The New Yorker,* rejoiced that Cather's stature was such that Princeton was willing "to forget and forgive her sex."[7] That attitude, the unspoken one of most of the male establishment, is no longer possible. Women applying to graduate schools today, and earning the most prized fellowships, are no longer willing to have their sex forgotten and forgiven. Nor are they unprepared to face down the response their request for feminist studies is bound to provoke, the response recorded for all time by Joanna Russ:

> That's not an issue.
> That's not an issue *any more*.
> Then why do you keep on bringing it up?
> You keep on bringing it up because you are crazy.
> You keep on bringing it up because you are hostile.
> You keep on bringing it up because you are intellectually irresponsible.
> You keep on bringing it up because you are shrill, strident, and self-indulgent.
> How can I possibly listen to anyone as crazy, hostile, intellectually irresponsible, shrill, strident, and self-indulgent as you are?
> Especially since what you're talking about is not an issue.
> (Any more)[8]

Let us face the fact: the spirit has largely gone from our studies. That at least is my experience, and the experience of most of those I speak with. It is not only that the sparks strike less and less often. It is not only that we are losing our audience, while hugging to ourselves the importance of our endeavors. Deep within most of us is a sense of futility, and a desire to search for new approaches to literature to rescue it from its currently moribund state. Feminism is not the only prescription, but it it an enlivening one. And those who have examined everything from the meaning of meaning to the metatext may discover that this apparently frivolous discipline offers them, in our own time, the key to new vitality. Is there one of those Modern Masters whose problems with women and his own concept of feminity have not been as important as they have been ignored? Can Frank Kermode find nothing missing from his accounts of the modern world?

1979

ENDNOTES

1. Robert Graves, *Goodbye to All That* (Garden City, N.Y.: Anchor Books, 1957), pp. 292–293.

2. Jonathan Culler, *Ferdinand de Saussure* (New York: Penguin Books, 1977), p. xv.

3. Gerald Graff, *Literature Against Itself: Literary Ideas in Modern Society* (Chicago: University of Chicago Press, 1979), p. 7.

4. Jonathan Culler, *Structuralist Poetics: Structuralism, Linguistics, and the Study of Literature* (Ithaca, N.Y.: Cornell University Press, 1975), pp. vii–viii. Culler has, of course, long since recognized feminism.

5. José Ortega y Gasset, *The Dehumanization of Art*, quoted in Graff, *Literature Against Itself*, p. 8.

6. Graff, *Literature Against Itself*, p. 8.

7. Louise Bogan, "American-Class," *New Yorker*, August 8, 1931; reprinted in James Schroeter, ed., *Willa Cather and Her Critics* (Ithaca, N.Y.: Cornell University Press, 1967).

8. Joanna Russ, "Reviews and Responses," *Frontiers* (Fall 1979), 4:68.

15

Women, Men, Theories, and Literature

LET ME begin with a confession, since it is the quickest way to annunciate a problem alive to most of us who teach English. In addition to being a professor of English literature at Columbia University, I write what is known as popular literature. Personally, I find this nomenclature disheartening: if there is a professional Association of Popular Culture (and, indeed, there is one), does that mean that most of us are, in the work to which we have devoted our lives, engaged in unpopular culture? Recently the *CEA Critic*, a publication of the College English Association, ran an article that asked forthrightly, "Masterpieces or Garbage"?[1] The implication, as we need no deconstructionist to tell us, is that our choice is between teaching masterpieces, which no one reads except under duress, or teaching garbage, an enterprise drearily self-explanatory. It is, however, as both a teacher of masterpieces and a producer of "garbage" that I tell the following anecdote.

An evening class in popular culture—to be more exact, in the detective novel—somewhere on the West Coast (exactly where I do not know, for reasons that will soon become clear) held its final session and voted on its favorite novel. They determined (this is clearly one of the advantages of popular culture) that they would call up the author of their favorite work. Amazed as I was to hear from them, I was even more amazed to discover that their classroom boasted a telephone connected for long-distance dialing. (I have been a full professor for nearly a decade, but Columbia allows me only local calls.) They called as my husband and I were, in our decorous way, retiring at midnight. I am not certain whether the authors of popular culture are expected to stay up all night as a regular thing or whether the class had rather lost track of the nation's time zones. In fact, so astonished was I that I should have believed I had dreamed the whole thing had my husband not been there. We have been married a long time, but we do not yet dream the same dreams.

Since I am a literary type, two quotations immediately came to mind when I had hung up. The first is from a speech J. Hillis Miller delivered two years ago at an ADE seminar:

> I believe in the established canon of English and American literature and in the validity of the concept of privileged texts. I think it is more important to read Spenser, Shakespeare, or Milton than to read Borges in translation, or even, to say the truth, to read Virginia Woolf.[2]

What he would think of reading Heilbrun I hardly dare contemplate.

The second quotation is from popular culture, Salinger's *Catcher in the Rye,* to be exact. The young hero explains:

> I read a lot of classical books, like The *Return of the Native* and all, and I like them. . . . What really knocks me out is a book that, when you're all done reading it, you wish the author that wrote it was a terrific friend of yours and you could call him up on the phone whenever you felt like it. That doesn't happen much though. (p. 25)

Torn as I am between my devotion, as a teacher, to masterpieces and my pleasure at the vitality of a popular-culture class that telephones an author, I do not think the choice before us, if we wish to bring excitement back to the classroom, is so violent a one as opting for "garbage." Inhibited by more than time zones, we may be unable as well as unwilling to telephone our favorite authors; yet we can, I believe, restore excitement to the classroom if we bring to bear on "masterpieces" the insights of critics who, in Stanley Fish's words, "challenge the assumptions within which ordinary practices go on."[3] I shall argue, moreover, that feminist criticism—whether practiced by women or, as is increasingly the case, by men—is probably the most powerful challenge to ordinary practice now at hand.

Let me begin with a new book by Robert Kiely, professor of English at Harvard. He is discussing three stories: "The Dead," by Joyce; "The Shadow in the Rose Garden," by Lawrence; and "The Legacy," by Woolf. In each story, Kiely tells us, "an apparently happy and ordinary marriage undergoes a sudden and violent rupture." He continues:

> The story of marriage becomes an entirely different matter for the modern writer when he begins to treat it as a plot with two authors. . . . Plot defined as the anticipated design of a single imagination seems no more appropriate than marriage defined in a similarly rigid and single-minded fashion. The husbands in the three stories are "obtuse" narrators of marriage plots over which they ultimately discover they have only limited control. The story has been lived simultaneously by wives with chapters in mind that the husbands have not even begun to imagine. The crisis occurs when "texts" of the two marriage plots are brought together. There is no *corpus delicit*, no naked intruder under the marriage bed to be thrashed or chased trouserless out of the window. The confrontation is a verbal one, a clash not of events but of languages that have derived from differing situations and fail to merge.[4]

I need hardly point out to you that the idea of two "texts" in marriage sounds like the latest in feminist criticism or psychology. And so it is. Nine years ago Jessie Bernard revealed that, if you talk to both partners in a marriage, instead of only the one who knows she is in trouble, you discover that there is not one marriage but two: his and hers. They do not agree even on what we have fondly thought to be facts: where money is spent, how often they make love, how often they converse, and about what (*The Future of Marriage* [New York: World, 1972]). Kiely may not have heard of Jessie Bernard and all her works; he is writing of three authors of masterpieces he has loved and read and taught since his graduate school days. Yet he is asking the same critical questions currently being raised with such exciting effect by feminist writers and teachers.

Let us now turn to another contemporary critic, Tony Tanner, in *Adultery in the Novel*. (Baltimore: Johns Hopkins Univ. Press, 1979). In the passage I want to consider, Tanner begins by quoting the New Testament story of the woman taken in adultery. He continues:

> The scribes and Pharissees (society in this context) set up a situation in which the woman is brought forward as a classified object to be looked at and talked about; they have depersonalized her (a woman taken in adultery) and reified her (she is "set" in the midst). Christ refuses to look and, initially, refuses to talk. That is, he refuses to participate in this purely specular attitude to the woman and to discuss her as a category. By doing this he restores the full existential reality to the situation that society seeks to deny. By treating the woman as spectacle and category, the representatives of society attempt to alienate her from her own being and to separate themselves from her by adopting the role of being the community from which the woman by her offense has isolated herself. Christ refuses to participate in their discourse, and when he does speak it is to them directly. This has two effects. It thrusts them back into their own interiority (they are "convicted by their own conscience"), and it dissolves the group identity within which they have concealed themselves.
>
> In this way Christ disperses the social stare that petrifies the wrongdoer, just as he uncongeals the legal language that seeks to imprison her in a category. . . . This is a subtler act than driving out the moneylenders, for this time Christ has banished the whole language and attitude of social "accusation" from the temple. He then speaks to the woman directly, as an individual. . . . What Christ has done is enforce a reconsideration of the context in which the woman's act should be considered. (pp. 21–22)

We may all of us, once the shock of perceiving Jesus as a feminist critic is past, agree that such a discussion is interesting and provocative, at least to those among us whom it does not make profoundly angry. But we are in trouble when this deconstruction of the canon —this placing of the woman, without punishment, outside her assigned place, this connecting of her sin with male sin—leaves the realm of discussion and enters the realm of discourse. By "discourse" I mean those exchanges within which power is actually exerted (as when Foucault states in *the order of things* that "every educational system is a political means of maintaining or modifying the appropriation of discourses, with the knowledge and power they bring with them.")[5] So a member of the MLA writes to Joel Conarroe, its executive director, expressing his views on a recent convention at which he was disturbed by an alleged "feminist takeover." These observations, Conarroe comments, "struck me as wondrous strange. Because feminists, after decades of not feeling welcome at the party, have set up a lively table near the middle of the room, are they suddenly dominating? Taking over? . . . That several meetings are devoted to [feminism] is surely not a sign of a takeover but an indication that this area is where energy, as well as research projects, can be found at this particular time" (*MLA Newsletter,* Spring 1980, p. 2).

My point is easily taken. With such discourse we may be in trouble, but we have also brought excitement back into the classroom, and not, let me add, by discussing detective novels or science fiction. Indeed, the struggle between the more theoretical critics and the old-style humanists like the man who wrote to Joel Conarroe has reached, for an academic contest, the status of the world series. But let Geoffrey Hartman describe the situation:

> In the past few years . . . a new battlefront has emerged. Critics, whether journalists or academics, send their wit and vocabularies charging against "deconstruction," "structuralism," "revisionism," and other foreign-sounding heresies. The sudden blaze of attention as when a war first breaks out, has even reached America's favorite parlor game, "The Dick Cavett Show," which devoted two of its recent sessions to literary criticism. . . . Now people are fighting about criticism . . . as if there were a politics of that subject too. One critic, Gerald Graff, has taken on the so-called Yale school no fewer than four times . . . ; an Australian critic emblazons his essay in *The London Review of Books* with the title "The Deconstruction Gang"; Alfred Kazin [in *The New Republic*] deplores "the triumph of deconstructionism" . . . while William Pritchard, in *Hudson Review,* talks of a "hermeneutical mafia" that contaminates good English prose . . . In England literary theory has become the focus of a heated public debate. "Structuralism and Dry Rot" was the headline of an attack in *The Observer.*[6]

Hartman goes on to comment on the whole situation, but I want to extract only one further sentence from his argument: "Marxism, structuralism, psychoanalysis, deconstruction—all regard language as a powerful and complex social force that limits or even undermines the autonomy of the individual." The word "feminism" is notable by its absence. Yet not even Hartman would deny that language has been a powerful social force, male, that undermines the autonomy of the individual, female. He just feels awkward with aspects of feminist criticism that lead to what he has called, in another connection, "the gendrification of literature" ("Shakespeare Gendrified," *New York Times Book Review,* March 22, 1981, pp. 11, 18–19).

If we retreat for a moment from Geoffrey Hartman to structuralism, we find ourselves with the linguistic model of Lévi-Strauss, which accounts for "social reality within the framework of a general theory of communication. Kinships and marriage rules ensure the 'exchange' of women between groups, as economic rules ensure the circulation of goods, and linguistic rules that of messages."[7] What is the feminist response to this? I quote from the latest in feminist criticism, an article by Nancy K. Miller entitled "Emphasis Added: Plots and Plausibilities in Women's Fiction," which appeared this year in *PMLA,* January 1981, 96(1):3. Women writers, she tells us, are writers whose texts manifest themselves as fantasies within another economy:

> In this economy, egoistic desires would assert themselves paratactically alongside erotic ones. The repressed content, I think, would be, not erotic impulses, but an impulse to power: a fantasy of power that would revise the social grammar in which women are never defined as subjects; a fantasy of power that disdains a sexual exchange in which women can participate only as objects of circulation.

What we discover is that women who have been the objects circulated wish now to become themselves subjects, themselves enabled to use circulation rather than be circulated. Let me put this another way, since Nancy Miller, with whom I teach (more about that in a moment), is a semiotician with an extended vocabulary, and I am a humanist generally given to standard if not basic English. As human beings we all make fictions of our lives, those of us who write books, or read them, and those who tell only ourselves the stories of the lives we shall lead. But that fiction has already been inscribed for women: they are to be married, to be circulated, to mediate between the man and his desire for a son, between male groups. In most French novels, for example, women's destiny encompasses two possible destinations, which Nancy Miller has called the euphoric and the dysphoric; that is, marriage or death.[8] The erotic destiny is all there is.

In England male novelists, almost from the beginning, began to imagine fictions of women as opposed to the stories of male adventures: so inscribed, might the fictions of women yet reveal more exciting texts than the male fictions offered? Samuel Richardson thought so, as did many of his famous followers of both sexes. The English novel, having discovered female fictions, seldom deserted them: from Thackeray to Wilkie Collins, to Meredith and Gissing, through Henry James, Hardy, and Lawrence, to E. M. Forster and Angus Wilson, English male writers, as I have mentioned elsewhere, found the female destiny more challenging than the male. Not only women writers— Nancy Miller is writing of French literature, where only women writers indulged in "a fantasy in another economy"—but men also began to write of women who erupted out of the economy of female circulation. Those of us who study modern British literature need not pause to validate feminist criticism. We have only to recognize what we have been doing.

I have recently taught two courses with Nancy Miller, a product of Columbia's Department of French and Romance Philology. As its austere title suggests, that department is the place of linguistic metacritics at their most esoteric. Miller, trained by the master, Michael Riffaterre, has brought all those high skills and intelligence to feminist criticism. I, trained in the school of Lionel Trilling to the strains of moral realism, still echo to what Forster called "the fag end of Victorian liberalism." Into this Trilling universe I have had to learn to inject the techniques of decoding that would enable me to understand how these liberal ideas, which I still honor, established themselves. In the (to me, at least) extraordinary dialogue that took place in the seminars between Miller and me and between us and our students, the dazzling Riffaterrian skills and the Trillingesque moral choices illuminated one another. Each of us—close, perhaps, to the fag ends of our specialties —became literally, and literarily, inspired to new and exciting work. Our excitement was increased by the knowledge that the economy of male domination, when deconstructed, when submitted to poststructuralist decodings by the most dazzling practitioners, reveals woman as the vital key. Poststructuralism, indeed, has taken over the feminine as one of its major metaphors, going beyond the impasse between feminism and structuralism, challenging what Derrida has called "credulous man who, in support of his testimony, offers truth and his phallus as his own proper credentials."[9]

My recommendation for returning excitement to the classroom is, admittedly, a radical one. I am suggesting that feminism, in the intellectual as well as the political sphere, is at the very heart of a profound revolution. Those who oppose feminism are in danger, furthermore, of imitating those creationists—from Darwin's time and our own—who question the validity of evolution. Like the creationists, the opponents of feminist criticism argue as protectors of a common body of "culture" as they have known it and as it shelters them.[10]

I have come to believe that we who teach literature can learn a great deal from Darwin and from the revolutionary effect of his work. As a commentator on Darwin explains:

> [the] world of 1857 was the only world a sane man, scientist or otherwise, could desire. As far as the biologists were concerned, it was a dependable world, the classical world, still, of fixed definitions. "To Aristotle," Herbert J. Muller writes, "definition was not merely a verbal process or a useful tool of thought, it was the essence of knowledge. It was the cognitive grasp of the eternal essences of Nature, a fixed, necessary form of knowing because an expression of the fixed, necessary form of Being." Into that satisfied and satisfying universe, the quiet, kindly unassuming Charles Darwin had dropped the bomb.[11]

I believe that many of us in the humanities are today engaged in challenging a world view. We are dropping a bomb into the stable world of literary masterpieces. In the words of Thomas Kuhn, Darwin changed the paradigm under which science operated, and "when paradigms change, the world itself changes with them." Kuhn has described the change that lies before us:

> Led by a new paradigm, scientists adopt new instruments and look in new places. Even more important, during revolutions scientists see new and different things when looking with familiar instruments in places they have looked before. It is rather as if the professional community had been suddenly transported to another planet where familiar objects are seen in a different light and are joined by unfamiliar ones as well. . . . In so far as their only recourse to that world is through what they see and do, we may want to say that after a revolution scientists are responding to a different world.[12]

Like Darwin, literary critics today are searching the earth for evidence of a "script" wholly unlike that written for us by the sacred literature. You will have noticed that, well over a century after Darwin, his discoveries and our right to teach them are being questioned. As Darwin himself wrote:

> Although I am fully convinced of the truths given in [*The Origin of Species*], I by no means expect to convince experienced naturalists whose minds are stocked with a multitude of facts all viewed, during a long course of years, from a point of view directly opposite to mine. . . .

But I look with confidence to the future,—to young and rising naturalists, who will be able to view both sides of the question with impartiality. (quoted by Kuhn, p. 151)

Max Planck would echo him years later: "a new scientific truth does not triumph by convincing its opponents and making them see the light, but rather because its opponents eventually die, and a new generation grows up that is familiar with it," (quoted by Kuhn, p. 151).

The excitement, I believe, lies in making that new generation familiar with our discoveries; in realizing that we have the chance both to read masterpieces—not, I hope, as narrowly defined as Hillis Miller wishes, but masterpieces nonetheless—and yet bring to the classroom the sense of wanting to call up the author. What Darwin can teach us is that, without acting or feeling like revolutionaries determined to overthrow the establishment, we can propose a new view of the world. Moreover, if we cease to think of the canon as creationists think of the Bible, that is to say, as a text that must be not only "privileged" but isolated and reified, we may even allow some popular and "emerging" literatures into our most conservative classrooms. We shall do so, not because we must turn to popular works as the only literature people are willing to read, but because the masterpieces have become so newly vital that they will continue to dazzle beside works more easily encountered.

1981

ENDNOTES

1. Donald E. Morse, "Masterpieces or Garbage: Martin Tropp and Science Fiction," in *CEA Critic,* (March 1981), 43(3):14.

2. J. Hillis Miller, "The Function of Rhetorical Study at the Present Time, in *The State of the Discipline, 1970s–1980s,* A Special Issue of the *ADE Bulletin* (Sept.–Nov. 1979), no. 62, p. 12. I have taken the quotation, however, from Sandra Gilbert, "What Do Feminist Critics Want? or, A Postcard from the Volcano," *ADE Bulletin* (Winter 1980), no. 66, pp. 16–23. This excellent article, essential to an understanding of the state of feminist criticism, is recommended to all who have not yet read it.

3. Quoted in Annette Kolodny, "Not-So-Gentle Persuasion: A Theoretical Imperative of Feminist Literary Criticism," Conference on Feminist Literary Criticism, National Humanities Center, Research Triangle Park, N.C., March 27, 1981, p. 7. The quotation is from Stanley Fish, *Is There a Text in This Class?* (Cambridge: Harvard University Press, 1980). See also Annette Ko-

lodny, "A Map for Rereading; or, Gender and the Interpretation of Literary Texts," *New Literary History* (1980), 9:45–55.

4. Robert Kiely, *Beyond Egotism: The Fiction of James Joyce, Virginia Woolf, and D. H. Lawrence* (Cambridge: Harvard University Press, 1980), pp. 87, 89.

5. Quoted in Alan Sheridan, *Michel Foucault: The Will to Truth* (London: Tavistock, 1980), p. 127.

6. Geoffrey H. Hartman, "How Creative Should Literary Criticism Be?" *New York Times Book Review,* April 5, 1981, pp. 11, 24, 26.

7. Joseu V. Harari, "Critical Factions/Critical Fictions," in *Textual Strategies: Perspectives in Post-Structuralist Criticism,* Josue V. Harari, ed., (Ithaca: Cornell University Press, 1979), p. 19.

8. See Nancy K. Miller, *The Heroine's Text* (New York: Columbia University Press, 1980).

9. Jacques Derrida, "Becoming Woman," Barbara Harlow, trans., *Semiotext* (E), (1978); vol. 3, no. 1; quoted in Miller, "Emphasis Added," p. 47.

10. See the proposed Family Protection Act, as well as articles on opposition to "secular humanism," *New York Times,* May 17, 1981, Sec. A, p. 1; and Marvin Perry, "Banning a Textbook," *New York Times,* May 31, 1981, Sec. E, p. 19.

11. Philip Appleman, "Darwin: On Changing the Mind," in *Darwin,* Philip Appleman ed. (New York: Norton, 1970), p. 634.

12. Thomas S. Kuhn, *The Structure of Scientific Revolutions,* 2d ed. (Chicago: University of Chicago Press, 1970), p. 111.

16
Feminist Criticism in Departments of Literature

IN BOOK Six of the *Odyssey,* Nausicaa, a princess, has gone down to the river to play ball and do the laundry. Why princesses should have done laundry or been inspired to do so by goddesses are questions undoubtedly worthy of discussion, but not in this essay. By whatever means, the goddess Athena had to get Nausicaa down to the river that she might discover Odysseus, rescue him, and enable him to continue his journey. The princess, therefore, throws a fast curve which wakes the sleeping Odysseus. Where am I, he wonders in Greek hexameters (here translated by Robert Fitzgerald):

> He pushed aside the bushes, breaking off
> with his great hand a single branch of olive,
> whose leaves might shield him in his nakedness;
> so came out rustling, like a mountain lion,

rain drenched, wind-buffeted, but in his might at ease. . . .
Odysseus had this look, in his rough skin
advancing on the girls with pretty braids;
and he was driven on by hunger, too.
Streaked with brine, and swollen, he terrified them,
so that they fled, this way and that. Only
[Nausicaa] stood her ground, being given
a bold heart by Athena, and steady knees.
She faced him, waiting. And Odysseus came
debating inwardly what he should do.

It is more or less my thesis that, in the allegorical form in which I have cast my tale, Nausicaa has for a very long time been standing there, with a bold heart and steady knees, and Odysseus has been wondering what to do, and until the last decade or so there has been remarkably little progress in this relationship.

But let us continue the tale, at least as far as it had, until recently, gone. Odysseus asks Nausicaa if she will help him (there is a certain amount of discussion between them about why, if he is so valiant and triumphant a chap, he looks such a wreck at the moment, but that question is sidestepped). She promises to help. After this, she meets him only once again; as they part, she says:

"Fare well, stranger; in your land remember me
who met and saved you. It is worth your thought."

And Odysseus answers that his only thoughts are for getting home:

"But there and all my days until I die
may I invoke you as I would a goddess,
princess, to whom I owe my life."

Yet, as the commentator W. B. Stanford puts it, "Nausicaa is never mentioned again in Homer. There is no evidence that Odysseus kept his rather extravagant promise all his life."[1] Indeed, it is astonishing the degree to which Nausicaa, with so small a part in the *Odyssey*, has continued to trouble the minds and hearts of men. Speculations and fantasies of what became of her, or what Homer might have wanted to become of her, divide themselves into two kinds of narrative.

The first narrative contrives to marry her off, if not to Odysseus, whom she clearly found attractive, then to his son, Telemachus. The men who write these marriage plots—Sophocles, Hellanicus, Goethe, Kazantzakis—are as uncomfortable with Homer's story as they would be if Elizabeth Bennet had remained unmarried at the end of *Pride and Prejudice*. Between Goethe and Kazantzakis comes Joyce, whose Nausicaa will be lame and simpering, her accomplishment to inspire the modern Odysseus to an act of autoeroticism. Whatever the story, Nausicaa, like a woman from the Old Testament, is woven back into the patrilineal succession.

The second narrative, also contrived by men, enables Nausicaa to seize the pen from Homer, and, borrowing many lines from the *Iliad*, write the *Odyssey* herself, changing it from a wholly masculine text to a text both feminine and masculine, antimachismo, if not androgynous. Samuel Butler was the first to put forward this revolutionary thesis: in his book on the subject, Butler, no feminist, points to the amazing vividness with which Nausicaa and her mother are described, to the preponderance of women in the work (compare Odysseus' visit to the underworld with Aeneas'), and to the unfailing loyalty of women to women. He offers many other arguments, to be sure, including a list of errors no male author could possibly have made, and these are all taken up eventually by Robert Graves who, in a novel entitled *Homer's Daughter*, argues just as vehemently, and in a more overtly feminist fashion, for Nausicaa's authorship of her own story.

TODAY, THOSE women who propound feminist literary criticism require, as did Nausicaa, a bold heart and steady knees to face that ferocious, god-like figure, the established Literature Department hiding its masculinity behind an olive branch. They need also to reassure their powerful but anxious male colleagues that they intend neither to go on retelling the old marriage plot, nor to seize the pen from male authors and rob all most cherished literature of its patriarchal emanations. Feminist critics wish only to suggest that in these days of falling enrollments, growing antihumanism, diminished government support, and rising student interest in job-oriented learning, it would be helpful if Odysseus were to redeem his promise to Nausicaa. For feminist criticism, taken straight in prudent doses or, better still, filtered throughout all literature courses, can restore to our classrooms and curricula some of the literary excitement they now so often lack.

The rewards of feminist criticism are not far to seek. At the pedagogical level one finds them in the vibrant classrooms of the many colleges and universities in which it is taught and at the level of critical practice, in the stunning work of some male critics who might shun the label of feminist, and of some who now emphatically do not. I mention the male critics before the female to counter two of the worst fears aroused by feminist criticism: men fear that it will somehow feminize the whole profession (thereby degrading it); women fear that, practicing feminist criticism, they will be ghettoized (and therefore also degraded). It was reported to me recently that a male professor at a prestigious women's college announced openly in a faculty meeting that it was bad enough to teach at a women's college without the added shame of its having a women's studies program. Translated, this means: one honors oneself only by teaching men and literature from the old, familiar centrist, that is to say male, point of view; we must, for economic reasons, teach women; let us therefore introduce them to the established world of texts and interpretations, while not allowing them to alter our perspective as it has been given to the world in the curriculum.

So pervasive is this attitude, bluntly stated or not, that I wish to discuss, as frankly as possible, the fears aroused by the idea of feminist criticism. Like all fears, they have their conscious and unconscious elements, and, like all fears of bogeys, they are based entirely on misconceptions. Let me begin by listing some male critics who have recently published feminist criticism: Tony Tanner, Wayne Booth, Robert Kiely, Lawrence Lipking, Robert Scholes, Terry Eagleton, Jonathan Culler—professors from the universities of, respectively, Oxford, Chicago, Harvard, Northwestern, Brown, Oxford, Cornell. In naming them, I feel rather like Jacques d'Amboise, the ballet dancer with the New York City Ballet, who more than a decade ago began a movement called sandlot ballet to convince the American public that for a boy to be a dancer was not to bring into question, not so much his sexuality, but that for which sexuality is a code word: his place in the power structure.

But the fears of men are not always greater than the fears of women. They too tremble lest, in practicing feminist criticism, they isolate themselves from the centers of power, and—what seems even worse in the literary world—from that approach to great literature which men have always enjoyed and taught. So a woman student, studying some great classic, is dismayed to hear another woman student analyze the long-dead, long-famous author's ideology concerning gender. She wants the idols in the sacred precincts she has entered to remain unaltered, that she may adore them and protect them from the dangers doubters bring. It does not occur to her that these texts, like temples and cathedrals that have become museums, will have failed in their essential purpose if life's questions are not, daily, brought to them. What we must recognize about feminist criticism is that it is not destructive. It seeks not to assault literature, but to reinterpret literature as it has been inscribed, however paratactically, by women, or as it has been written, if not by women, then at least in a spirit not adverse to women's rejection of gender and sexual ideologies. In carrying out this task, feminist criticism resembles, more than anything else, comedy.

ELAINE SHOWALTER writes that, "of all the approaches to English studies, feminist criticism is the least understood. Members of English departments who can remember what Harold Bloom means by *clinamen,* and who know the difference between Tartu and Barthian semiotics, will remark that they are against feminist criticism and consequently have never read any."[2] She then offers as an example of the sort of villain the feminist comedy educes a critic who published "A Case against Feminist Criticism" in *Partisan Review.* This gentleman (all males in comedies are gentlemen, even the villains, perhaps especially the villains) used a single feminist work as an example of feminist deficiency in "intellectual honesty" and "rigour." He defined feminist criticism as "the insistence on asking the same questions of every work and demanding ideologically satisfactory answers to those questions as a means of evaluating it." He ended by saying: "We ought to demand that [feminist criticism] be minimally distinguished by intellectual candour and some degree of precision." This comedic gentleman, however, made his case so recklessly, using intimation instead of honesty and rigor, that the feminist critic under attack brought charges for libel, and the *Partisan Review* had to print a retraction in the following issue. Does not our *Partisan Review* critic sound like Lady Bracknell in *The Importance of Being Earnest,* advising Jack to get at least *one* parent before the season is quite over?

And, indeed, feminist criticism which has, like Wilde's hero, a necessary impulse to be earnest, is also, like Wilde's hero, capable of wit, amusement, laughter, and the amazed delight of shared discovery. Let us think once again of Athena in the *Odyssey.* When Odysseus at last reaches Ithaca, he is wary. Can he trust Athena not to be mocking him, not to have led him astray? Stanford describes Athena's answer to Odysseus. I help you, Athena tells him, because you are so civilized, so intelligent, so self-possessed. Stanford then offers us a disquisition on the Greek words used for these admirable qualities which are, noticeably, the opposite of the macho virtues. The first word, "civilized"—used, Stanford tells us, nowhere else in Homer—implies "personal attentiveness, kindness, and gentleness, in contrast with boorishness and selfish indifference to other people's feelings." The second word "intelligent," "implies a quality approximating to what is called feminine intuition, that gift of instantaneous insight into the essence of a complex matter, which both ignores and baffles logical analysis." The third word, "self-possessed," describes a person "who does not allow his impulses and thought to lead to wrong words and actions." Athena, who from the beginning admired Odysseus for these qualities hardly to be described as manly, had earlier disguised herself as a little girl to tell him of the importance to his endeavors of the queen, Arete, when he goes to visit the Phaeacians. Athena equips him, in short, with a knowledge of female wisdom which will serve him well to include in his discourse.

Let me offer two more instances of male critics whose arguments defend feminist criticism either directly or by analogy. First, the analogy: Professor Robert Scholes is writing as general editor of a series of book-length studies of science fiction:

> It is an interesting feature of literary history that during [this century] a body of fiction has flourished which privileges the type over the individual, the idea over the word, and the unexpected over the plausible even. This body of work, which has come to be called . . . "science" fiction, has had some recognition from serious critics but still hovers between genuine acceptance and total dismissal in literary circles.
>
> Schools now offer courses in science fiction. . . . But it is rare to hear of works of science fiction integrated into "regular" courses in modern literature. . . . What is needed is a criticism serious in its standards and its concern for literary value but willing to take seriously a literature based on ideas, types and events beyond ordinary experience.[3]

My analogy, needless to say, derives from feminist criticism's being based on ideas, types, and events which, though not in general beyond ordinary experience, are nonetheless beyond the ordinary experience of certain men. I have never, as it happens, fought for the integration of the detective novel into regular courses in literature (though I write the things), but I am aware that if I did I would have less difficulty than I have encountered advocating feminist criticism. The latter more obviously demands the reconstruction of ideologies that are, for many, and especially for male professors, persuasively comfortable.

MY SECOND example is taken from an essay by a bearded scholar at the University of Toronto, Professor S. P. Rosenbaum. He writes, in New Literary History, of the need for a literary and historical account of the Bloomsbury Group: "The theory of [modern] literary history has been of the great-man variety: the earlier twentieth century is the age of Joyce or Lawrence, Eliot or Pound. (Even a great-woman theory of literary history might be an improvement on these simplifications; the failure of historians and anthologists of modernism to recognize, until quite recently, the movement for the emancipation of women as a defining characteristic of modernism shows what can happen when historical contexts are ignored.)"[4]

Freud wrote that there had been three major revolutions which displaced man from the center of the universe. Copernicus, who said the earth was not the center of the galaxy; Darwin, who said man was not the object of creation; Freud, who said man's conscious reason was not the controlling force in his life. The changing status of women makes a fourth in this remarkable series. To be sure, it is a revolution of a different sort, beginning as political, social, and economic change, rather than as a startling new insight into the order of the universe. But who can believe that it will not, indeed has not already, radically shifted our mental coordinates? Who can believe that it does not require us radically to reexamine our views of culture as well as of society? Who doubts that such reexamination can be, indeed is, a source of great excitement both to members of our profession and to our students?

Jonathan Culler asks whether we "can pose the question of the distinctiveness of literature while also demonstrating the centrality of literary structures to the organization of experience." Literature can, as he tells us, illuminate and situate the problems raised by any other discipline by "offering a perspective that consists primarily of awareness of rhetorical structures and forces, awareness of textuality."[5] The study of literature cannot survive if it cannot so illuminate human experience; and human experience cannot today be illuminated without attention to the place of women in literature, in the textuality of all our lives, both in history and in the present.

To those great Odysseuses, the Literature Departments, I suggest that for them, as for Odysseus, help may come where it is least looked for, in the wisdom and trust of a young woman and her queen mother. Nor are goddesses to be ignored. If you remember the advice of Athena concerning both the redeeming qualities essential in survivors and the unexpected sources of help in the struggle, you will find your way home, and no longer sit, like Odysseus at the beginning of the *Odyssey,* "the sweet days of his life time . . . running out in anguish."

1983

ENDNOTES

1. W. B. Stanford, *The Ulysses Theme* (Ann Arbor: University of Michigan Press, 1968).

2. Elaine Showalter, "Toward a Feminist Poetics," in *Women Writing and Women Writing about Women,* Mary Jacobus ed. (New York: Barnes & Noble, 1979).

3. Robert Scholes, "Editor's Foreword," in Frank McConnell, *The Science Fiction of H. G. Wells* (New York: Oxford, 1981).

4. S. P. Rosenbaum, "Preface to a Literary History of the Bloomsbury Group," *New Literary History* (1980–81), vol. 12.

5. Jonathan Culler, *The Pursuit of Signs: Semiotics, Literature, Deconstruction* (London: Routledge & Kegan Paul, 1981).

17

Presidential Address

ONE—THAT wonderfully neuter, transcendent, hegemonic one—always begins a presidential address by referring to past presidents. All presidents express, one way or another, the impossibility of representing, in their single persons, so heterogeneous an organization as the MLA. I shall quote only one past president.

"Though in principle I am speaking as the voice of the MLA," Helen Vendler began her fine address in 1980, "and expressing its concern, I have noticed in reading past presidential speeches that presidents are helpless to do other than to express their own hopes, couched in various literary frames of reference, in addresses tending toward the homiletic."[1] Here I paused to wonder if I would indeed be delivering a homily. My desk Webster defines a homily as "a tedious exhortation on some moral point." Clearly, I would be delivering one.

Two additional statements in Vendler's presidential address have encouraged me: she said, "We owe it to ourselves to teach what we love" (350), and she said also, "Love is shown, as Harold Bloom has made us recognize, as much by revolutionary reaction and reappropriation as by gratitude and imitation" (346). You will already have guessed that I am going to speak tonight not just as the president of the MLA but as a woman president, to ask what effect the fact that women are one third of our membership, and more than a third of our professional colleagues, has had or is likely to have on our association and our profession. I speak both to women and to men. I speak to men about their inevitable problems with "revolutionary reaction and reappropriation" where they might have expected "gratitude and imitation." I speak to women of the need we have long felt to articulate—and here I again borrow Vendler's words, though from a different occasion—our "own balance between danger and decorum in imagery of rebellion (which usually lost) against tradition (which usually won),"[2]

Before 1973, there were eighty-two presidents of the MLA, two of them women. These two women presidents made it, as some of their kind still tell us they have done, on their merits and saw no reason why other women could not do likewise. These two women presidents, furthermore, had in their unmarried state apparently chosen the life of the mind over the life of the body. Only in imagination could women, in Nina Auerbach's words, live "her unacted parts," dream "herself into forbidden roles." For most of us, "whether actual or metaphorical, maternity alone was the seal of respectable female maturity."[3] Here I shall let Vendler speak for me again: "The long exposure of most women to the more primitive experiences still remaining in civilized life—menstruation, intercourse, pregnancy, miscarriage, childbirth, nursing, toilet training, and child-rearing—make any woman feel as if she has spent ten to fifteen years in a Cro-Magnon cave" ("Adrienne Rich," 261). Vendler, writing about the poems of Adrienne Rich, spoke of childbearing, still the prescribed female destiny for her generation, Rich's and mine. Today, we women speak of the body but not alone of childbearing. We have learned to recognize, in Auerbach's words, "an adult woman without reference to children." We are not men, nor primarily mothers. Yet we know, as Jane McCabe puts it, that while we join men in this association and profession, "it simply feels different to be a woman and will continue to feel different, even in the most liberated society."[4] I suspect, though I can speak only for myself, that the seven women presidents since 1973 would all agree with that. I, the seventh, speak to you then as a woman but as a woman declaring, I hope honorably, her intentions to examine the recent female intrusion on the male hegemony in which I have passed my professional life.

This intrusion must be examined first as a matter of gender. Is gender, as the most exalted of our male theorists tell us, merely a property of linguistic discourse? If I offer you a total of fifteen words, thirteen from Whitman and two from Dickinson, am I invoking more than a figure in linguistic discourse? Whitman's thirteen words are, "I celebrate myself and sing myself/And what I assume, you shall assume." Dickinson's two words are, "I'm nobody."

If major theorists believe the difference here to be wholly linguistic, what of the linguistic errors still clinging to the word feminist, which has wandered widely from its proper place in discourse? So Hilary Spurling, in her second volume of Ivy Compton-Burnett's biography, tells us that Ivy's lifetime companion "was a feminist pioneer in practice, if not in theory, firmly established by the 1920's at the top of a profession staffed otherwise through her working life almost exclusively by men."[5] It is immediately obvious, I think, that by that definition of *feminist,* those two early women presidents of the MLA would also have qualified. And, of course, they do not. For the very heart of feminism and, I suspect, of our theories of gender has to do with solidarity and identification with other women: how many of us are there, and do we greet one another as peers and comrades? For a woman to be a feminist, I would suggest, is to be where women are and to value the presence of women there. And to see to it, if one does not find oneself where women are, that women are soon where one is.

We women in the MLA are now in a retrospective mood. Some of us are full professors, wooed as outstanding men have ever been wooed by major academic departments. By chance, the result of anonymous submission, the October 1984 issue of *PMLA* is entirely composed of articles by women. (A year earlier, to no one's surprise, an issue was all male.) If we lift our eyes beyond our profession, the sight of Geraldine Ferraro still dazzles. Yet Elaine Showalter offered a paper entitled "Women's Time, Women's Space: Writing the History of Feminist Criticism" to the English Institute last year. She spoke not only of the successes of feminist criticism, its impact on the profession, but also, wryly, of those prominent male critics who have ignored fifteen years of feminist criticism right under their noses. Presumably for these critics, "feminist criticism takes place in a women's time that is outside modernity."[6]

With male critics such as these, we women seem locked in a fruitless dialogue, early characterized in a poem by Maxine Kumin:

I am tired of this history of loss
What drum can I beat to reach you?
To be reasonable
Is to put out the light.
To be reasonable is to let go.[7]

In the early days of feminism, we women of the MLA alternated between terror and amazement: terror at what might befall us, amazement at what we had done. Here is Helen Vendler on Adrienne Rich:

Four years after she published her first book, I read it in almost dis-believing wonder; someone my age was writing down my life. I felt then, as I feel now, that for each reader there are only a few poets of whom that is true, and by the law of averages, those poets are usually dead or at least far removed in time and space. But here was a poet who seemed, by a miracle, a twin: I had not known till then how much I had wanted a contemporary and a woman as a speaking voice in my life. (237)

Of course, we do not today read only women poets, but we have begun to read as women, a different matter, and new for most of us. As Rich has written, evoking the experience of most of us who are today academics,

I had grown up hearing and reading poems from a very young age, first as sounds, repeated, musical, rhythmically satisfying in themselves, the power of concrete, sensuously compelling images. But poetry soon be-came more than music and images; it was also revelation, information, a kind of teaching. . . . And of course I thought that the poets in the anthologies were the only real poets, that their being in the anthologies was proof of this. . . . I had no idea that they reflected the taste of a particular time or of particular kinds of people. I still believed that poets were inspired by some transcendent authority and spoke from some ex-traordinary height. I thought that the capacity to hook syllables together in a way that heated the blood was the sign of a universal vision.[8]

Rich has led us to the realization that the male and the universal are not synonymous, that beautiful poetry can lie, and is no less beautiful for that.

In 1971 Adrienne Rich addressed the MLA as part of the second forum held by the Commission on the Status of Women in the Profession, which had itself been formed in 1969. I speak then, you will have noticed, also retrospectively, of fifteen years of women actively participating, as women, in the MLA. In her address, Rich said three things that continue to echo for women in the profession. She said, "It is no longer such a lonely thing to open one's eyes," and "The awakening of consciousness is not like the crossing of a frontier—one step, and you are in another country."[9] It is today a much less lonely thing than it was in 1971 to open one's eyes; I might even say that, however belatedly one does so, there are others visible in the new country. We have today something like a frontier, something like a country. There are now enough of us to constitute a women's space, into which one can cross. Emigration is never easy; it is, indeed, always full of pain. But because we now know that there can be no feminism, no life for women as women unless there are numbers of us, we have lessened the loneliness by creating another country.

The third statement of Rich's I wish to recall tonight is, "Every woman writer has written for men" ("When We Dead," 38). Today I believe that we women write as much for women as for men, and it is in no small part Rich's writings that have made this so. We have been astonished, let me admit, to discover how exciting this realization is. The fact remains that we are writing for men too. How can we not? In Elaine Showalter's recent retrospective on feminist criticism, she observed that "virtually all American feminist critics of the first wave were trained by men (as far as I know, I am the only one in this group to have had a woman dissertation director)."[10] For many of us, one of the men we trained with became for us part of what Alice Jardine has called the "writing couple":

> For there would appear to exist a seeming historical necessity for the heterosexual woman who wants to create, to write (and be read) to couple herself, in fact or fantasy, if only temporarily, with a man who also writes or wrote; a famous man in her life or in her writing.[11]

Jardine mentions "Virginia and Leonard, Lou Andreas and Friedrich, Julia and Philippe, Simone and Jean-Paul"; those of us who are Americans can come up with other couples, many only in fantasy or of shorter duration than Jardine's, that nonetheless fit her definition.

The advent of the first modern woman president of the MLA may have marked, however, writing couples who do not fit Jardine's model. We have begun to produce women mentors in impressive numbers. Beyond even that, as Gilbert and Gubar wittily tell us,

> Recently, casually, and almost comically, Harold Bloom declared that "the first true breach with literary continuity will be brought about in generations to come if the burgeoning religion of Liberated Woman spreads from its clusters of enthusiasts to dominate the West. Homer will cease to be the inevitable precursor and the rhetoric and forms of our literature then may break at last from tradition." Bloom seems to be speculating provisionally about some future catastrophe, yet it is possible to argue that what he describes in such ironically apocalyptic terms is an event that has already occured.[12]

We women have often waited for some response from the men of our profession, but we have not always known clearly what response we wanted. We have taken a long time to assess the dangers inherent in the male academic or literary world we inhabit. I am more inclined than some of my feminist colleagues to welcome what have come to be called "male feminists" and to read and hear with pleasure accounts of conversions undergone by some men who have suddenly read literature anew, as though through a woman's eyes. I appreciate that, as Wayne Booth has observed, in viewing certain texts in this feminist way, men may actually give up some of their pleasure in them. I admire the daring of male feminists and have been sympathetic to their accounts of the discomfort that sometimes follows their forays into feminism. But I would like to ask them to move beyond their attempts to understand feminism from a woman's point of view and to examine how it feels to be a man in the hegemony that feminism has brought to their attention. We have had little enough account of this. Hélène Cixous has remarked, "Men still have everything to say about their sexuality."[13] But they have not spoken of their difference; it is as though their condition were the universal condition.

Male feminists have told us that their wives' experience has affected them. But I question whether the couple Jardine has described will ever be the model for male understanding of feminism. Rather, I think, it is the father-daughter relationship that will prove significant. And I want to emphasize that I do not speak metaphorically; I am referring here not to male mentor and female "daughter" but rather to the actual daughters of actual men. I have long observed that it is through their daughters, rather than through their wives, that men first begin to question the powers of the patriarchy. Politicians with daughters at the Democratic convention were a notable spectacle, and most of us have read accounts of how crowds reached out and touched Geraldine Ferraro and how many in these crowds were fathers who had brought daughters especially that they might touch her.[14] Men with daughters, then, may more readily move to examine their own roles and the roles of other men in the masculine precincts of their own professions.

We women must still heed the words of Adrienne Rich: "I am not warning against reading men's books, learning whatever men have to teach, but against the danger of identification with the male mentor to the exclusion of other women."[15] More, we must, as Nancy Miller has told us, learn to interpret the many stories that "stage the inter-weaving of structures of power, gender, and identity inherent in the production of mimetic art." Miller offers the example of Arachne, who created a "realistic representation of the ancient heroines of the oldest Western stories of seduction and betrayal, the female figures poised at the violent intersections of sexuality and textuality." We women schol-ars must not, like the Athena Miller describes for us, "mutilate the text" of a feminist scholar or "destroy its author by beating her over the head with the shuttle—[our] shared emblem."[16]

Jonathan Culler has recognized that for feminists there is "an urgent question: to minimize or to exalt sexual differentiation?" He suggests, following the example of deconstruction, "the importance of working on two fronts at once, even though the result is a contradictory rather than unified movement."[17] This means, for feminists—indeed for all women in the profession—that, to quote Myra Jehlen, in asserting difference we "implicitly deny the possibility of any all-encompassing and all-representative wholeness, and assert that the particular is not part of a larger whole that completes it, but is already complete in itself." We must accept, Jehlen tells us, "that contradiction is the norm, and synthesis its transient deformation."[18]

We must recognize that, for the earlier women presidents of the MLA, whatever their personal accommodations to the male world in which they flourished, their professional personas required that they meld into a male "whole" in which their womanhood would be un-noticed and inoffensive. We have only recently learned that the distinguished philogist and folklorist who was the first woman president of MLA helped organize a women's military company when she was in college, was the first woman elected to the Nebraska Sports Hall of Fame, and was the beloved of Willa Cather.[19] But for the later presidents, and the women members of MLA, it has become possible to live "on two fronts," accepting contradiction as the norm. As Catharine Stimpson has warned us,

> To measure what is the flesh, the natural, the humanly given, and what are the mediating forces of personality, convention, culture is like weighing water with open hands. The "semantics of biology"—the ways in which we codify, interpret, and experience our carnality, our mortality, the world of storm, stones, and chromosomes—defy an easy reading.[20]

So too, we now see that the texts of our Western tradition defy easy gendered reading. A few months ago I heard an eminent member of our association, Geoffrey Hartman, analyze with great intensity and acuity those few verses from Genesis where Jacob wrestles with the angel.[21] Humanist, agnostic, and profoundly suspicious of religious institutions as I am, I have nonetheless always felt that story to be as weighted as any in our entire culture with an extraordinary mythic power. Those few verses from Genesis have moved many of us, including Barthes, who says that the confusion in the telling of this story—what Barthes calls "this amphibology"—is not due to ineptitude on the part of the original tellers but is intimately bound up with the "paradoxical structure of the contest." In this struggle, Barthes tells us, "the weakest defeats the strongest," and God, in this story, "acts against nature."[22]

Here are the three central verses of the biblical story: "And Jacob was left alone; and there wrestled a man with him until the breaking of the day. And when he saw that he prevailed not against him, he touched the hollow of his thigh; and the hollow of Jacob's thigh was out of joint, as he wrestled with him. And he said, Let me go, for the day breaketh. And he said, I will not let thee go, except thou bless me.

Hartman enumerated for us the wonders of this story: why does the fight begin? why are those in the biblical patriarchal drama off in the shadows? The story, Hartman says, turns on a blessing: what can be won rather than seized or expended. Most enigmatic of all, even beyond the confusion of the pronouns, is that this story is in no way necessary to the biblical narrative. Everything about Jacob, Hartman tells us, "is betwixt and between." Jacob is one of those trying to assume a larger destiny, desiring a grounding. Because Jacob is in Scripture, and not in literature, he cannot proclaim, "Call me Israel." He must engage in an enigmatic struggle, capable of many interpretations. The Bible can dare to go wrong.

I believe as critics we must dare to go wrong; there are at least two women critics of record (and more unrecorded) who believe Hartman himself to have gone badly wrong in his analysis of the story of Philomela and Procne. In this story, where Philomela is raped by Tereus, the husband of her sister, Procne, and has her tongue cut out to silence her, she weaves an "account of her violation into a tapestry which Sophocles calls 'the voice of the shuttle.' " Hartman calls this the archetypal story of the artist.[23] Patricia Joplin has answered his assertion in an article called "The Voice of the Shuttle Is Ours."[24] Jane Marcus also argues that Hartman misses the message, that this is a story not of general artistic truth but of womanhood, of those women artists who have woven the stories of the female violation, as Arachne did, into forms of art much resented by the oppressor.[25] Feminist criticism finds an archetypal metaphor in these weavings, the retribution that follows their revelation, and the confiscation of such stories by the patriarchy.

Hartman, if he has usurped the story of woman's weaving of the truth, has, I believe, helped to give women the story of Jacob. I am not the first to feel this a women's story. Emily Dickinson seized this account as her own a century ago, writing seven poems that, in the words of Cynthia Griffin Wolff, "are explicit recastings of the moment when Jacob struggled with the Lord—and many more touch lightly upon that unique moment by their use of the words 'wrestle,' 'grappel,' and 'strive.' " Dickinson, Wolff continues,

> accepted Jacob's wrestle with the Lord as a moment of unparalleled importance. In surprising and uncanny ways, this Archetype even echoed elements central to her own personal experience. It was as if history had deliberately waited for this moment . . . so intimately was Jacob's legend fitted for Dickinson's telling.[26]

Dickinson wrote of Jacob, "And bewildered Gymnast/Found he had worsted God."

But at the end of her life, Wolff tells us, Dickinson wrote, "pre-empting at the last even the power of God to bless: 'Audacity of Bliss,' said Jacob to the Angel 'I will not let thee go except I bless *thee*'— Pugilist and Poet, Jacob was correct."

Women's texts have, for the most part, been woven in secret ways, hard to decipher, dangerous if discovered by the wrong people, or merely misread, misunderstood. Yet the wrestling of Jacob, in those three verses thrust so unaccountably into a narrative of brotherly rec-onciliation, seems to me to be also a women's text, to speak of the suddenness and decisiveness of the struggle that attends any intrusion into the patriarchal world. If we read those confused pronouns as fem-inine, if we perceive the blessing demanded as from, or to, women, we are no more preemptive than Hartman when he interprets Procne's story as that of the genderless, presumed-male, artist. We women in-trude on the narrative of male hegemony, as Jacob did, to be wounded and to demand a blessing. We may change our name, we may even discover that we have acquired the highest sanction. This story is ours, as Emily Dickinson has told us. If, as Joplin writes, "the story of Phi-lomela's emergence from silence is filled with the tension of *feminist* poetics" (24), so is the story of Jacob. If Philomela can well be the male artist, so both figures in the struggle of Jacob and the angel can be female. We have therefore another archetype, not only of women wrestling within the profession for acknowledgment but of each woman wrestling with the angel of the female past, with all female refusal to acknowledge the new state of women. Each of us struggles with this angel, and each of us, though she has wounded us, must refuse to let her go "except thou bless me."

1984

ENDNOTES

1. Helen Vendler, "Presidential Address 1980," *PMLA* (1981), 96:344–350.
2. Helen Vendler, "Adrienne Rich," *Part of Nature, Part of Life* (Cam-bridge: Harvard University Press, 1980), p. 238.
3. Nina Auerbach, *Romantic Imprisonment: Women and Other Glorified Outcasts* (New York: Columbia University Press, 1985).
4. Jane McCabe, "A Woman Who Writes," *Anne Sexton: The Artist and Her Critics,* J. D. McClatchy, ed. (Bloomington: Indiana University Press, 1978), p. 223.

5. Hilary Spurling, *Secrets of a Woman's Heart: The Later Life of Ivy Compton-Burnett 1920–1969,* 2 vols. (London: Hodder, 1984), 2:9–10.

6. Elaine Showalter, "Women's Time, Women's Space: Writing the History of Feminist Criticism," English Institute, Cambridge, Mass., September 2, 1983, p. 5.

7. Maxine Kumin, "September 22," *The Privilege* (New York: Harper, 1965), p. 82.

8. Adrienne Rich, "Blood, Bread, and Poetry: The Location of the Poet," *Massachusetts Review* (1983), 24:524.

9. Adrienne Rich, "When We Dead Awaken," *On Lies, Secrets, Silence* (New York: Norton, 1979), pp. 35, 48.

10. Showalter, "Women's Time," p. 16.

11. Alice Jardine, "Death Sentences: Writing Couples and Ideology," *Poetics Today.*

12. Sandra Gilbert and Susan Gubar, "Tradition and the Female Talent," in *Literary History: Theory and Practice,* Herbert L. Sussman, ed., Proceedings of the Northeastern University Center for Literary Studies, p. 6.

13. Hélène Cixous, "The Laugh of the Medusa," Keith Cohen and Paula Cohen, trs., *Signs* (1976), 1:877n.

14. Jane Perlez, "Crowds Reach Out to Touch Ferraro," *New York Times,* September 9, 1984, late ed., sec. 1, p. 32.

15. Rich, "Comment on Friedman's '"I go where I love": An Intertextual Study of H. D. and Adrienne Rich,'" *Signs* (1984), 9:736.

16. Nancy K. Miller, "Arachnologies," unpub. essay.

17. Jonathan Culler, *On Deconstruction* (London: Routledge, 1983), pp. 172, 173.

18. Myra Jehlen, "Against Human Wholeness: A Suggestion for a Feminist Epistemology," unpub. essay.

19. Sharon O'Brien, " 'The Thing Not Named': Willa Cather as a Lesbian Writer," *Signs* (1984), 9:580.

20. Catharine R. Stimpson, "Feminism and Feminist Criticism," *Massachusetts Review* (1983), 24:287.

21. Geoffrey Hartman, "The Struggle for the Text," English Institute, Cambridge, Mass., September 2, 1984.

22. Roland Barthes, "The Struggle with the Angel," *Image-Music-Text,* Stephen Heath, tr. (New York: Hill, 1977), pp. 132, 135.

23. Geoffrey Hartman, "The Voice of the Shuttle," *Beyond Formalism* (New Haven: Yale University Press, 1970), p. 337.

24. Patricia Klindienst Joplin, "The Voice of the Shuttle Is Ours," *Stanford Literature Review* (1984), 1:22–53.

25. Jane Marcus, "Liberty, Sorority, Misogyny," in *Representation of Women in Fiction,* Carolyn G. Heilbrun and Margaret R. Higonnet, eds. (Baltimore: Johns Hopkins University Press, 1983), p. 88.

26. Quoted from Cynthia Griffin Wolff's manuscript on Emily Dickinson and Jacob. Wolff's study, *Emily Dickinson,* was published by Knopf in 1986.

18

The Politics of Mind: Women, Tradition, and the University

I HAVE been a member of the Columbia University community for more than thirty-five years, and I can only consider myself to be speaking as what Lionel Trilling called an opposing self,[1] opposed to culture, in this case the culture of the university. Lionel Trilling was the most powerful and honored presence during most of my years at Columbia: as much as anyone, he defined, both for his department and for the wider community beyond it, what he honored as the life of the mind. But history has moved, times have changed, the politics inherent in that phrase "the life of the mind" have emerged. We have come to recognize the degree to which the life of the mind is organized to reflect the politics of mind, particularly the politics of a wholly male-centered culture and university. The numbers of women in universities today, and the whole question of the canon, has come under a scrutiny which Trilling could scarcely have forseen. It is unfortunate that the very phrase "the life of the mind," which has for so long represented all that was desired from education, and all that women, excluded from education, had come to cherish as an ideal, what Virginia Woolf called "the strange bright fruits of art and knowledge," has become a kind of "buzz word" for something disembodied, unconnected with gender, or race, or the differing cultures and aspirations in our rapidly changing world.

In 1971 at the Library of Congress, Trilling delivered the first Jefferson Lecture in the Humanities, entitled "Mind in the Modern World." He spoke of the marvelous "life of the mind," and of how that proud concept was being undermined by, among other things, affirmative action. His deep concern with the threat to the "life of the mind" from affirmative action was phrased in his usually forthright and vigorous way. He called attention to

> the silence of our colleges and universities about what is implied for their continuing life by the particular means our society had chosen to remedy the injustice [of inequality]. I have in view the posture toward colleges and universities which of recent years has been taken by the Department of Health, Education, and Welfare. [It] has responded with its directive that institutions of higher education which receive government funds shall move at once toward bringing about a statistically adequate representation on their faculties of ethnic minority groups and women. The directive does not pretend that this purpose is to be accomplished without a change in the standards of excellence of the academic profession.[2]

Trilling does not deny the importance of the goals inherent in affirmative action, his point is only "that the academic profession does not debate it." "Surely," he continues, "it says much about the status of mind in our society that the profession which is consecrated to its protection and furtherance should stand silent under the assault, as if suddenly deprived of all right to use the powers of mind in its own defense" (29).

Trilling could hardly have anticipated the direction events have taken in this decade: reactionary forces have attempted to consolidate the defense of "the life of the mind" with other objectives, including the promotion of "old fashioned values" and the protection of a narrowly demarked "legacy" or "intellectual heritage," in ways that, I think, he would not have welcomed. Trilling was right in observing that it is the reluctance of the academic community to debate these points which most threatens the life of the mind.

My thesis, then, is that women particularly have a great deal to contribute to the life of the mind in the University, but that they have been prevented from doing so because much of what passes for the life of the mind is, in fact no more than the politics of mind. The life of the mind is a synonym for what is referred to as the universal—treated, revered, accepted as though it had been engraved somewhere as eternal and unchanging truth. But we must ask, what is lost to this "life of the mind," to mind itself, to colleges and universities, to that proud contemplation of texts and culture to which Lionel Trilling devoted his life, when women are excluded from taking their full part.

There are additional reasons for considering at this time the importance of women to the essential life of a university, to its life of the mind in the most creative and vital sense. One is the extraordinary fact that there are almost no all-male colleges or universities left in the United States or, for that matter, in England. (That all the original, all male, colleges at Oxford now have women undergraduates is a phenomenon little noticed or commented upon in this country. The loss to these colleges has not been to the life of the mind, but to the life of the playing fields. The athletic, hearty and rather mindless young men who made up about a third of these famous colleges are no longer there, their absence fundamentally affecting the quality of undergraduate life, though probably not the quality of the life of the mind.) Many women, on the other hand, for reasons faculties of coeducational institutions ought to take more seriously than they do, still prefer to attend all-women colleges. This has a great deal to do with the life of the mind.

Feminism has now reached a retrospective stage. We are very far from the early years when rather unsophisticated methods started feminist literary critics on the heady road toward reinterpretation. Feminism itself has developed new critical strategies for reading literature, and has elaborated theoretical models which place literature and cultural forms within a complex set of ideological and social arrangements. Despite this, often the most sophisticated male readers of cultural texts, even those who in their own work underscore the material and symbolic conditions that produce a politics of mind, resist the broader implications of feminist theory. Thus we discover these words from a prominent male scholar, my colleague, Edward Said: "Nearly everyone producing literary or cultural studies makes no allowance for the truth that all intellectual or cultural work occurs somewhere, at some time, on some very precisely mapped-out and permissable terrain, which is ultimately contained by the State. Feminist critics have opened this question part of the way, but they have not gone the whole distance."[3] Women, it seems, are likely to be condemned both if they do go all the way, and if they don't.

We must recognize the unique force of feminist criticism in revising the assumption and deflating the platitudes of our cultural and literary life, in or out of universities, but particularly within them. More than a few male academics, however, remain fearful of what they conceive to be a feminist threat. That is, I think, most unfortunate, for men in the university have everything to gain and little to lose from feminist criticism. Of course, they must put aside the fear of feminization in a profession that has always risked appearing effete, and in which the codes and flourishes of masculinity have long been fetishistically clung to.

Why are men so afraid? "I think the answer to this question," Christine Froula, a young feminist critic, writes, "has to do with the fact that woman's voice threatens to discredit that masculinist culture upon which [men have] modeled their identity."[4] Many works of the canon have constructed their "speech on the bedrock of women's silence." "Men very commonly express the fear that feminist criticism will invert that hierarchy in which they have invested so much—will, in other words, silence *them* as patriarchal discourse has silenced women. . . . But woman speaking does not reverse the conditions of her own silencing. She does not demand that men be silent; she asks only that men cease speaking in such a way as to silence her" (178).

All the jokes in literature about women-dominated marriages, all the horrible wives in Dickens, Trollope, and others speak to the male fear of hierarchical reversal. If men are not boss, women will be. But this is what men fear, not what women want. Women ask men only to "grant women's voice an equal position with male discourse, rescuing it from the now inevitable reactive position of either assimilation or opposition."[5] Women do not ask for a new harmony with the major theme always in the soprano range, but for counterpoint.

Feminist criticism is another way of knowing. Uniquely, it addresses the longest established binarism of our culture, a binarism seen as most in need of protection by those who fear change, new ideas, and the loss of power and control. It is no accident that the new right, here and around the world, and the religious fundamentalists with whom they are almost coextensive, are driven first of all by the need to return women to their traditional place of powerlessness in society.

What men have to gain by reconstituting the category of woman is not only the risk and excitement that is the reward of challenging long-held convictions, or the satisfaction of declining to dismiss them because they are discomforting. What men have to gain is the heady sense of encountering the future; what they lose is the heavy sense of insisting upon the unexamined rectitude of the past. We may all gain a way to conceive difference without opposition; we may, with equal daring, challenge the ancient male-female binarism as an intellectual imperative.[6] Nor should we allow this challenge to be met by the accusation that it overturns old "values," old morality. Old values and old morality are most often defended by those who benefit from them, and fear to share those benefits.

All women who have ever read a classic or undertaken an intellectual pursuit have imagined themselves as men. What alternative was there? Women in universities and outside of them have always "read with a double consciousness—both as women and as the masculine reader they have been taught to be."[7] Might not men gain now by learning to read, not with a double consciousness, but consciously as men in relation to women? The male establishment at universities might consider that the discomfort they feel before women's texts is the discomfort women have long lived with, and have never quite learned to take for granted, though some have been more thoroughly trained to this, as to restrictive clothing, than others. In literature and out, femininity has existed only as a representation of masculine desire: "men appear unwilling to address the issues placed on the critical agenda by women unless those issues have first been neutralized . . . to the already known, the already written . . ." (Owens 62). Women challenge the degree to which all male modern texts are narratives of mastery; women may suggest other narratives, other modes of relationship.

Yet we live in a time when the already read and the already written are being hailed as revitalizing our "legacy," when men like Secretary of Education William Bennett and retired Yale President A. Bartlett Giamatti bemoan the loss of some fetishized tradition. We may notice that men in fundamentalist societies fear the loss of virginity in unmarried women: sexual experience for women, like the not-already-read books written by women, or with women as their protagonists, seem horribly to threaten the male claim on paternity and authorship. Virgins are held sacred, and terribly fragile; and female writings are declared ephermeral, charming, but altogether too sensitive for the manly business of literary authority. Lynn Sukenick quotes Hugh Kenner, who writes: "Lady novelists have always claimed the privilege of transcending mere plausibilities. It's up to men to arrange such things. . . . Your bag is sensitivity, which means, knowing what to put into this year's novels . . . the with-it cat's cradling of lady novelists."[8] Other men broach the matter more forthrightly: Anthony Burgess finds Jane Austen's novels to be failures because she "lacks a strong male thrust," and for William Gass women writers "lack that blood congested genital drive which energizes all great style." Norman Mailer says a good writer must have balls.[9] These gentlemen express with clarity the phallocentric values of our universities, a set of assumptions we have not sufficiently debated, and which Bennett and Giamatti would have us take for granted, marking all debate as destructive.

"What characterizes good teaching in the humanities?" Bennett asks, and triumphantly answers himself: "First, and foremost, a teacher must have achieved mastery of the material."[10] Bennett does not only mean that the teacher should have read the material, but that he should have incorporated it into his conception of the universe. More importantly, mastery means that one knows what questions to ask, and more important still, what questions not to ask. Giamatti is in no doubt about this last criterion. He says that today "students of literature are increasingly talking only to ourselves and no one else is paying any attention."[11] We are hardly surprised to learn that the two villains are feminism and theory, which are largely to blame for the failure of the many eager students of literature to come properly to love what has, by theorists, feminists, and their ilk, been snatched from them. It does not occur to either of these gentlemen that what marks the immortality of the literature we all love and cherish is precisely that it continues to require new questions. We love what we are in dialogue with; the rest we endure, or protect out of fear. Universities are not, or should not be, merely museums for the display of culture. They ought to be theaters for its ongoing creation and recreation.

Blaming feminists, new-fangled theorists, and women writers are all ploys in the oldest game in town—older than Hawthorne, who bewailed the scribbling women who stole his audience, older than Aristotle, who classed women with slaves and animals. What is surprising is that, in an age when youth is most notably responsive to inspiration electronically conveyed, the life of the mind seems to consist in asking the same canonical questions of the same canon. Bennett is not loath to tell us what that canon includes: his list, ranging from Homer to Faulkner, embraces, with a nod toward the second half of this century, the Birmingham speech of Martin Luther King, Jr., and the works of Jane Austen and George Eliot. The devoted canonists, forced by some pressure they see as faddish but must reluctantly pretend to acknowledge, will always choose Jane Austen or George Eliot if they must include a woman writer. The unthreatening aspect of these two writers is, of course, a delusion: but it requires a more probing and indeed theoretical reading to discover the not-already-read in these apparently conventional novelists. Once permitted, albeit reluctantly, to enter the canon, such new arrivals deserve to be met with new non-canonical questions. But, of course, they probably will not be. Who is prepared to suggest that Elizabeth Bennett in *Pride and Prejudice* did not absolutely triumph in capturing Darcy and Pemberley?

There is a scene in *The Mill on the Floss* when Maggie visits her brother Tom at his school, run by Mr. and Mrs. Stelling. Tom has said to her: "*you'll* be a woman some day," and Maggie, not much liking the crossness of the women she knows, answers: "But I shall be a *clever* woman." "O, I dare say," Tom responds, "and a nasty conceited thing. Everybody'll hate you."[12]

> They were presently fetched to spend the rest of the evening in the drawing-room, and Maggie became so animated with Mr. Stelling, who, she felt sure, admired her cleverness, that Tom was rather amazed and alarmed at her audacity. . . .
>
> 'What a very odd little girl that must be!' said Mrs. Stelling, meaning to be playful, but a playfulness that turned on her supposed oddity was not at all to Maggie's taste. She feared Mr. Stelling, after all, did not think much of her, and went to bed in rather low spirits. Mrs. Stelling, she felt, looked at her as if she thought her hair was very ugly because it hung down straight behind.
>
> Nevertheless it was a very happy fortnight to Maggie—this visit to Tom. She was allowed to be in the study while he had his lessons, and in her various readings got very deep into the examples in the Latin Grammar. The astronomer who hated women generally caused her so much puzzling speculation that she one day asked Mr. Stelling if all astronomers hated women, or whether it was only this particular astronomer. But, forestalling his answer, she said:

'I suppose it's all astronomers: because you know, they live up in high towers, and if the women came there, they might talk and hinder them from looking at the stars.'

Mr. Stelling liked per prattle immensely. (133)

What Maggie is puzzling about, as the literary critics Mary Jacobus and Nancy Miller have observed, is "the maxims that pass for the truth of human experience. These maxims, and the encoding of that experience in literature, are organizations, when they are not fantasies, of the dominant culture."[13] George Eliot herself tells us this later in the novel, describing, one cannot but feel, those who insist that to rescue women from the generalities that have confined them is to work against time ratified "values." The "man of maxims," Eliot writes,

> is the popular representative of the minds that are guided in their moral judgment solely by general rules, thinking that these will lead them to justice by a ready-made patent method, without the trouble of exerting patience, discrimination, impartiality, without any care to assure themselves whether they have the insight that comes from a hardly-earned estimate of temptation, or from a life vivid and intense enough to have created a wide fellow-feeling with all that is human. (435)

The historian Joan Scott recently observed at a celebration at Smith College that "There is in [the literature about higher education for women] a persistent and striking undercurrent of concern with sex and gender, with the impact education will have on the sexuality of women and on that system of gender relations deemed 'natural' to human society." She quotes a doctor who, in 1873, attributed those cases of "female degeneration" he had seen to co-education:

> Put a boy and girl together upon the same course of study, and with the same lofty ideal before them . . . and there will be awakened within them a stimulus unknown before, and that separate study does not excite. The unconscious fires that have their seat deep down in the recesses of the sexual organization will flame up through every tissue, permeate every vessel, burn every nerve, flash from the eye, tingle in the brain, and work the whole machine at highest pressure.[14]

This sounds fine to me; the worried doctor, however, was concerned with the fate of the womb. We in universities today seem more concerned with the fate of the Legacy, which threatens to dissolve or disintegrate under this "highest pressure." We now worry, not that mental and physical exertion will desex women, but that the exertion of female questions may desex our legacy.

The questions women wish to ask of the canon are certainly not questions only about women. We women within the university wish to examine the exclusion not only of women from culture—although that should not be forgotten—but those less obvious "exclusions that keep us outside the desire for theory and the theory of desire."[15] Diana Trilling has noted that: "It is when we close the book on Emma Woodhouse's marriage that we let ourselves be fully aware of the pleasure we took in the energies that will probably no longer be exercised: the wise Mr. Knightley will curb them as unsuited to a wife, attractive as he found them before marriage."[16]

Universities are not unlike Mr. Knightley: they have found attractive the energies of the young women who will increase its pool of intelligent applicants, and who will encourage young men to choose that college where such intelligent young women are to be found. But, like Mr. Knightley, having taken the young women to its institutional bosom, it wishes to confine the energies it found so attractive to the already designated duties of a girlfriend or co-ed, or eventually of a consort. Where the university must change is in allowing the energy of women to be exercised fully and to its own ends. Nothing is perhaps so wasted in our culture as the energies of its women; Diana Trilling wisely pointed to "the cruel disparity there has been in literature, as in life, between female promise and female fulfillment." If we look back over all the women in the literature in the established canon, including what Mr. Bennett sees as imperative for a student of the humanities, we cannot fail to notice that female energy is the least prized and the most wasted resource, even, perhaps especially, in the novels of Jane Austen and George Eliot. Yet how often is that question of blunted energy raised in a course like a survey course in literature, or a graduate course in Victorian prose writers, or a course on the Romantics? Women who are at the margin of the society and of the University no longer wish only to examine that marginality; rather, they profoundly desire to alter the nature of discourse that defines margins and centers, to make the condition of the oppressed not merely a fact in the study of domination, but a living part of the legacy of western civilization.

Women within the University need not only to pass from the margin to the center of intellectual life, they need help from the University in confronting the problems of being female in our culture, and especially in the culture of the University at this time. There is a sign in my local newspaper store reading: "By the time you know all the rules you're too old to play the game." Men in today's university might well complain that by the time they know the rules, women have changed the game. But rules always change with time, and women, like men, need help from one another as these rules inevitably change.

Women need help in the University in other ways besides challenging the canon or daring to see our heritage as other than male-centered (or other than racist or classist, since it also comes to that). The woman student faces special problems. As likely as her male counterpart—perhaps likelier—to have mixed feelings about a female authority figure, she is at the same time eager to show herself worthy of the club she has been allowed to join. Deliberately or not, women are raised to be untroublesome, and to many women, young and old, it seems profoundly boorish to question the nice gentlemen who have let them into their university. As E. M. Forster put it, it is hard, after accepting six cups of tea from your hostess, to throw the seventh in her face.[17] Women fought for a century or more to gain a university education, and they are slow to realize that they are no longer pounding on the doors, but, on the contrary, finding that the door they lean on gives way so readily that they collapse across the threshold. There is, furthermore, a tendency for an accomplished woman to think of herself as a special case, not as a member of a group called "women," a situation intensified by the unfortunate fact that, in any revolution, those who fight are seldom those who win. The young women who now receive the rewards scarcely understand what the struggle was all about. How could they, for they will never find themselves so equal as they seem in college. Unfortunately that makes it difficult for the college to prepare them to cope with the inevitable inequalities of work, marriage, child-rearing, and aging.[18] If the men who teach them refuse to bring openly into discussion the place of females in our culture, the young women will rest in an attitude of gracious appreciation, bathed in the comforts of male authority, marvelously unprepared for the life that awaits them, including the life of the mind. To this might be added that young men themselves would benefit from knowing what the female destiny has been and may be, and from questioning, not so much their attitude toward women as their attitude toward themselves and the presumptions of their maleness.

Women in the university would welcome from devotees of the legacy an enlightened understanding of why non-canonical texts must be read, and canonized texts approached with new questions. Here I can offer a personal example. The period, as we say, that I specialize in is modern British literature. When I was in graduate school thirty years ago, that was a totally male literature, and has largely remained so. In earlier years, the peculiarity of this never occurred to me. That I was forbidden to teach Virginia Woolf or even mention her without fear of raucous laughter struck me as in the nature of things. In American literature, similarly, Gertrude Stein was a joke, or part of a limerick I remember finding particularly funny: There are geniuses three named Stein/There's Gertrude there's Ep and there's Ein;/Gertrude's writing is junk/Ep's statues are punk/And nobody understands Ein.

More recently I heard this joke from about the same time: a critic was asked to review *A Skeleton Key to Finnegans Wake,* and he refused, saying that what Joyce needed was a lock, not a key. I don't agree with the sentiment here expressed, but I noticed it because it is the only joke I can remember hearing about the proliferation of studies of Joyce. When Woolf began to be studied, and written about, and to have her letters and other writings published, the result was a howl of laughter that echoed from *New Yorker* cartoons to newspaper articles discussing the "cult" of Virginia Woolf. (We have also, of course, had "cults" of contemporary women poets like Sylvia Plath.) It is the usual no-win situation: either a woman author isn't studied, or studying her is reduced to an act of misplaced religious fanaticism. All these are gambits to ensure non-recognition of women authors. We must read Gertrude Stein and Virginia Woolf because they are writers of the first importance for an understanding of our world: it is really that simple. Tender buttons as well as phalluses can organize a vision.

I well remember the love I felt for modern British literature in all my early academic years. The period was close to contemporary then, and it spoke exactly of the way we felt: it spoke us. Taught to read as a man, I did not notice that I was nowhere in most of the texts by which I believed myself gloriously empowered. Neither bird-girl with feathers, nor arrogant young sinner among prostitutes, I read as I had been taught to read, failing to identify myself as other than a reader, male, of texts also male, but pretending to be neuter, universal. Today I find the same literature equally compelling, but I can perceive, not only that words like "collegiality" camouflage the inevitable maleness of our university culture, but also certain connections, like those between the fear of women and the attraction of fascism, the disdain of women and the ease of imperialism. Hugh Kenner, who has called my period the Pound era, has also said that *Ulysses,* like *Paradise Lost,* is the pivotal work of its time.[19] I believe this last to be true, including in the sense that the important voices are those that have turned from Joyce as T. S. Eliot turned from Milton. This is not to say that Joyce and Milton are not among the greatest writers we have in our legacy. It is to say that we must learn to ask new questions of them. It is to say, further, that Virginia Woolf and Gertrude Stein have asked those questions in ways that soon reveal themselves when they are read with the same intensity with which Kenner and his colleagues have read Joyce and Pound and Eliot.

If we look back over the history of the English novel, we cannot but be struck by the centrality of women within it. Most of the women who study the English novel feel empowered by this fact. Simply to name Richardson, Defoe, Thackeray, Collins, Meredith, Hardy, Gissing, James, Lawrence, Forster is to perceive that woman's grip upon the imagination of most male English novelists is intense, almost, one might guess, as though the limited condition of women, their inability to fulfill, in James' words, the demands of their imagination, spoke to male novelists of something close to their own experience, to their own fears. Yet how often is the English novel studied from that perspective? Similarly, the most cursory study of nineteenth-century literature indicates that George Sand was perhaps the greatest single influence upon many of the major male English authors. But how many courses in the Victorian age even mention George Sand, let alone study her writings and her life?

Down to this very day, women's place in culture has been what might be called a Lacanian "contained spectacle," existing only as an embodiment or representation of male desire. Because half our student population is female, but not only because of this, reclaiming and restoring the life of the mind requires us to confront that central cultural fact, as yet unexamined in the legacy that men like Bennett and Giamatti would hand on to us. Their legacy, their literature has served men well. Yet we often fail to notice in the texts we study how much they embody both fear of women and the need to protect conventional masculinity. Feminist criticism provides the essential analytic methods to use if one wishes seriously to engage the gender basis of our culture. Yet how infrequently has such analysis been admitted in the discourse of the University. Courses in History that deal at length with the Scientific Revolution, the Industrial Revolution, the French and Russian Revolutions, and the Revolutions of 1848, scarcely touch upon the revolution in the status of women. If the Universities neglected to debate affirmative action when it was first imposed upon them, they have declined to debate the assumptions about gender which they have accepted far longer and more readily.

So today, each time we take up—and often enough we do not even bother to take up—Milton's Eve, or Shakespeare's Lady Macbeth, or Jane Austen's Emma, or George Eliot's Maggie Tulliver, or Charlotte Brontë's Lucy Snowe, or Henry James' Isabel Archer, or D. H. Lawrence's Lady Chatterley, we do not ask them to speak themselves; we do not ask of them what we ask of the Underground Man, or Pip, or Tom Jones, or Lear, or Beowulf.

And we must ask women within the University to speak for themselves also. We must permit women, without shaming them as foolish, or strident, or shrill, or unsexed, to enter, with respect, the ancient discourses. Carlyle met Margaret Fuller with certain assumptions, upon which he later commented. She is, he wrote, "a strange lilting, lean old maid, not nearly such a bore as I expected."[20] When he said this of her, Margaret Fuller was thirty-six; she would be dead at forty. We know how much Carlyle was amused when she told him wearily that she had decided to accept the universe. "She'd better," he said (87). But in the end we shall learn that she need not accept the universe he took for granted; we may even hope that her appearance, her marital status, and her age will not be the primary aspects with which we engage, that the ways she questions the universe will come to seem as essential to understanding the humanist legacy as the questions of Plato, Augustine, Joyce, and T. S. Eliot have always seemed.

1986

ENDNOTES

1. Lionel Trilling, *The Opposing Self* (New York: Viking, 1955).

2. Lionel Trilling, *Mind in the Modern World: The 1972 Jefferson Lecture in the Humanities* (New York: Viking, 1972), p. 27.

3. Edward Said, *The World, the Text, and the Critic* (Cambridge: Harvard University Press, 1983), p. 169.

4. Christine Froula, "Pechter's Specter: Milton's Bogey Writ Small; or Why Is He Afraid of Virginia Woolf?" *Critical Inquiry* (1984), 11:178.

5. Kristen Kahn, student paper, fall 1986.

6. Craig Owens, "The Discourse of Others: Feminists and Postmodernism," *The Anti-Aesthetic: Essays on Postmodern Culture,* Hal Foster, ed. (Port Townsend, Wash.: Bay Press, 1983), pp. 57–82.

7. Judith Fetterley, *The Resisting Reader: A Feminist Approach to American Fiction* (Bloomington: Indiana University Press, 1978), p. xii.

8. Quoted in Lynn Sukenick, "On Women and Fiction," *The Authority of Experience: Essays in Feminist Criticism,* Arlyn Diamond and Lee R. Edwards, eds. (Amherst: University of Massachusetts Press, 1977), pp. 28–44.

9. Burgess and Gass quoted in Sandra Gilbert and Susan Gubar, *The Madwoman in the Attic* (New Haven: Yale University Press, 1979), p. 9.

10. William J. Bennett, *To Reclaim a Legacy: A Report on the Humanities in Higher Education* (Washington, D.C.: National Endowment for the Humanities, 1984).

11. A. Bartlett Giamatti, Speech before the Signet Society, Harvard University, 94th Annual Dinner, April 11, 1985.

12. George Eliot, *The Mill on the Floss* (Cambridge: Riverside Press, 1961), p. 130.

13. Nancy K. Miller, "Emphasis Added: Plots and Plausibilities in Women's Fiction," *PMLA* (1981), 96:36–48.

14. Joan Scott, "Women's History as Women's Education," address, Smith College, April 17, 1985.

15. Elaine Marks, "Breaking the Bread: Gestures Toward Other Structures, Other Discourses," *Bulletin of the MMLA* (1980), 13(1):55.

16. Diana Trilling, "The Liberated Heroine," address, Columbia University, April 1978, published in *Partisan Review* (1978), 45(4):501–522.

17. E. M. Forster, *The Longest Journey* (New York: Knopf, 1961), p. 75.

18. Gloria Steinem.

19. Hugh Kenner, *Joyce's Voices* (Berkeley: University of California Press, 1978), p. xii.

20. Paula Blanchard, *Margaret Fuller: From Transcendentalism to Revolution* (New York: Delacorte, 1978), p. 257.

V

DETECTIVE

FICTION

Introductory Note

"THE DETECTIVE Novel of Manners" was written for a collection of essays on the novel of manners which has not yet appeared. It represents an important, earlier moment for me when I finally faced the full implications of the English class system and English imperialism in the novels I had long been teaching, as well as in detective fiction. Lest I appear unforgivably naive in saying this, let me mention that these themes are relatively new to literary studies. In my case, the anglophilia which had been a central part of my life from my earliest reading days loosened its hold on me. I suddenly seemed to see through much that had been so appealing to me in the past. The changes in England itself, of course, had a good deal to do with this. That said, I ought perhaps to admit that P. D. James and John Le Carré, both staunchly English, are among my favorite writers of detective fiction.

They, of course, have no illusions about the England they inhabit and write of.

"Gender and Detective Fiction" was the keynote address at a symposium on Detective Fiction held at Wesleyan University.

The essay on Dorothy Sayers, Lord Peter, and Harriet Vane combines and rewrites parts of two papers prepared at the request of the Dorothy L. Sayers Society in England. I attended their celebration of the fiftieth anniversary of *Gaudy Night* at Somerville College, Oxford, and spoke about that novel, it's reflection of Sayers' own experience of Oxford and its manifold importance for American readers. I was subsequently asked to write an introduction to a volume of *The Dorothy L. Sayers Historical and Literary Society,* and offered them my thoughts on Harriet Vane. I decided not to include here my two essays on Dorothy Sayers from earlier years, both of which originally appeared in *The American Scholar:* "Sayers, Lord Peter, and God," in 1972, and "Dorothy L. Sayers: Biography Between the Lines," ten years later. The first of these has been reprinted in a volume collection of Sayers stories called *Lord Peter,* and is outdated; the second, while still accurate, was essentially a criticism of a biography of Sayers, with ideas I have published elsewhere.

19

The Detective Novel of Manners

UNTIL THE day before yesterday, I would have defined the Detective
Novel of Manners with ease and certitude: its roots were the British
Golden age, late Victorian and Edwardian, when the only people worth
writing about spent sunny afternoons at garden parties and cricket games,
with an occasional amateur foray into the world of unexpected and
quite unacceptable crime. Its setting was among intelligent people,
comfortably surrounded by examples of dull rectitude, living a life readily
evoked and encompassed in a recognizable community, in which murder was as outrageous as it was unusual. This Detective Novel of Manners was never set in a world of criminals devoid of upper-class moral
or social principles; its major story never encompassed those outside
the bounds of the gentry, aristocracy, professional, or upper-middle
classes. I would have said, in short, that the detective novel of manners

consisted precisely of that: manners, displayed in a world where certain modes of behavior were trustfully anticipated, and murder or any other crime was reprehensible chiefly because it amounted to a betrayal of that trust. Definitions of the novel of manners, such as those that the writers of the introduction to this volume quote and to which they take exception—where questions of "social convention" predominate—these certainly suit the detective novel of manners if not the novel of manners generally. The study of "character," the nature of the "self," are hardly foremost in the detective novel of manners.

What I have determined since yesterday is that the DNOM, unlike the novel of manners in general, is dependent upon class, particularly as class is embodied in British culture, and cannot survive without it. From the adventures of Sherlock Holmes to those of P. D. James' Adam Dalgliesh, the detective novel of manners has depended upon and been inconceivable without the clear class demarcations of English society: prep schools, public schools, university, small villages with their clear, unquestioned social hierarchy, and above all everybody's knowing his or her place. Whether English class distinctions were as clear in life as they appear in literature I am not historian enough to say, but my reading of modern British literature and my experience of England after World War II certainly suggest that class was palpable in that society. Noel Annan, in an article on the Leavises and the Bloomsbury Group whom they despised and attacked, mentions that "If we are to isolate the most important element in Leavis's make-up, we must use the referent in British society which provides so many clues to British behaviour. We must observe class differences."[1] Annan continues:

> Bloomsbury addressed themselves to the English clerisy, to the elite who had been educated at public schools and at Oxbridge, together with any who had climbed the educational and social ladder and had assimilated to the upper middle class. The eclecticism of their approach to literature and their hatred of insularity made them assume that any educated person spoke and read French and also probably German, and was thoroughly acquainted with Russian literature in translation. That he had read the Greek and Latin classics in the original went without saying. . . .
>
> Leavis, on the other hand, was the son of a piano-dealer in Cambridge who was a vigorous rationalist and republican. He came, therefore, from lower-middle-class non-conformist stock, and went to the local grammar school. (33)

One need hardly add that both the Leavises detested detective fiction, DNOMs most of all, and that Dorothy Sayers is unique in receiving critical attacks as violent as those the Leavises mounted against Bloomsbury and especially Virginia Woolf.

Today, when England has many immigrants from its lost Empire who are not native, not white, and not imbued with centuries'-old class feeling, when even Oxbridge graduates affect the lower-class accent of the Beatles, we must remember that the detective novel of manners was born and flourished at a time when everyone in England was white, most were Protestant, the richest were Church of England, and all belonged naturally to the class in which they had been born, a class marked not only by pedigree but also by distinctions of speech, height, dress, and demeanor. (As Annan notes, that some few men, by means of scholarships, or some women, by means of marriage, might move up within the class structure was, in great part, made possible exactly by the specific mannerisms that characterized each class.) A reviewer of a biography of Anthony Eden, comparing Eden's wealthy boyhood with his abandoned family estate remarks that:

> what had been spacious and elegant was now gaunt and vacantly lonely.
> . . . Was not this ruin symbolic of a society's failure to grasp the kind
> of economic adjustments required by the harsh environment of the 20th
> century? The disappearance of Britain's world power is one of the most
> remarkable and, for some, melancholy features of this century. The
> causes—strategic, economic, demographic, social, psychological—are so
> complex and tangled that they have yet to find their Gibbon.[2]

With the disappearance of Britain's world power went, as a kind of footnote, the disappearance of the DNOM. Insofar as it persists, for example, in Adam Dalgliesh, who went to public school and publishes poetry, or in the characters of a writer like June Thomson, it pictures the historical remnant of the British class system. P. D. James writes of what remains and is sharply aware of what is gone, but she is not nostalgic; John Le Carré writes of what is gone, and his public school and University graduates, like their real life counterparts, become spies for the Communist world. The DNOM ends with British world power.

Think for a moment of Sherlock Holmes. He has been to public school and university. He is entitled, by class, to consult with royalty and to enter the most exclusive clubs. He has an unearned income. He is, unmistakably, inevitably, a gentleman. That he is so talented at imitating other classes, and disguising himself as someone less endowed, underlines the distinctive qualities that must be assumed for purposes of identification. (Recall how much easier it was for a man to pretend to be a woman in those days, as in *Charlie's Aunt*. When the sexes dressed totally differently, and women in voluminous and inhibiting garments, one had only to put on women's clothes to become a woman; in the days of unisex wear—T-shirts and blue jeans—the male is less easily disguised.) Holmes' cases and clients are so embedded in the class system that there is scarcely a Holmes story that would be possible in today's world. There are many reasons for the continued popularity of the Holmes stories, but one certainly is the historical evocation of a world for which no one but a fundamentalist could have nostalgia, but which, because it is unconsciously honest about the class arrangements, is true to its own time. Nostalgia has no part in it; what is operating is the eternal fantasy of the time machine.

Class is at the very heart of the detective novel of manners, and the detective novel ceases to be a DNOM precisely when class ceases to operate. The American school of tough guys walking mean streets created by Hammett, Chandler, MacDonald, and others does not produce DNOMs, not because no one in them has any manners, but because everyone can be anyone: as Tocqueville long ago noted, if a gold watch chain marks a gentleman, in America one can get a brass watch chain and claim to be a gentleman. The very concepts of noblesse oblige and behaving honorably toward ladies, however more honored in the breach than in the observance, are hallmarks of the behavior of a gentleman and would be simply funny in an American tough guy detective novel. Julian Symons, who admires the American detective novel while castigating the likes of Sayers with leftist scorn, nonetheless sets a recent story published in the *Ellery Queen* magazine in 1987, in a home of the upper classes, complete with snotty lady, servants, and a proper tea.[3] Class is the clue. Not to put too fine a point on it, as they used to say in British detective fiction of the golden age, I have reluctantly come to recognize a simple and disturbing fact: the detective novel of manners is a novel of the white middle and upper classes.

The Iran-Contra hearings of recent memory are not unconnected with this point. Even while they continued daily to fascinate, trouble, and astound me, I read Robin Winks' new book *Cloak & Gown: Scholars in the Secret War, 1939–1961*, which is about the development of the secret service and the beginnings of covert actions by the United

States.[4] Winks, himself no mean analyzer of the detective novel (and a member of the Yale faculty), here recounts how the agencies responsible for America's covert operations were founded and almost entirely staffed by men who were among Yale's most prestigious alumni, many of them members of Skull and Bones or other exclusive Yale clubs. Clearly, for a time, men highly placed socially, and working through networks of those similarly endowed, hoped simultaneously to maintain their elite ambience and to develop covert actions. I found this history compelling and shocking, as was the author's intention. Nor could one read it without recalling the upper-class Cambridge network from which emerged in England McLean, Burgess, Philby, Blunt, and others, no doubt, with as yet less familiar names. The upper classes in both countries, the elite, deserted their house parties and other elegant pursuits and went in for spying (though in the case of the Americans, it was mostly spying for the home side).

Winks' covert actions are no longer run by Skull and Bones chaps from Yale, understanding each other, but by the likes of Oliver North, a born-again Christian altogether outside of the world that inspired the classical detective novel, the one with "manners." Which is to say, that the detective novel of manners is finished, or if appearing in spectral form, giving the clues of its own demise in the rapidity with which it dates. The novels of Dorothy Sayers, which may be called the epitome of the detective novel of manners, are not dated: they are historical manifestations of a real time, when the upper classes were the model to which the middle classes aspired, when the British Empire was (apparently) intact, and the classes were accepted naturally, as though ordained by heaven. Sayers' novels, like Conan Doyle's, are documents as historical as Austen's novels, or Trollope's, or Pym's, and if we read them now from nostalgia, they were written not from nostalgia but from conviction and confidence. They are the product of a certain class, race, and empire that is done forever.

The heir to the true detective novel of manners, as opposed to its imitators, is John Le Carré, who has written best of the manners of a dissolving class and faith. In *Tinker, Tailor, Soldier, Spy*, Le Carré's hero, George Smiley, must determine which of the men within the inner circle of England's highest spy operation is a "mole," a double agent working for the Russians. The mole turns out to be a graduate of Eton and Cambridge, who has come to hate England: "He spoke not of the decline of the West, but of its death by greed and constipation. He hated America very deeply, he said, and Smiley supposed he did. Haydon also took it for granted that secret services were the only real measure of a nation's political health, the only real expression of its subconscious."[5] Haydon goes on to explain how "in the war it scarcely mattered where one stood as long as one was fighting the Germans."

> For a while, after '45, he said, he had remained content with Britain's part in the world, till gradually it dawned on him just how trivial this was. How and when was a mystery. In the historical mayhem of his own lifetime he could point to no one occasion; simply he knew that if England were out of the game, the price of fish would not be altered by a farthing. He had often wondered which side he would be on if the test ever came; after prolonged reflection he had finally to admit that if either monolith had to win the day, he would prefer it to be the East. (356)

Smiley, when he has finally caught Haydon, feels little more triumph than Marlow feels in *Heart of Darkness* when he had found Kurtz and watched him die. "Leaving King's Cross, [Smiley] had had a wistful notion of liking Haydon and respecting him: Bill was a man, after all, who had had something to say and had said it" (366)—an exact quotation, conscious or not, from *Heart of Darkness,* that early analysis of imperialism. And when Le Carré came to write *The Little Drummer Girl,* only his naive heroine was from an English-speaking country, without principle or purpose. The rest is the struggle of the Middle East, Israel against the PLO: class, empire, and the playing fields of England are quite out of it. Compare this to the easy racism of Sayers' novels, the anti-Semitism and anti-black assumptions. Sayers was without nostalgia. She wrote of a world she believed was the best there was, one that could happily be assumed to endure.

Adrienne Rich, writing of the poetry she had been taught was universal but which she had come to recognize as white, male, and upper class, nonetheless knows that it is often beautiful despite its lying claims to being universal. So it is with the detective novel of manners in its true form.

What we have today are not true detective novels of manners: they are imitation, they are nostalgia, and they succeed, I believe, only when their narration is able to encompass simultaneously the lost world and a new world, understood and welcome. Hanna Charney writes that the "detective novel of manners shapes its own society, where understanding of social and moral norms is expected" (xi). "The illusion," Charney claims, "depends on the cooperation of reader and narrator" (xii).[6]

True enough. And for the nostalgic reader, like the nostalgic writer, the detective novel of manners that persisted beyond the time of the English system of class and race and gender is a nostalgic fake, depending on the cooperation of reader and narrator to pretend that they are not indulging in something similar to the Harlequin romance. Let us take a favorite example of Charney's, Robert Bernard's *Deadly Meeting,* an academic novel published in 1970.[7] It serves Charney as an example of the closed society of the detective novel of manners. Encouraged by her book to read it, I was amazed to discover an English department wholly male, with a chairman openly racist. There is a scene set at an MLA convention at which all the participants are men, with the exception of nuns in clerical garb. True, an English woman medievalist of advanced years is imported as a temporary stopgap. But the book assumes that all applicants for faculty positions will be men; in short, what is called a detective novel of manners is in fact a true exercise in nostalgia for the reader, and a misreading of "manners" for the writer. Class, gender, race must be firmly in place for the detective novel of manners to be written. Less than two decades after its publication, this socalled DNOM jolts the reader with its inaccuracies. True writers of DNOMs are never inaccurate or dated: they are historical. That both Austen and Sayers, in their differing ways, criticized and subverted the gender and social arrangements of their society in no way disproves this rule.

Are there, then, no detective novels of manners being written today? Let me, before answering that question, swerve from a discussion of class, imperative to the creation of a true DNOM, to gender, a much more slippery concept, though certainly connected to class and, like class, barely detachable from the DNOM. A feminist since the dawn of the women's movement, I have recently been forced to realize how upper class (perhaps upper-middle class), white, and privileged a revolution feminism was in its second-wave beginnings. Recently, the women's movement has had to expand to become as aware of class and race as of gender, or, as I prefer to put it, of gender as it is played out among other cultures, races, societies, and classes. Students of mine in graduate school, now much more ethnically diverse than was the case a decade or two back, are studying literature through the lenses of class and race as well as gender, and discovering what Woolf knew in the late thirties: that imperialism, patriarchy, and fascism are intimately related. This is a concept properly terrifying to the middle and upper classes of America and Europe. In England, which gave birth to the DNOM, feminism is often feared by the upper, educated classes, who see it as lesbian—that is, opposed to the heterosexual plot on which the class system and patriarchy generally rested; devoted to the third world, and thus opposed to white supremacy in any form; and Marxist, or opposed to the power of private wealth. The question of how gender affects, reforms, and rewrites the class system upon which the DNOM depends remains to be answered. As Virginia Woolf might have put it about the DNOM before World War I, "behold, literature was an elderly gentleman in a grey suit talking about duchesses."[8]

Perhaps the least discussed aspect of the DNOM is the position and role of women in these novels. Nothing so distinguishes the English detective novel from the American as the presence in the English novels of women of extraordinary vitality, intelligence, and individuality. This, of course, reflects a similar development in the English mainstream novel, particularly if, as should happen, Henry James is included in that canon.

I have written elsewhere about the development of the independent woman in the British DNOM, reaching from Wilkie Collins through the women writers of the golden age, and including prominent male writers like Nicholas Blake and Dick Francis. Even Sherlock Holmes encounters a woman who defeated him, perhaps uniquely in the canon, who wore men's clothes when convenience dictated, and remained for him *the* woman, suggesting that even this bachelor and reputed misogynist honored women of independent mien who had the intention and ability to control their own lives. There is no question, however, of the class of these independent women from Collins to the death of Sayers: they are all upper, or upper-middle class. That class divisions are occasionally flouted, as when Lord Peter's sister married a policeman, serves to emphasize the enormity of such a break with tradition. What is clear is that the class structure of the DNOM allowed the emergence of women in a way that neither the American detective novel nor English and American imitations of the DNOM were able to do. Robert Bernard's *Deadly Meeting* fails because it mistook a passing condition for solid structure, and did not perceive the changing attitudes that were already undermining what turned out to be an ahistorical rendition: the sort of book that, when women write it, we call old-fashioned.

That John Le Carré is not a writer of DNOMs is evident; that P. D. James is not is less so. She has fashioned after her first novel, as Le Carré did after his, a world she recognizes and portrays as in a state of social transformation. While her detective is upper-middle (the son of a parson), and some of her characters are upper-upper, these last come to sticky ends, wishing for death and expecting destruction. Compare her novels with those of Ngaio Marsh, for example, whose detective is the brother of an ambassador, chillingly upper class, if gracious, and whose social world, as someone said of Jane Austen's, lies still beneath her class. P. D. James, though she is profoundly influenced by DNOMs, as Henry James was by Austen, is notable for getting into the minds of her male characters in a way no DNOM ever did, portraying against their expressed principles their deep resentment of women and often their efforts to manipulate women sexually, to use or avoid them.

Not only is Dorothy Sayers the best representative of the DNOM, but in *Gaudy Night,*[9] her most feminist novel and the one most rigorously attacked by the Leavises, she presents, without for a moment threatening the class structure, a rare community of women. I have heard many men sneer at this community, but for women it remains after fifty years encouraging and unique. In *Gaudy Night,* Sayers is writing, as Lee Edwards put it, of and for "an elite, an heroic cadre, a class of educated women (to use Virginia Woolf's phrase) whose education and intelligence demand that they choose, and that they understand their choice and its consequences."[10] She is not writing of those who have no choice. Choice is, indeed, the whole point of *Gaudy Night.* And choice is available only to those with the money and condition to make it. (That most women with the money and condition choose not to choose is true, but not the subject I am pursuing here.) P. D. James has written: "Like all good writers [Sayers] created a unique and instantly recognizable world into which we can still escape for our comfort, hearing again with relief and nostalgia her strongly individual, amused and confident voice." But, she adds "those of us who first enjoyed and were influenced by Dorothy L. Sayers in our youth, . . . still read her with something more than nostalgia."[11] American women read her with something more than nostalgia, since they can scarcely be nostalgic for something they have never had, nor even had the pos-

sibility of having in the years before 1970: the community of women
scholars in Shrewsbury College in *Gaudy Night*.

Nina Auerbach has written: "the women of Shrewsbury—unlike
many manless women in literature . . .—are not defined by negation;
they are seen vigorously, in terms of what they have, not of what they
lack . . . No other academic novel that I know of captures so well
the fun that peers out from the methodological rigor and high seri-
ousness of academic life, and the exhilarating privilege of belonging
to it."[12] In the years following the publication of *Gaudy Night*, it continued to tell the only story available in which women lived lives defined not by negation, not by their lack of men, but by their commitment to and love for the work they had chosen, and their friendship
and respect for one another. It is of the utmost importance to remember that the solution to the mystery of *Gaudy Night* does not involve
massive ingenuity, but only a freedom on the part of the investigators
from the internalization of sexual myths. It is, I believe, for this reason
that it is not only necessary but wholly correct historically that Lord
Peter should solve the mystery. For it is women, even women like
Harriet Vane, who internalize the long-lived theories of women's de-
pendence upon men, and the accompanying doubts of female capac-
ities, more than do highly intelligent and sensitive men, rare as these
may be. Were Sayers writing today, Vane would be her own detective.
But Sayers' novel is historically accurate about the complex ambiguities
of educated women even as she created the only example of a true
women's community.

Lord Peter, in propounding his solution to the mystery, understood
the uniqueness of the Shrewsbury community. He says: "[T]he one
thing which frustrated the whole attack from first to last was the remarkable solidarity and public spirit displayed by your college as a
body. I think that was the last obstacle that X expected to encounter
in a community of women. . . . there was not a woman in this Common Room, married or single, who would be ready to place personal
loyalties above professional honour" (ch. 22). And when, in Lee Edwards' words, "Annie attacks . . . the Shrewsbury community, she
does so in the name of the old ideology of love."[13] But no one in the
book attacks the ideology of class: quite the contrary. Sayers' vaunted
defense of each person's doing her or his "proper job" was another
way of reinforcing the Victorian concept of each adhering to the position in which it had pleased God to place one.

Let me here compare two episodes, one written by Virginia Woolf, the other by Sayers. Woolf, you will remember from *A Room of One's Own,* was wandering, lost in her thoughts, at Cambridge:

> It was thus that I found myself walking with extreme rapidity across a grass plot. Instantly a man's figure rose to intercept me. Nor did I at first understand that the gesticulations of a curious-looking object, in cut-away coat and evening shirt, were aimed at me. His face expressed horror and indignation. Instinct rather than reason came to my help; he was a Beadle; I was a woman. This was the turf; there was the path. Only the Fellows and Scholars are allowed here; the gravel is the place for me. Such thoughts were the work of a moment.[14]

Here is Dorothy Sayers, from a letter to an Oxford friend written during the Easter break of 1913:

> The exam was so funny—I was the only woman taking it, and sat, severely isolated like a leper, in one corner of the T-room at the Schools, while the men occupied a quite different branch of it. The first day while looking for my desk, I wandered into the men's part of the room, whereupon the old chap who sees you settled (not the invigilator but the door-keeper sort of person) rushed at me with wildly waving arms and a terrified expression, and shooed me away to my seclusion like an intrusive hen.[15]

You will have noted that Woolf, in 1928, and Sayers, in 1913, both knew "by instinct" what the trouble was at Cambridge and Oxford alike: they were women. Yet Woolf's book was designed to challenge the class system, not only on behalf of women, but on behalf of working-class men whose chance to become great English writers was almost as bad as if they had been born female. Sayers' book, a genuine DNOM, wishes to readjust the positions and expectations of women already enabled to receive an Oxbridge education.

Do I mean to assert that there will be no more DNOMs? Yes, unless we allow the definition to be so rubbery that it will fit any community with a clearly defined set of manners, in which case we should have DNOMs about the Mafia or about the members of municipal trade unions. The stories, for example, of whistle blowers, who go against the mores of their tribe, are profound and moral stories, but they are not DNOMs. The essential ingredient in DNOMs is class, and the unthinking acceptance of one's own class not only as having leisure, money, a certain education, and a clear path to the corridors of influence and power but also as deserving these privileges and seeing them as productive of a good world, perhaps the best possible world. The feminist element in true DNOMs has perhaps been one of the attractions of this genre for the current generation of writers of detective fiction. If women writers are drawn to Peter Wimsey, his feminism is a large part of his appeal. The same can be said of the heroes and heroines of writers like Nicholas Blake, before he reverted to conventional English misogyny, Dick Francis, Robert Parker, and P. D. James. P. D. James has not only created a female private eye, Cordelia Gray, who is classless, however much her tasks may lie with the upper-middle classes, but also Kate Miskin, an equally classless policewoman from James' latest, *A Taste for Death*. Similarly, the women police detectives, private eyes, and amateur sleuths created now and in recent years by women writers have been influenced by the English DNOMs, but these authors are not writing in that outmoded genre. It is questionable whether even a dyed-in-the-wool reactionary could write in that genre; even the most narrow minded of the rich must perceive, if only dimly, that they are no longer the class that runs their world, and that entrance to any world—jet set, Brahmin, or Mayflower descendent—is possible to those with enough money, ambition, and what even the elegant today call chutzpah.

As for the traditional, tough-guy, nonfeminist, anti-woman American detective novel, that has never been a DNOM, and, of course, never will be. If those who eschew this genre of violence still write detective novels of moral people able to conceive of a moral universe, fighting for what seems right even when the system offers no rewards for such courage, they may be in the process of creating a new genre. The ancestry of that genre may include the DNOMs, but as with most ancestors, the influence will be fleeting, and more and more difficult to recognize as time goes by.

1987

ENDNOTES

1. Noel Annan, "Bloomsbury and the Leavises," *Virginia Woolf and Bloomsbury: A Centenary Celebration,* Jane Marcus, ed. (Bloomington: Indiana University Press, 1987), p. 32.

2. Gaddis Smith, "A Gentleman and a Scapegoat," review of Robert Rhodes James, *Anthony Eden, New York Times Book Review,* August 23, 1987, p. 12.

3. Julian Symons, "The Borgia Heirloom," *Ellery Queen* (November 1987), pp. 52–56.

4. Robin W. Winks, *Cloak & Gown: Scholars in the Secret War, 1939–1961* (New York: Morrow, 1987).

5. John Le Carré, *Tinker, Tailor, Soldier, Spy* (1974; New York: Bantam, 1975), p. 355.

6. Hanna Charney, *The Detective Novel of Manners: Hedonism, Morality, and the Life of Reason* (Rutherford, N.J.: Fairleigh Dickinson University Press; London and Toronto: University Presses, 1981), p. xi.

7. Robert Bernard, *Deadly Meeting* (New York: Perennial Library-Harper, 1986).

8. Virginia Woolf, *Orlando: A Biography* (1928; New York and London: Harvest-Harcourt, 1956), p. 280.

9. Dorothy L. Sayers, *Gaudy Night* (London: Gollancz, 1935).

10. Lee R. Edwards, *Psyche as Hero: Female Heroism and Fictional Form* (Middletown, Conn.: Wesleyan University Press, 1984), p. 295.

11. P. D. James, Foreword to James Brabazon, *Dorothy L. Sayers* (New York: Scribner's, 1981), pp. xiii, xvi.

12. Nina Auerbach, "Dorothy L. Sayers and the Amazons," in Auerbach, *Romantic Imprisonment: Women and Other Glorified Outcasts* (New York: Columbia University Press, 1985), p. 188.

13. Edwards, *Psyche as Hero,* p. 186.

14. Virginia Woolf, *A Room of One's Own* (New York: Harcourt, 1929), pp. 7–8.

15. Dorothy L. Sayers, Letters, MS, Sophia Smith Collection, Smith College, Northampton, Mass.

20

Gender and Detective Fiction

IN 1973, more as scholar than sleuth but, as Robin Winks has so well demonstrated, inevitably as both, I published a book called *Toward a Recognition of Androgyny*. The term "androgyny" was very new then, and shocked a great many reviewers who would be marvelously ho-hum in a few years. By now androgyny has become a media event, and I have gone on, as a scholar, to discuss and teach gender in a much more sophisticated way, with all proper references to Lacan, semiotics, and psychoanalytic history, but I have never discussed androgyny in connection with the detective story. I would like to do that here, because it has recently occured to me that there is a kind of gender division in detective fiction that has become quite unrealistic since, say, 1970, but which never carried very much conviction.

I was led to the decision to discuss gender and the detective story by a sudden bout of housecleaning. As those of you who have grown children well know, getting them to leave home is child's play compared to getting them to take their possessions with them. After a decade of storing objects about which children feel sentimental enough to keep in your space but not sentimental enough to store in their own, most parents rebel. Come and get it, they say, or out it goes. Recently, as most of the accumulation was going out, I rescued two paperbacks originally published in 1940 and 1964, entitled *The Boys' Book of Great Detective Stories* and *The Boys' Second Book of Great Detective Stories,* both edited by Howard Haycraft. The first volume's preface began thus: "This is a book for modern boys in their teens—for those active, growing, adventurous young minds that demand more robust fare than 'children's books.' At such an age boys turn naturally to the detective story." The collection begins with Poe and ends with Sayers, including Agatha Christie in between. Haycraft no doubt knew then what moviemakers know today: that girls will reverberate to stories about boys, but neither wants stories about girls. But is this really true with the detective story?

The English detective story from the very beginning, and the American detective story lately, is remarkably androgynous in the work of its more interesting practitioners. And what do I mean by androgynous? I mean the opposite of sexual stereotyping. Here is how the psychologist Sandra Bem describes the androgynous person, who, interestingly enough, is characterized by an ability to cope. Those who are stereotypical males and females are unable to act when they do not know what the appropriate action is. Placed in an unprescribed situation, they sink into bewilderment and inaction. As Bem writes:

Even if people were all to become psychologically androgynous, the world would consist of two sexes. . . . Thus, being female typically means that you have a female body build; that you have female genitalia; that you have breasts; that you menstruate; that you can become pregnant and give birth; and that you can nurse a child. Similarly, being a male typically means that you have a male body build; that you have male genitalia; that you have beard growth; . . . that you can impregnate a woman and thereby father a child. Precisely because there are biological givens which cannot be avoided or escaped, except perhaps by means of very radical and mutilating surgery, it seems to me that psychological health must necessarily include having a healthy sense of one's maleness or femaleness. But I would argue that a healthy sense of maleness or femaleness involves little more than being able to look into the mirror

and to be perfectly comfortable with the body that one sees there. . . .
But beyond being comfortable with the body, one's gender need have
no other influence on one's behavior or life style. Thus, although I would
suggest that a woman ought to feel comfortable about the fact that she
can bear children if she wants to, this does not imply that she ought to
want to bear children, nor that she ought to stay home with any children
that she does bear. Similarly, although I would suggest that a man ought
to feel perfectly comfortable about the fact that he has a penis which
can become erect, this in no way implies that a man ought to take the
more active role during sexual intercourse, nor even that his sexual partners ought all to be female.[1]

Let us notice that subordinate phrase "except perhaps by means of
very radical and mutilating surgery." We have recently come to understand that the entire phenomenon of transsexualism is the result of
defining sex roles as absolutely distinct, as at opposite ends of the old
masculinity-feminity scale. Transsexuals are the ultimate victims of
stereotypical gender behavior. The best example of this is from *Conundrum* by Jan Morris, who, before she became a woman, had been
an adventurous journalist who had, among other exploits, more or less
run up Mount Everest in sneakers. Jan Morris writes:

> The more I was treated as a woman, the more woman I became. If I
> was assumed to be incompetent at reversing cars, or opening bottles,
> oddly incompetent I found myself becoming. . . . My lawyer, in an
> unguarded moment one morning, even called me 'my child'; and so,
> addressed every day as an inferior, involuntarily, month by month, I
> accepted the condition. I discovered that even now men prefer women
> to be less informed, less able, less talkative, and certainly less selfcentered
> than they are themselves, so I generally obliged them. . . . If the
> condescension of men could be infuriating, the courtesies were very
> welcome. . . . I did not particularly want to be good at reversing
> cars. . . .
> My view of life shifted too. I was even more emotional now. I cried
> very easily, and was ludicrously susceptible to sadness or flattery. . . .
> Let me see what everyday inessential sensations I conceive as specifically
> female. First, I feel small, and neat. I am not small in fact, at 5'9" and
> 133 lbs., and not terribly neat either, but femininity conspires to make
> me feel so. My blouse and skirt are light, bright, crisp. My shoes make
> my feet look more delicate than they are, besides giving me, perhaps
> more than any other piece of clothing, a suggestion of vulnerability that
> I rather like. When I walk out into the street I feel consciously ready
> for the world's appraisal, in a way that I never felt as a man. . . . And
> when the news agent seems to look at me with approval, or the man

in the milk-cart smiles, I feel absurdly elated, as though I have been given a good review in the *Sunday Times*.[9]

Let us compare to this an account of how a "real" woman, in this case Marcia Yudkin, feels:

I have to confess that, in the sense in which transsexuals use the phrase, I do not feel myself to be "really a woman." I feel myself to be "really" just a person, sex unspecified. Of course, I know that I am female, just as I know that I am 5'6", have brown hair and blue eyes, and am 25 years old; but I do not let any of these facts define me and I prefer to be in circumstances where others do not define me by those physical facts. . . . I do not consider myself a "woman in a woman's body," as I should if the transsexuals' versions of womanhood as an inner reality which can match or fail to match biological facts were correct for everyone. This intuition too contradicts some philosophers' insistence that women are essentially women rather than human beings who happen to be of the female sex.[3]

This is an American woman speaking. But for many years, it was the English, even so unlikely a one as D. H. Lawrence, who supported what has come to be called androgyny. Here is Lawrence, quoted appropriately enough by Dorothy Sayers:

Man is willing to accept woman as an equal, as a man in skirts, as an angel, a devil, a baby-face, a machine, an instrument, a bosom, a womb, a pair of legs, a servant, an encyclopedia, an ideal or an obscenity: the one thing he won't accept her as is a human being, a real human being of the female sex.[4]

The English novel, and certainly English mysteries, have accepted "androgyny" from the beginning. Indeed, the English detective novel has always boasted androgynous males, though they would certainly not have welcomed the phrase. When women as writers of crime novels entered the field of detective fiction in large numbers in the 1920s, they followed the males in making their detectives charming and effete.

These women writers' male detectives were even more gentlemanly, upper class, and languid than their predecessors. This, while arousing all good revolutionaries to considerable and understandable ire, was, of course, a put-on. Criminals and others were lured into thinking that anyone that effeminate must be incompetent. For a number of years the women authors paraded their carefully dressed, gentlemanly heroes through case after case, as sales soared and the form became one of the most popular of genres, particularly with intellectuals. I need not remind you of how much money Agatha Christie made, nor of her detective, Poirot, who might be called many things, and frequently was, but "manly" was not one of them. Manliness, indeed, was left for the Watsons in the outfit. Let me merely point out, in passing, that the English, in their detective fiction from Holmes on, were the first, but perhaps not the last, to equate manliness and stupidity.

The United States has been slow here as elsewhere to move away from sexual stereotyping. It is a fact that Americans divide children by gender earlier and more emphatically than any other culture. Not only have our male writers produced tough detectives, they have produced women who are stereotyped and usually either dead or man-eaters as well. Robert Parker is one of the rare exceptions. Spenser is tough, to be sure, but he is also tender, and his views on women and poetry would terrify Rambo as well as the moral majority.

It is, however, women detective writers with women detectives who have brought about the greatest change. Carol Brenner, with whom I discussed this matter a short time ago—you all know, I am sure, that she runs that wonderful bookstore Murder Ink, and is both extensively knowledgeable and enormously kind about mysteries of all persuasions—Carol mentioned that when Amanda Cross began publishing her novels in 1964 there were very few female detectives available in the novels on the shelves at Murder Ink. By 1972 we had, among others, the wonderful Cordelia Gray from England in P. D. James' *An Unsuitable Job for a Woman*. Today there are more than anyone but Carol and perhaps Marilyn Stasio and Michele Slung can keep up with, and most of them are American. Sara Paretsky's V. I. Warshawski, whose latest and most marvelous adventure is called *Killing Orders*, is a woman private eye, period. She is one of those women who has crossed the line from amateur to professional detective, she earns her living at it, and she's good at it. Lynne Jacobi, in Dorothy Uhnak's *False Witness*, is high up in the D.A.'s office, a public rather than a private eye, and a fine example of how an androgynous female can beautifully succeed in crime fiction. So, too, Carolyn Wheat's Legal Aid lawyer Cassandra Jameson avoids stereotypical thought as assiduously as most American male novelists, detective or straight, embrace it.

This move toward androgyny and away from stereotypical sex roles— away, more importantly, from the ridiculing and condemning of those who do not conform to stereotypical sex roles—has, I am proud to say, found greater momentum in the detective story than in any other genre, and has recently gone further in the United States than elsewhere. It is the sad truth that despite the efforts of the English women detective writers and a good many of the men, including Dick Francis, the English have recently embraced our machismo rather than our, or their own, androgynous tradition. Of course, this move toward androgyny in crime writing or anywhere else is not an easy one. The same Sandra Bem who did the studies of androgynous individuals tried, together with her husband, to raise their children free from what she calls "gender-schematic processing." To inculcate beliefs and values that deviate from the dominant culture, Bem tells us, one must begin to undermine the dominant ideology in the children before the ideology can undermine them. Bem and her husband tried with their own children to undermine the gender-schematic process, which assigns sex by all sorts of external signs rather than the single anatomical sign. They found this inspiriting if uphill work. Bem reports:

> Before we read our daughter her first volume of fairy tales, we discussed with her the cultural beliefs and attitudes about men and women that the tales would reflect, and while reading the tales we frequently made such comments as, "Isn't it interesting that the person who wrote this story seems to think that girls always need to be rescued?" If such discussions are not too heavy-handed, they can provide a background of understanding against which the child can thoroughly enjoy the stories themselves, while still learning to discount the sex stereotypes within them as irrelevant both to their own beliefs and to the truth.[5]

The Bem son, aged four, met up with phallocentrism in a more literal way. He decided one day

> to wear barrettes to nursery school. Several times that day, another little boy told Jeremy that he, Jeremy, must be a girl because only girls wear barrettes. After trying to explain to this child that wearing barrettes doesn't matter and that being a boy means having a penis and testicles, Jeremy finally pulled down his pants as a way of making his point more convincingly. The other child was not impressed. He simply said, "Everybody has a penis; only girls wear barrettes."[6]

I recommend the entire article to you; for after all we are all faced with those who see that everyone (who matters) has a penis; and we must all be pre-programmed against the sexual stereotypes of fairy tales. Unfortunately, most of the theorists and critics of the crime story have observed women's emergence in the contemporary detective novel rather as one responds in the early stages of any infiltration. The hope is that if one doesn't notice the invaders, and especially if one doesn't encourage them, they will go away.

I have served for two years running on a Mystery Writers of America committee to pick the best biographical or critical work on a mystery writer. Please do not think that my only or even major criterion was that the winning book be enlightened on the subject of "gender schematic processing." Both years the committee was intelligently and readily unanimous; the first year the prize was given to a biography of James Cain, the second year to a wonderfully well-written study of Le Carré, neither author noted for his original views on women. Le Carré is a bit better than Cain, but in any case, the question never arose. I mention all this to suggest that I am far from asking for a new party line in detective criticism. At the same time, one wishes someone would notice that women have not just been writing more books lately—"the ladies, God bless them"—but that they have done a certain amount to transform the genre. I have two shelves of academic, ponderous (I'm afraid) books on crime writing, and there are but a few of them that consider the new androgynous writers at all; when women are taken up, it is in a separate section, as though to say, Hey, fellows: look! The girls have a softball team too. No one has noticed that crime writing is changing in an important way.

There is, of course, a gender bias even to their not noticing. Dick Francis and Robert Parker, to stick to two of my favorite male novelists, have gone far along the road of anti-stereotyping, and they have both been honored by fame and fortune and awards. But androgynous women in male novels with a tough and resourceful hero are not as threatening, or unfamiliar, or dangerous as androgynous females in novels by women. And this fact has marked the whole history of androgyny, as many commentators have noticed. Men may acquire "feminine" characteristics, but woe unto the woman who becomes "masculine." One need think no further than the theories of Jung and Norman O. Brown. Aggressive women frighten everyone: it's an idea we've been taught to be uncomfortable with; furthermore, we have defined men not as wonderfully human, but as "not women."

There is a plethora of books, romances and westerns, designed for those who want no surprises. These books relax the reader precisely because everyone knows what to expect, of men, women, and the plot.

I am not altogether certain that the American classics by that sainted trio Hammett, Chandler, and Ross Macdonald do not always satisfy the same unexamined and unchallenged assumptions. Parker interests me and many others because, in that same tradition, he does challenge them. And recent writers, women and men, have begun to challenge them too. I think that this openness about the prison of gender is one of the detective novel's great claims to fame and has been ever since Holmes' Irene Adler put on men's clothing for her own purposes. I think, since I am throwing so many scandalous opinions around here, that the English, who began by being courageously androgynous, are passing that torch on to Americans who today have shown wonderful new possibilities for the genre.

It's a safe guess that every detective novelist has been asked why he or she writes detective stories and not "real" novels. There are many answers, but I think an important one has never been stated flat out: that with the momentum of a mystery and the trajectory of a good story with a solution, the author is left free to dabble in a little profound revolutionary thought. In my opinion, detective fiction, often called formula fiction, has almost alone and with astonishing success challenged the oldest formulas of all.

1986

ENDNOTES

1. Sandra Bem, "From Traditional to Alternative Conceptions of Sex Roles," in *Beyond Sex-Role Stereotypes: Readings Toward a Psychology of Androgyny*, Alexandra G. Kaplan and Joan P. Bean, eds. (Boston: Little, Brown, 1976), p. 60.

2. Jan Morris, *Conundrum* (New York: Harcourt, Brace, 1974), pp. 149, 150, 153, 157.

3. Marcia Yudkin, "Transsexualism and Women: A Critical Perspective," *Feminist Studies* (1978), 4(3):103.

4. Dorothy L. Sayers, "Are Women Human?" in *Unpopular Opinions* (London: Victor Gollancz, 1946), 114.

5. Sandra Bem, "Gender Schema Theory and Its Implications for Child Development: Raising Gender-aschematic Children in a Gender-schematic Society," *Signs* (1983), 8(4):612.

6. *Ibid.*

21

Sayers, Lord Peter, and Harriet Vane at Oxford

MUCH OF the Oxford that would appear in *Gaudy Night* in 1935 was already evident to the Dorothy Sayers who had attended Oxford twenty years earlier and wrote to her friends about it. That life seemed to her then, as it was to seem to her readers later, close to perfection—something to do with community, and scholarship, and the public life which could be seen as not separate from, but part of, the private life; love and work were not antithetical, but joined, as they had long been for men. The mature artist of twenty years later who would understand and recreate exactly the quality of Oxford's gift to women is clearly adumbrated in the prewar undergraduate.

In his biography of Sayers, James Brabazon quotes from her correspondence during the summer vacation of 1913. Sayers wrote from her home in the rectory at Bluntisham to Muriel Jaeger, called Jim, that she was very frustrated because her normal technique of "vehemently disagreeing with everybody" did not arouse the response she hoped for, but merely resulted in people going rather quiet and polite. "Oh Jimmy, I miss our loud-voiced arguments . . . hang it all, what were tongues made for?" All her life, Brabazon adds, "Dorothy was a steam-roller in arguments and all her life she was to look for people who would stand up to her and give her back as good as they got."

At the library of Smith College there is a small collection of Sayers letters which the curator of rare books has allowed me to quote from. Most of these were written during vacations from Oxford, and after graduation, to a classmate named Catherine H. Godfrey and called "Tony." I have chosen to quote from them with the greatest restraint, but I think these passages do clearly show Sayers' love of Oxford, and strike one or two notes that will be heard again in *Gaudy Night*. She writes in Easter week, 1913, obviously in response to a letter from Tony:

> Hear! Hear! I'm simply dead sick of telling people about Oxford, and how many there are of us at Somerville and how many dons there are, and why have I got to do an exam in German when my subject's French, and do I see much of the Prince of Wales, and do we have lectures with the men, and is there a tennis court at Somerville, and what is the name of our Head, and what time are lights put out at night, and how do we get milk when we make our own tea, and may we go to the theatre, and have I made any particular friends, and what sort of people live in my passage, and have I one room or two, and will the new buildings be finished when we get back, and do the maids wear caps and aprons, and when was the college founded and are there more women students at Oxford or Cambridge? I suppose people have to ask questions.

Later, in the same letter, she complains about a friend from Girton who is visiting her, and who claims to have, like one of the women mentioned in *Gaudy Night,* a mind above clothes. Alas, the friend from Girton is also

> very keen on socialism and suffrage and eugenics and God knows what— but I have observed that she is enormously taken up with the fact that her cousin the Bishop of Ely has been exalted to the House of Lords, and never ceases talking about it, though with an elaborate affectation of contempt. So much for socialism! I do wish to goodness people would be sincere about things.

Slightly later in that vacation, Sayers writes to Tony:

Do you know—you're the only person to whom I dare confess it—for a bit after I got home, I was simply homesick for Oxford—not for college—but for that curve in the High and Radcliffe Square by moonlight, and for the people in the street and the stories about Varsity life. Talking about moonlight, on several occasions we amused ourselves by going to Wadham after dinner, and sitting in the Warden's garden under the pale rays of the tranquil moon! It was ripping. Wadham is such a perfectly shaped little college, and the garden is full of dark old trees.

And she concludes her letter, as our minds veer forward twenty-two years, with: "I'm afraid I shan't be able to get up for the opening of the new buildings? Shall you be there?"

Commenting on an exam where she was the only woman, she wrote: "Readman turned up on the second day with a damaged leg and a general air of heroic suffering and wild disorder about the hair. He is always getting himself smashed up—I think he drives a young motor. He really did look rather bad, poor chap." Just like someone's nephew twenty-two years later.

During a leave in 1914, she wrote to Tony of how she was passing the time. I quote this to counter the often-heard comment that Sayers took up religion when she gave up Wimsey. "At present I am deep in the writing of an allegorical epic of which I have completed the first canto. I began it last vac; and it is distinctly Christian in tone." (Something Sayers was to write many years later, in her introduction to her translation of the *Inferno,* seems to me also to have remarkable bearing on the moral center of *Gaudy Night:* "We must abandon any idea that we are the slave of chance, or environment, or our subconscious; any vague notion that good and evil are merely relative terms, or that conduct and opinion do not really matter; any comfortable persuasion that, however shiftlessly we muddle through life, it will somehow or other all come right on the night. We must try to believe that man's will is free, that he can consciously exercise choice, and that his choice can be decisive to all eternity." This, she tells us, is the "Christian and Catholic view of ourselves as responsible rational beings.")

But back to 1915, and the end of Sayers' undergraduate Oxford years. She writes to Tony from Bluntisham: "This is decidedly the deadliest hole in Christendom. . . . So here's the following—you must imagine it set to a resounding tune:

Sitting by the window pane
Growling at the falling rain
Burdened by the dismal fields a-wash with yellow water,
Drearily, wearily
Here's a song for you and me
And every one who's glad to be
Alma Mater's daughter.

It's O it's O for Oxford
With the rain on Keble Road
And we're going to be late
For it's after eight
I heard it strike as we passed the gate
Though the Doctor snarl and swear
And bid us all be blowed
It's O it's O for Oxford
And the rain on Keble Road.

This continues for many verses, ending up:

But it's O it's O for Oxford
And the rain along the High
College and hall
And Frowning wall
And loud bells echoing over all,
The stout old town
Where the days go bustling by
And it's O it's O for Oxford
With the rain along the High!

She concludes her letter: "I mean to use the chorus of this some day—put better verses to it, and make it less topical, because I like the refrain." When one loves a college as much as Sayers loved Somerville, and if one is a writer, one will write of it someday, in a novel as profound and enduring as *Gaudy Night*, if one is talented and lucky. (One may also write of it too soon if one has hated it—an example might be *Dusty Answer*, but that is a wholly different story.)

And so back to *Gaudy Night* and 1935. The final letter I wish to quote from is addressed to a Mr. Hopkins, the nephew of Gerard Manley Hopkins, who had apparently sent her his enthusiastic praise of that novel. In one passage of her reply she wrote: "The fact that in *Gaudy Night* Peter is never seen except through Harriet's eyes makes the difference [from the other books in which she had appeared] perhaps a little more acceptable; also, I feel that it really did become a more important thing *to him* than it had seemed at first—but perhaps this is only rationalizing the *fait accompli!*"

Also, "Lord Peter, who has, I think just about got back from his honeymoon, sends you much gratitude, and says he remembers you perfectly. He has a vivid recollection of behaving with intolerable affectation at Chilswell, and wonders how Bridges ever put up with him. He was writing a good deal of minor verse himself at the time, and has a horrible notion that he probably read it aloud; also, that he aired a number of callow opinions about G. M. Hopkins' metres, which he now blushes to think of. He is greatly looking forward to seeing the new volume you have in hand. . . . With many thanks from both Peter and myself, yr.s, DLS."

At another point in the same letter she writes: "Incidentally, it was kind of you not to point out at the same time that I had mis-spelt your uncle's name—I quite thought I had verified this, but evidently it was only a thought. I will have it put right in the next edition." This exchange surely recalls a passage from *Gaudy Night* when Harriet says: "The tenth [reader] writes me a letter, and I promise to make the correction in the second edition, but I never do." In this case, Sayers did. All editions after the first carried the correct spelling of "Manley."

Gaudy Night is Sayers' most memorable novel not least because of the remarkable way it renders the new-found equal love between men and women. As Sayers portrayed love in the engagement of Harriet and Peter, she did not do so through any capitulation of Harriet's such as popular fiction and great literature have long offered us. Rather, Peter gains her consent in the words of the great, long-male, ceremony of the granting of degrees. I think the idea for this was planted when Sayers attended the Encaenia in 1914, and wrote to her friend Tony about it. The letter describing the ceremony is very long indeed, and contains many points that were to be echoed in *Gaudy Night*. She concludes with the moment when the Vice-Chancellor "addressed the assembled doctors in a sing-song little speech, beginning something about 'Does it please you doctors of the University that so-&-so should be admitted to such and such degree—Placentne?' and then he took off his cap and said 'Placent' without leaving time for anyone to make an objection if he wanted to."

Thus the ceremony of engagement to marry she later portrayed between a man and woman was borrowed from a ceremony that concluded a period of rigorous, individual achievement. But there is more to it even than that. For perhaps the most important aspect of the relation between Harriet and Peter in *Gaudy Night* is not that Peter is seen only through Harriet's eyes. More significantly still, he is seen in the novel as an object of female vision, as a sexual being so regarded as he walks toward them by the members of the Senior Common Room of Shrewsbury College. Only Colette has also accomplished this rare feat of brilliantly rendering the male as sex object.

But, important above all this, is the fact that Peter changes in the course of the novel. There is only one story that I know of in all of Western civilization where the hero of the story is a woman, and the man she loves changes along with her, to become worthy of their new love. That story is "Psyche and Amor" by Apuleius, and it is an extraordinary aspect of that tale that Amor matures and changes as Psyche undergoes her difficult tasks, and that together they produce—I have always taken this as a prophetic note—not the son, the male heir, it is assumed throughout the tale Psyche is carrying, but a daughter, named Joy. We remember that Lord Peter has told us that the only sin sex can commit is to be joyless.

Did Sayers know the tale of Psyche and Amor? She probably knew it, but certainly she did not consciously follow it. By a strange insight, however, she told, in the most important novel of her career, a story similarly unique in its own culture, of a female hero coming to self-awareness and autonomy, and sharing equally with the male protagonist the perilous journey to self-development.

SAYERS HAS told us a great deal about the creation and ultimate refinement of the character of Lord Peter Wimsey. We are, however, rather left to infer that Harriet Vane, having served "in the conventional Perseus manner" as a maiden to be rescued by the ever more popular Lord Peter, was neither created nor done away with through any particular forethought. It was, we are told in Sayers' own account of the writing of *Gaudy Night*, Peter who was to be married off and got rid of, or, alternatively, to be made into a "complete human being."

Sayers confesses that she could not at once "marry Peter off to the young woman he had . . . rescued from death and infamy, because I could find no form of words in which she could accept him without loss of self-respect." We have seen that in *Gaudy Night* she found the solution to that problem. Nevertheless, Sayers neglects to mention, perhaps because she never recognized, that the complete human being she was creating was Harriet Vane, and that it was Harriet far more than Peter who, once fully portrayed, had to be married off and got rid of. However she may have hidden her need to write about Harriet, Sayers was primarily compelled, not to make Peter more human, but to create a woman, autonomous, intellectual, unwomanly and, ultimately, lovable. It was Harriet who, once presented in that amazing autonomy, could then be married off and done away with. Sayers says she did not do away with Peter, because "a lingering instinct of self-preservation, and the deterrent object-lesson of Mr. Holmes's rather scrambling return from the Reichenbach Falls, prevented me from actually killing and burying the nuisance." This is pure camouflage, a brazen pulling of the wool over her eyes and ours. Once Harriet's independent role and character had been fully played out, Sayers put her back into the proper womanly, wifely position in *Busman's Honeymoon* and abandoned her to the fate of a married woman, a fate delineated further in "Talboys." Peter, meanwhile, returned as the detective he had always been, diverting himself in detection even during his honeymoon and even during Harriet's childbirth scene. Sayers' need to create a wholly independent woman had been happily assuaged.

HARRIET VANE first appeared in *Strong Poison*. Let us examine her carefully. Here is a woman who has, metaphorically speaking, killed and abandoned her lover when she outgrew him. So realistic, so "unfeminine" is her scorn of him that she is, literally, tried for his murder, a fate society might well mete out to a woman who treats a man as men have ever treated their women lovers. Peter, that ideal man, recognizes her right to have had a lover as equal to his own (a far from common view at that time), and rescues her, not so much from the charge of murder as from the charge of unwomanly conduct. She cannot accept him in his Perseus role, and proceeds in what may be the most extraordinary, because uncritical, portrait of an independent woman in all literature, to enact her belief that "the best remedy for a bruised heart is not, as so many people seem to think, repose upon a manly bosom. Much more efficacious are honest work, physical activity, and the sudden acquisition of wealth." Because readers anticipated romance and the inevitable abandonment of this declared independence, they failed to be shocked by how unusual Harriet was. She travels alone, is not given to "groupy" activities at Oxford, and works there, independently, not only as a detective, but as a member of a rare community of female scholars and colleagues who are, no more than she, refugees from a male bosom. In all the novels in which she appears, furthermore, she fairly flaunts her independence, scorns women who flutter around gigolos or otherwise bother much about men, and befriends women so independent that they might even be seen as outside the marriage game altogether. Harriet, indeed, cannot be sentimental enough to like someone because she has once liked them, or because they are ill, and she is a positive bundle of arrogant and wholly defensible opinions. *And,* she dines alone in restaurants without ever discussing the pros and cons of a question still hotly debated in a recent major New York newspaper.

Sayers, who invented an extraordinary life for herself, needed, I am certain, to create once and for all a woman as independent and, in the light of proper womanly behavior, as outrageous as she. Harriet Vane is close to a unique creation in a literature where women writers before 1970 have rarely, if ever, given us women characters as independent as themselves. Sayers was determined to create Harriet Vane, and then to marry her off and get rid of her, as women characters have ever been got rid of. Their stories end with marriage, wifedom, and motherhood. The tale about killing off Peter was folderol. Sayers couldn't kill him off until Harriet had been created. Only then could she go on to the other work—theology, religious drama, the translation of Dante—which Lord Peter's earnings, that "sudden acquisition of wealth," had enabled her to do. Although Lord Peter appeared with his family in a few stories set during World War II, after *Busman's Honeymoon* Sayers wrote no more detective novels.

1986

Index

GENDER AND CULTURE
A series of Columbia University Press
Edited by Carolyn G. Heilbrun and Nancy K. Miller

In Dora's Case: Freud, Hysteria, Feminism
  Edited by Charles Bernheimer and Claire Kahane
Breaking the Chain: Women, Theory, and French Realist Fiction
  Naomi Schor
Between Men: English Literature and Male Homosocial Desire
  Eve Kosofsky Sedgwick
Romantic Imprisonment: Women and Other Glorified Outcasts
  Nina Auerbach
The Poetics of Gender
  Edited by Nancy K. Miller
Reading Woman: Essays in Feminist Criticism
  Mary Jacobus
Honey-Mad Women: Emancipatory Strategies in Women's Writing
  Patricia Yaeger
Subject to Change: Reading Feminist Writing
  Nancy K. Miller
Thinking Through the Body
  Jane Gallop
Gender and the Politics of History
  Joan Wallach Scott
The Dialogic and Difference: "An/Other Woman" in Virginia Woolf and Christa Wolf
  Anne Herrmann
Plotting Women: Gender and Representation in Mexico
  Jean Franco
Inspiriting Influences: Tradition, Revision, and Afro-American Women's Novels
  Michael Awkward
Hamlet's Mother and Other Women
  Carolyn G. Heilbrun
Rape and Representation
  Edited by Lynn A. Higgins and Brenda R. Silver
Shifting Scenes: Interviews on Women, Writing, and Politics in Post-68 France
  Edited by Alice A. Jardine and Anne M. Menke
Tender Geographies: Women and the Origins of the Novel in France
  Joan DeJean

Gender and Culture Readers